SOCIOLOGICAL WISDOM

WILLIAM E. THOMPSON
Texas A&M University—Commerce

MICA L. THOMPSON
Texas A&M University—Commerce

ROWMAN & LITTLEFIELD
Lanham • Boulder • New York • London

Executive Editor: Nancy Roberts
Assistant Editor: Megan Manzano
Executive Channel Manager, Higher Education: Amy Whitaker
Interior Designer: Integra, Inc.

Credits and acknowledgments for material borrowed from other sources, and reproduced with permission, appear on the appropriate page within the text.

Published by Rowman & Littlefield
An imprint of The Rowman & Littlefield Publishing Group, Inc.
4501 Forbes Boulevard, Suite 200, Lanham, Maryland 20706
www.rowman.com

6 Tinworth Street, London SE11 5AL, United Kingdom

Copyright © 2020 by The Rowman & Littlefield Publishing Group, Inc.

All rights reserved. No part of this book may be reproduced in any form or by any electronic or mechanical means, including information storage and retrieval systems, without written permission from the publisher, except by a reviewer who may quote passages in a review.

British Library Cataloguing in Publication Information Available

Library of Congress Cataloging-in-Publication Data
Names: Thompson, William E. (William Edwin), 1950- author. | Thompson, Mica L., 1980- author.
Title: Sociological Wisdom: Things Are Not What They Seem / William E. Thompson, Texas A&M University Commerce, Mica L. Thompson, Texas A&M University Commerce.
Description: Lanham: Rowman & Littlefield, [2020] | Includes bibliographical references and index.
Identifiers: LCCN 2019014921 (print) | LCCN 2019017709 (ebook) | ISBN 9781538127896 (ebook) | ISBN 9781538127889 (pbk: alk. paper)
Subjects: LCSH: Sociology. | Human behavior. | Social groups.
Classification: LCC HM435 (ebook) | LCC HM435.T46 2020 (print) | DDC 301—dc23
LC record available at https://lccn.loc.gov/2019014921

∞™ The paper used in this publication meets the minimum requirements of American National Standard for Information Sciences—Permanence of Paper for Printed Library Materials, ANSI/NISO Z39.48–1992.

Dedicated to Jaxon

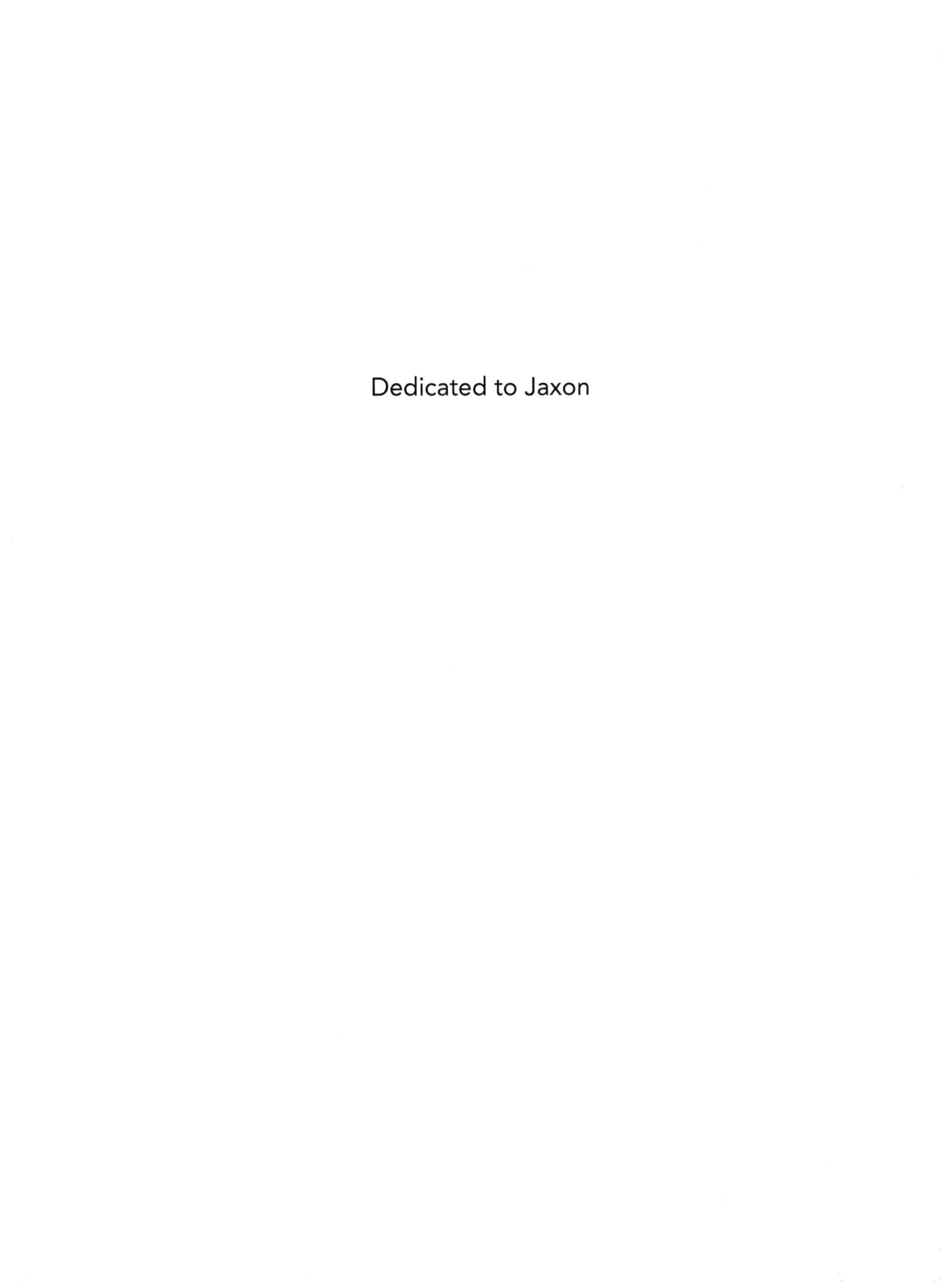

Brief Contents

Preface — xi
Acknowledgments — xiii
About the Authors — xv

01 Sociological Wisdom 1
#ThingsAreNotWhatTheySeem
DISCOVERING SOCIOLOGY — 1

02 Sociological Wisdom 2
#AnalyzeWithYourBrainNotWithYourHeart
DOING SOCIOLOGY — 29

03 Sociological Wisdom 3
#There'sNoSuchThingAsAnUnculturedPerson
UNDERSTANDING SOCIETY AND CULTURE — 57

04 Sociological Wisdom 4
#WhenYouWereBornYouWereNotYetYou
BECOMING YOU: A SOCIAL BEING — 81

05 Sociological Wisdom 5
#TheWorldRevolvesAroundTheSunAndNotYou
INTERACTING IN EVERYDAY LIFE — 105

06 Sociological Wisdom 6
#TheWorldIsAMessyPlace
ORGANIZING OUR SOCIAL WORLD — 131

07 Sociological Wisdom 7
#SomeRulesAreMadeToBeBrokenButSomeAren't
CONTROLLING SOCIAL BEHAVIOR — 155

08 Sociological Wisdom 8
#TheOnlyDifferenceThatMattersIsTheDifferenceThatMatters
EMPHASIZING DIFFERENCES — 179

09 Sociological Wisdom 9
#NothingEnduresButChange
CREATING SOCIAL CHANGE — 205

10 Sociological Wisdom 10
#NothingLastsForever
SUSTAINING THE PLANET — 231

11 A Final Note
#SociologicalWisdomOnlyHasValueIfItIsApplied — 257

References	269
Further Readings	293
Index	301
Credits	311

Contents

Preface — xi
Acknowledgments — xiii
About the Authors — xv

01 Sociological Wisdom 1
#ThingsAreNotWhatTheySeem
DISCOVERING SOCIOLOGY — 1

- SOCIOLOGICAL WISDOM — 3
- THE SOCIOLOGICAL IMAGINATION — 4
- LIFE IN A GLOBAL SOCIETY — 6
- COMMON SENSE VERSUS COMMON NONSENSE — 11
- THE IMPORTANCE OF SCIENCE — 12
- THE STRUCTURAL FUNCTIONALIST PERSPECTIVE — 20
- THE CONFLICT PERSPECTIVE — 22
- THE FEMINIST PERSPECTIVE — 23
- THE SYMBOLIC INTERACTIONIST PERSPECTIVE — 24
- SOCIOLOGICAL WISDOM: TAKING AN INTEGRATED APPROACH — 26

02 Sociological Wisdom 2
#AnalyzeWithYourBrainNotWithYourHeart
DOING SOCIOLOGY — 29

- HOW WE KNOW THINGS ARE NOT WHAT THEY SEEM — 30
- SOCIOLOGY AND SCIENTIFIC KNOWLEDGE — 35
- THEORY-BUILDING PROCESS — 36
- SCIENTIFIC METHOD — 40

ETHICAL ISSUES IN SOCIOLOGICAL RESEARCH	42
TYPES OF RESEARCH	43
QUANTIFYING SOCIAL LIFE	45
QUALITATIVE STUDIES	48
KEEPING IT SCIENTIFIC	50

03 Sociological Wisdom 3
#There'sNoSuchThingAsAnUnculturedPerson
UNDERSTANDING SOCIETY AND CULTURE — 57

TYPES OF SOCIETIES	59
COMPONENTS OF CULTURE	60
ETHNOCENTRISM AND CULTURAL RELATIVISM	71
IDEAL VERSUS REAL CULTURE	75
SUBCULTURES AND COUNTERCULTURES	76
POPULAR CULTURE	78

04 Sociological Wisdom 4
#WhenYouWereBornYouWereNotYetYou
BECOMING YOU: A SOCIAL BEING — 81

NATURE AND NURTURE	83
DEVELOPING A SOCIAL SELF	85
AGENTS OF SOCIALIZATION	87
SOCIALIZATION OVER THE LIFE COURSE	94
DESOCIALIZATION AND RESOCIALIZATION	100

05 Sociological Wisdom 5
#TheWorldRevolvesAroundTheSunAndNotYou
INTERACTING IN EVERYDAY LIFE — 105

PERSONAL SPACE AND NONVERBAL COMMUNICATION	106
STATUSES AND ROLES	114
SOCIAL NETWORKS	119

PATTERNS OF SOCIAL INTERACTION	122
MEDIA AND TECHNOLOGY: REDEFINING SOCIAL INTERACTION	125

06 Sociological Wisdom 6
#TheWorldIsAMessyPlace
ORGANIZING OUR SOCIAL WORLD — 131

SOCIAL GROUPS	132
LEADERS AND LEADERSHIP STYLES	138
FORMAL ORGANIZATIONS	141
BUREAUCRACIES AND US	142
SOCIAL INSTITUTIONS	143

07 Sociological Wisdom 7
#SomeRulesAreMadeToBeBrokenButSomeAren't
CONTROLLING SOCIAL BEHAVIOR — 155

RANGE OF TOLERANCE	157
RELATIVITY OF DEVIANCE	159
DEVIANCE AND STIGMA	160
THE POWER OF MEDIA	162
CYBERPORN, CYBERSEX, AND INTERNET ADDICTION	163
POPULAR EXPLANATIONS OF DEVIANCE	165
SOCIOLOGICAL THEORIES OF DEVIANCE AND CONFORMITY	167
SOCIAL CONTROL	177

08 Sociological Wisdom 8
#TheOnlyDifferenceThatMattersIsTheDifferenceThatMatters
EMPHASIZING DIFFERENCES — 179

IMPORTANCE OF SOCIAL CLASS	180
SOCIOECONOMIC STATUS	183

RACE, ETHNICITY, AND MINORITY GROUPS	187
SEX AND GENDER	193
AGE AND AGEISM	196
INTERSECTIONALITY	201

09 Sociological Wisdom 9
#NothingEnduresButChange
CREATING SOCIAL CHANGE — 205

SOCIAL CHANGE	207
SOURCES OF SOCIAL CHANGE	209
COLLECTIVE BEHAVIOR	215
SOCIAL MOVEMENTS	222
RESISTANCE TO CHANGE	225

10 Sociological Wisdom 10
#NothingLastsForever
SUSTAINING THE PLANET — 231

FORCES OF NATURE	232
DEMOGRAPHY	234
POPULATION GROWTH	235
URBANIZATION AND SUBURBANIZATION	238
ECOLOGY AND THE ENVIRONMENT	244
WHERE DO WE GO FROM HERE?	254

11 A Final Note
#SociologicalWisdomOnlyHasValueIfItIsApplied — 257

References	269
Further Readings	293
Index	301
Credits	311

Preface

Warning: If you believe Santa Claus comes down people's chimneys on Christmas Eve; the Easter Bunny lays chocolate eggs; and illusionists saw people in half and magically put them back together, this book may not be for you, and you may not want to read any further—or perhaps this book is especially for you, and you should proceed with caution. In either case, you have been warned.

Sociological wisdom can be shocking, upsetting, unsettling, and possibly even bad for your health. It is potentially exciting, exhilarating, liberating, and most certainly infectious and addictive. Thinking sociologically is simultaneously a blessing and a curse. Once you develop your sociological wisdom, you cannot easily turn it off. You will never attend a wedding, funeral, meeting, family reunion, birthday party, or any other social event without analyzing it in a way that you have never done before. Attending class, shopping, driving in traffic, visiting friends, meeting strangers, and all other routine daily activities will take on entirely new meanings. In today's global world, with the internet, social media, twenty-four-hour reality television, docudramas, bloggers, tweeters, hackers, and a vast array of other ways to disseminate information to millions of people in nanoseconds, it is more important than ever to study human behavior, social groups, and society utilizing critical thinking skills and careful analysis associated with sociological wisdom.

In this book, we introduce you to 10 wisdoms of sociology:

Things are not what they seem;
Analyze with your brain, not with your heart;
There's no such thing as an uncultured person;
When you were born, you were not yet you;
The world revolves around the sun and not you;
The world is a messy place;
Some rules are made to be broken, but some aren't;
The only difference that matters is the difference that matters;
Nothing endures but change;
Nothing lasts forever.

Then, we add a final note: *Sociological wisdom only has value if it is applied.* This book can help you develop these sociological wisdoms and apply them on a daily basis in order to better understand and navigate the world in which you live. Welcome to sociology.

W. E. Thompson
M. L. Thompson

Acknowledgments

The authors would like to thank Marilyn, Brandon, and Jaxon for their support and encouragement during the writing of this book. We also want to thank Joe Hickey for his many contributions to the manuscript. Special thanks go to Nancy Roberts and others at Rowman & Littlefield for their vision, help, and encouragement in this process. We also thank reviewers, copyeditors, and all others associated with this project.

Note to Readers
You may notice when reading this book that we have adopted the now commonly accepted practice of using plural gender-neutral pronouns with singular nouns. This practice violates the traditional rules of grammar we learned as students and have practiced as teachers and authors throughout our careers. We must admit that at first it was awkward for us to embrace this practice but as Sociological Wisdom 9 tells us, "nothing endures but change."

About the Authors

William E. Thompson was born and raised in Tulsa, Oklahoma, and was the first member of his family to receive a high school diploma. He received his bachelor's degree from Northeastern State University, a master's degree from Missouri State University, and a PhD from Oklahoma State University. Professor Thompson has authored and coauthored more than 40 articles in professional journals, including several reprinted in sociology textbooks and readers. He has coauthored Society in Focus, now in its 9th edition, a textbook on juvenile delinquency, which is going into its 11th edition, and a textbook entitled *Deviants and Deviance: A Sociological Approach*, and he has coedited an anthology on juvenile delinquency. Thompson also is the author of *The Glass House*, a nonfiction account of his mother's two-year battle with cancer and the lessons about life and living learned from her death and dying; and in 2012, authored *Hogs, Blogs, Leathers, and Lattes: The Sociology of Modern American Motorcycling*. For fun and relaxation, Thompson plays the drums and rides motorcycles.

Mica L. Thompson earned her bachelor's degree from Oklahoma State University and her master's degree in sociology from Texas A&M University–Commerce. She has more than 15 years of public school teaching experience and teaches "Introduction to Sociology" and "Deviant Behavior" at the university level. Her research interests include qualitative methods, feminist theory, education, and popular culture. In addition to having collaborated on articles published in professional journals, Mica is co-author of *Society in Focus* (8th and 9th editions). Mica is the author of a blog about mindset titled "The Flipside of ME," which can be found at theflipsideofme.com.

Sociological Wisdom 1

#ThingsAreNotWhatTheySeem

DISCOVERING SOCIOLOGY

IF YOU ARE LIKE MOST PEOPLE, you probably enjoy a good magic show. When you are watching, you must temporarily suspend the knowledge that what you are watching is not in fact magic, but deception. Most good magicians rarely use the word "magic," calling themselves illusionists rather than magicians. Illusionists use clever hand motions, pretty assistants, and a constant barrage of words to distract their audiences from realizing what is actually taking place. Peter Berger (1963:23) contended, "The first wisdom of sociology is this—*things are not what they seem.* [emphasis ours]" Nowhere is the first wisdom of sociology more meaningful than during a magic show.

What does a magic show have to do with our daily lives? More than you might think. Admittedly, there are some times in life when what you see is what you get, and things are pretty much what they seem. No doubt, you have heard, and probably even said yourself, "It is what it is." But even this statement implies a certain amount of social consensus that you and at least one other person agree upon what you consider to be objective reality. Upon examination, however, what if other people enter the picture and argue, "It is *not* what you have determined it is?" It is only when people give meaning to what is happening around them that their reality comes into existence. Although giving meaning to an event seems highly personal and something that takes place within an individual's mind (as we have been encouraged to believe from psychology), giving meaning to human activities is an inherently social process. Many Americans have grown up with the old adage that at least two things in life are certain: death and taxes. But let's examine that expression for a moment, starting with death. What is death? At one time in American society, the difference between life and death was determined by whether or not a person was breathing. Literally, if a person could not fog a mirror held up to their nose and mouth, they were pronounced dead. Later, with the advent of the stethoscope, it was discovered that a person could stop breathing, but still be alive. The determination of death was dependent on the heart still beating. Once a person's heart stopped, they were dead. Lo and behold, however, we learned that a person's heart could stop and then be restarted; hence, they were still alive. Today, it is a fairly common operation to remove the heart from a living patient and replace it with one harvested from a dead one, or, in some cases, to implant a mechanical heart that will continue to beat long after a person is pronounced dead, as life and death today are linked to brain functioning and cellular growth rather than to heartbeat. In other words, the meaning of death has changed significantly over time, and thousands if not millions of people pronounced legally "dead" in earlier times would be considered "alive" by present standards. Death "is what it is," but as former President Bill Clinton once infamously opined, "It depends on what your definition of *is* is." Although it is true, at least today, that everybody dies, determining if and when that happens is very much a social process involving medical personnel, family members, and sometimes attorneys, judges, and the United States Congress. As for taxes, millions of people do not pay taxes, or at least not the amount of taxes they owe. Sociological wisdom tells us that more often than not, *things are not what they seem*.

"Remember, Stevens, things are rarely what they appear to be."

SOCIOLOGICAL WISDOM

Sociological wisdom is based on applying the basic principles of sociology to the world around us. *Sociology* is the systematic and scientific study of human behavior, social groups, and society (Thompson, Hickey, and Thompson 2019). Sociologists examine structural and institutional forces that shape our everyday lives, behaviors, and social values, and look at how we help create those social structures and institutions.

Sociology is an academic discipline, but this does not mean that it is simply "a thing to be studied. . . . Sociology is, first of all, a thing lived" (Lemert 2012:xv). Perhaps sociologist Peter Berger (1963:4) said it best when he wrote, "Sociology is not a practice but *an attempt to understand*." This requires that sociologists look at everyday events a little differently from the way most people view them.

Do you sometimes enjoy the peace and solitude of being alone? At other times do you like being with other people, celebrating your achievements or sharing your concerns? If you are like most people, the answer to both questions is probably "Yes." Although all of us enjoy some time alone, we also need and actively seek the company and security of other people. We congregate to establish families, groups, tribes, communities, nations, and many other organizations, some of which transcend national boundaries. This *social imperative* sets us apart from other animals, and though it is survival related, it transcends biological or instinctive drives to cluster for survival. As we form collectivities, we make both conscious and unconscious choices to sacrifice some of our individual freedoms, but at the same time we derive many social benefits from the process. This interdependence between society and the individual is the primary focus of sociology, and understanding it requires the development of a *sociological imagination*—a quality of mind that provides an understanding of ourselves within the context of the larger society (Mills 1959).

THE SOCIOLOGICAL IMAGINATION

We can better see the relationship between ourselves and the society in which we live by using our sociological imaginations. Sociologist C. Wright Mills (1959) contended this requires that we grasp the connection between *history* (events that have shaped an entire society's values and beliefs) and *biography* (an individual's life experiences within a particular society). This important link is often overlooked, but it is essential for sociological understanding because it places individual behavior in a larger social context. It reminds us that we, as individuals, are to some extent *products* of the particular society and historical period in which we live, but also acknowledges that we are *history makers* who help produce and change society by our actions. We can only guess what would have happened to the Civil Rights movement of the 1960s if the late Rosa Parks had given up her seat to the white man and moved to the back of the bus in Montgomery, Alabama, in 1955; or what might have transpired if she had refused to do so 30 years earlier, in the 1920s. Sociology teaches us that everything, from the most heroic and spectacular actions to the most mundane and taken-for-granted features of our existence, reflects the dynamic interplay between the individual and society.

Our sociological imagination allows us to see the important relationship between *personal troubles*, which affect an individual (e.g., being addicted to painkillers), and *social issues*, which reflect a problem for the entire society (e.g., the national opioid crisis) (Mills 1959). This distinction is a critical component of sociology because it enables us to see the *general* in the *particular* (Berger 1963). Sociologists study patterns of behavior in order to draw general conclusions about a social issue that transcend the effect of the problem or issue on any particular individual. For example, although painkiller addiction may have devastating consequences for the addict and their immediate family, sociology focuses on the larger problem of both legal and illegal drugs and their impact on society. This is not to say that sociologists are unconcerned about individuals and their lives, but sociology's emphasis is on the way individuals relate to others, people's positions in society, and the interdependence between society and individuals.

One goal of sociologists is to identify and understand general patterns of social behavior by studying the actions of specific individuals and groups. As a result of sociological studies, we know that nationality, race, age, gender, social class, sexual orientation, political preference, religion, and a host of other social factors greatly affect our viewpoints and actions. In making generalizations, however, we must be careful not to fall prey to overgeneralizations and inaccurate *stereotypes* (oversimplified ideas about a group) that can seriously distort our thinking and cloud our understanding. Consider some of the ways we think about and act toward people based on their race, age, sex, social class, and other characteristics, and how these thoughts and actions can be potentially damaging and even dangerous. Many of our stereotypes come from the mass media, especially television. Stereotypes also come from our myopic view of the world. The sociological imagination and locating individuals in a larger social context require us to understand that we live in a global society.

LIFE IN A GLOBAL SOCIETY

One of the most significant social consequences of the twentieth century was the transformation of a world of separate nation-states with unique histories, cultures, and social experiences into a massive global village. In the sixteenth century, the Portuguese navigator Ferdinand Magellan led a Spanish expedition that was the first to circumnavigate the globe. The treacherous journey took approximately three years. Today, ships can make the same journey in less than a week, and airplanes in less than 24 hours; communication satellites orbit the earth in less than two hours and send electronic signals around the world in seconds. In the time it takes most people to read this paragraph, 6 million texts can be sent via smartphones worldwide. Time is now measured in nanoseconds.

The world has changed, and understanding the nature of these changes is essential for developing a sociological understanding of our lives as well as the world around us. Nowhere is that change more apparent and powerful than in our ability to communicate information, transport people, and move huge sums of capital around the globe quickly. *Globalization* refers to the interconnectedness among people around the world. It is a "process whereby goods, information, people, money, communication, and fashion (as well as other forms of culture) move across national boundaries" (Eitzen and Baca Zinn 2011:1). Technological advances in communication, transportation, importation, and exportation have rendered the ideology and policies of *social isolationism* not only ridiculous, but also impossible. As one sociologist noted, globalization changes everything: "some social things may be reshaped or threatened . . . they can't any longer be taken for granted" (Lemert 2012:181).

Look around you. Two of the most popular brands of Japanese automobiles, Toyota and Honda, are manufactured in Ohio and Kentucky, whereas many General Motors cars are made from parts manufactured in Mexico and Canada. The bestselling American athletic shoes, Nike, are headquartered in Oregon but made in China and Indonesia. Designer clothes with European labels are made in Central and South America, as are some of the least expensive brands sold under American labels in huge discount stores in the United States. Harley Davidson, America's most iconic motorcycle, has manufacturing plants in six different countries, with plans to expand internationally.

The recognition that we live in a global society is an integral part of thinking sociologically and developing our sociological imaginations—that is, understanding ourselves in a larger social context. Global awareness also helps us to question cultural misconceptions and media stereotypes about people who live in countries with cultures very different from our own. It accentuates diversity and helps us challenge views that our particular way of doing things is the only way, or even the best way, of doing them. Although some social scientists support the *convergence hypothesis*, assuming that globalization is causing different cultures to continually become more alike, others emphasize that we must recognize that among cultures, and even within cultures, there remains a great deal of diversity (Domosh et al. 2011).

Imagine a world where everybody is exactly the same: everyone looks alike, acts alike, talks alike, and thinks alike. What a simple and uninteresting world it would be. Although it may sometimes be comforting to be around people with similar backgrounds and interests, the world is far more complex than that. We live in a world where variety is indeed the "spice of life." Globalization has increased mobility, providing in many places a social mosaic of people from different racial and ethnic backgrounds, nationalities, religions, and cultures.

How does this diversity affect you and me? It requires that we look at ourselves and the world in which we live a bit differently. Sociological research indicates that although most Americans acknowledge the importance of diversity, popular conceptions of it are ambiguous and reflect "political correctness" more than understanding (Bell and Hartmann 2007). We must realize that complex social issues cannot be viewed in simple terms of *right* or *wrong*, *black* or *white*, and *good* or *evil*, but require that we understand and consider other values, points of view, and ways of life that may be dramatically different from our own. Just as sociology makes generalizations about how common powerful social forces act on all of us, it also recognizes the importance of diversity for understanding social interaction and human society.

Sociologists are interested in how variables such as age, race, sex, and social class, as well as a host of other social characteristics, influence social interaction and shape the society in which we live. These and other aspects of social diversity are at the heart of the sociological enterprise. This appreciation for diversity quashes numerous misconceptions and stereotypes about various categories and groups of people, and leads us to question many aspects of social life often taken for granted. Questioning "common-sense" understandings is at the heart of sociology and sociological thinking.

Thinking sociologically is a form of *critical thinking* that involves objectively assessing ideas, statements, and information. It entails defining problems, looking beneath the surface of commonly held ideas, questioning assumptions, logically and systematically analyzing evidence, recognizing biases, avoiding emotional knee-jerk reactions to issues and arguments, forming reasonable solutions to problems, and developing tolerance for a certain amount of uncertainty and ambiguity (Ruggiero 2014). Simply put, *sociological wisdom* involves asking questions and questioning answers. It requires taking a closer and more critical look at our social world.

The subject of sociology is people and what we do in groups, organizations, and societies—subject matter familiar to all of us. Unfortunately, much of our understanding of the social world is individualized and limited to personal experience, hearsay, and our preconceived notions about the way we think things are and the way we might want them to be. Sociology looks beyond the commonly accepted understandings of human social action to discover different levels of meaning that may be hidden from the consciousness of everyday life. It may even require a bit of suspicion and skepticism about the way human events are interpreted both personally and officially.

This sometimes creates a problem for sociologists. If they study a commonly experienced social institution such as the family, for example, and find that children tend to adopt the religious and political views of their parents, many people respond with a resounding "So what? Everybody knows that." On the other hand, if sociological findings contradict a commonly held assumption—for example, when they reveal that child molestation is more likely to be perpetrated by a family member or a close friend of the family than by a stranger—they are likely to be met with skepticism, disbelief, or even anger. As one sociologist noted, applying sociological wisdom may make you "a rude, improper guest who crashes someone else's well-planned party" (Lemert 2012:224).

This "damned if you do, damned if you don't" dilemma is faced by virtually all who undertake the sociological enterprise. The study of sociology does not require that we abandon our values, thoughts, ideas, and accumulated knowledge, but it does necessitate being open-minded and tolerant of values, thoughts, ideas, knowledge, and experiences that may be dramatically different from our own. This allows us to see the *strange* in the *familiar*—an important aspect of thinking sociologically. This is not to say that sociologists are interested only in the bizarre or sensational aspects of human life. Quite the contrary. The sociologist is as interested in the priest as in the thief, in the hero as in the mass murderer, in the executioner as in the death row inmate (Berger 1963). But when we study these people and their roles sociologically—that is, systematically and scientifically—we find that many of our preconceived notions are inaccurate and that much of what passes for *common sense* is nothing more than *common nonsense*. Sociology differs from everyday observation because it uses systematic, scientific methods to obtain information for research and study. Sociological thinking requires looking beneath the surface to question what we think we already know about people and their roles in society. When we do this, more often than not we find that *things are not what they seem*.

Analyzing assumptions and challenging personal experiences can be quite unsettling; sociology often raises more questions than it answers. Those who demand concrete answers and absolute certainties may become frustrated with sociology. Those who enjoy the search for elusive answers to the riddles of social life, however, will find sociology very appealing.

Sociological wisdom also demands that we look beyond common-sense assumptions, media portrayals, and official data, to assess critically how such information is reported, collected, and interpreted. Any attempt to think sociologically about contemporary society must include a focus on mass media, social media, and new information technologies.

These media not only reflect our society but also play an important role in shaping and defining it. Now, more than ever, we need the critical thinking skills of sociology to analyze the "lies, distortions, and calculated fantasies" that have become part of "the normal content of mass communication" (Connell 2000:214).

We have emphasized the importance of critical thinking and realizing *things are not what they seem*. It is important, however, that we also stress that in order to have a happy, healthy life, there are times you need to look at something and say, "It is what it is." It is almost impossible to maintain healthy relationships if you are constantly looking at them through a critical eye. If you think that everybody is trying to deceive you, has ulterior motives, and cannot be trusted, you will find it difficult to develop and maintain meaningful relationships. Skepticism is good; too much crosses a line and becomes cynicism. This is one of the hardest parts of being a sociological thinker. You have to know how to adjust your sociological filter when dealing with your personal life. In the words of former president Ronald Reagan, "Trust, but verify."

COMMON SENSE VERSUS COMMON NONSENSE

It is surprising how many ideas that seem to reflect common sense are factually wrong. Sociologists have found that many widely held beliefs about the world, other people, and even ourselves are based on preconception, not fact. When sociologists take a look beneath the surface of our taken-for-granted world, we find that much of what passes for "common-sense" understandings in our society is nothing more than common nonsense. Here are a few examples:

Common (Non)sense: Following the adage that "Two heads are better than one," the more people in a group, the better decisions that group is likely to make because more alternatives will be considered.

Fact: Groups often become subject to *groupthink*, whereby the strong desire for consensus and group harmony causes members to ignore alternative solutions and go along with the group.

Common (Non)sense: The majority of people on welfare are members of minorities who have been on welfare for generations and are too lazy to get a job.

Fact: The largest category of welfare recipients comprises female heads of households with young children, and most of them have been on welfare for less than two years.

Common (Non)sense: The United States provides equal educational opportunities for everyone regardless of race, ethnicity, or socioeconomic status.

Fact: Members of racial and ethnic minorities and the poor still suffer from unequal and inadequate educational opportunities in many parts of the United States.

Common (Non)sense: In national elections in the United States, most voters vote, and winning candidates are elected by a majority of voters.

Fact: Often fewer than half of registered voters vote in national elections; although winners typically receive a majority of votes cast, they are usually elected by a minority of eligible voters and sometimes even by a minority of those who cast votes, as was the case in the 2000 and 2016 presidential elections, in which the losing candidates lost the electoral college but received the most popular votes.

These are but a few examples of how so-called common sense may be nothing more than common nonsense. Examples like these and countless others emphasize why, although some forms of common sense may be important for our everyday lives, it is important that we turn to science for facts and information that can help us better understand the world in which we live.

THE IMPORTANCE OF SCIENCE

Writings of philosophers, poets, and religious leaders of the ancient civilizations of Babylon, Egypt, India, and other parts of the world reflect substantial interest in interpreting social life. Most of the early writers, however, were less concerned with discovering what society *was* than with describing what it *should be*. Although social thinkers had long pondered the influence of society on human behavior, and the tenets of sociology probably have been practiced informally since humans first appeared, the term *sociology* was not coined, and the formal discipline of sociology did not emerge, until the early nineteenth century. Sociology was born in France, gained impetus in Great Britain and Germany, and eventually made its way to the United States as each of these countries experienced radical changes in social conditions and the intellectual explanations for them.

Prior to the Industrial Revolution, European society was characterized by a feudal system consisting of wealthy landowners (lords), who owned huge manors, and large numbers of peasants (serfs), who tilled the land and were thus economically tied to the lords and their manors for subsistence. As the lords died, were displaced, or drove one another off their lands, the manors were divided into small farms tilled by their new owners and their families, and small villages with an emerging merchant class developed as important economic centers and social communities.

One of the driving forces that led to the development of sociology in Europe was the dramatic social upheaval linked to the processes of *industrialization, urbanization*, and *immigration*. With the advent of new technology, especially steam-driven machines, factories developed, luring people from small villages and the less productive farms to more centralized locations to work for the new factory owners. Thus, *industrialization*, the transformation from a predominantly agriculture-based economy to a manufacturing one, was accompanied by rapid *urbanization*, the growth of large cities. These two factors were accompanied by massive waves of *immigration*, as increased mobility encouraged people to cross political borders to escape oppressive conditions or pursue perceived opportunities elsewhere.

New problems emerged, such as inadequate housing; inordinate wealth juxtaposed with abject poverty; crime; air, water, and noise pollution; and disease. Moreover, wherever industrialization, urbanization, and immigration have occurred, they have been linked to enhanced political awareness and demands for greater political, economic, and social participation. Consequently, nineteenth-century Europeans experiencing dramatic social upheaval sought explanations for, and workable solutions to, the day-to-day problems they were experiencing.

Scholars often describe the eighteenth century as the *Age of Reason* or the *Age of Enlightenment*, because during this time Western culture emerged into a new era of social thought. Over several centuries, and as a result of much struggle, the dominant way of explaining social events shifted from *theological* to *scientific*. Rather than attribute human behavior and social conditions to supernatural forces, people searched for logical, rational, and cause-and-effect explanations. As a result, universities replaced the church as the primary source of knowledge. The works of several nineteenth-century scholars provided the foundation for contemporary sociology. One of the first was Auguste Comte, often credited with being the founder of sociology.

Auguste Comte (1798–1857) grew up in the aftermath of the French Revolution. Observing the social turmoil of his native country, he believed the new scientific approach to problem solving that was sweeping Europe might also be applied to the study of society. He coined the term *sociology* and wrote *Positive Philosophy*, the first systematic sociological approach to the study of society. Comte's new science emphasized *positivism*, the use of observation, comparison, experimentation, and the historical method to analyze society.

Comte envisioned sociology as being much more than an intellectual enterprise. He dreamed of a utopian society fine-tuned by social engineers (sociologists) who would apply sociological knowledge to cure society's ills. In his later years, his devotion to sociology became so intense that he envisioned it almost as a religion, with sociologists the "high priests of positivism." Although later sociologists tempered Comte's idealistic and zealous vision, most continue to believe in sociology's promise as a vehicle for positive social change.

Harriet Martineau (1802–1876) grew up in England. Because she was raised in a Unitarian family, Martineau was better educated than typical women in British society of her time (Lengermann, Madoo, and Neibrugge 1985; Lengermann, Madoo, and Wallace 2007). In 1853, she translated Comte's six-volume *Positive Philosophy* into English and condensed it into two volumes, thus introducing sociology to England (Webb 1960). Although Martineau is most often referred to by scholars of the past as simply Comte's translator, she made her own contribution to sociology with *Society in America* (1837), one of the first and most thorough sociological treatises on American social life and one of the first to compare the system of social stratification in Europe to that in America. Because of her sociological work describing, explaining, and evaluating social norms, she is an important—yet often overlooked—founder of sociology. She took sociology from the realm of ideas to the arena of practice in *How to Observe Manners and Morals*, published in 1838 and one of the first books to focus on sociological research methods. In this writing, Martineau ([1838] 2015) looks at the patterns of behavior in society and the ideas behind those actions. She was a radical thinker who wanted progress, especially in the form of equality for women. Although Martineau introduced sociology to England, it was Herbert Spencer's controversial application of sociology that gained attention and support from wealthy industrialists and government officials in England and throughout Europe.

Observing the negative aspects of the Industrial Revolution in England—the struggle, competition, and violence—Herbert Spencer (1820–1903) developed a theoretical approach to understanding society that relied on evolutionary doctrine. To explain both social structure and social changes, he used an *organic analogy* that compared society to a living organism made up of interdependent parts—ideas that ultimately contributed to the structural functionalist perspective in sociology. Using the phrase "survival of the fittest" even before Charles Darwin's landmark *On the Origin of Species* ([1859] 1964) was published, Spencer's *social Darwinism* concluded that the evolution of society and the survival of those within it were directly linked to their ability to adapt to changing conditions. According to Spencer, a free and competitive marketplace without governmental interference was essential so that the best and the brightest would succeed and in turn help build a stronger economy and society. Spencer opposed welfare or any other means of helping the weak or the poor, believing such efforts would weaken society in the long term by helping the "unfit" to survive. These ideas appealed to wealthy industrialists and government officials, who used Spencer's theory to scientifically support policies and practices that helped them maintain their wealth, power, and prestige at the expense of those less fortunate.

Karl Marx (1818–1883) was trained in history, economics, and philosophy, but his ideas reflect sociological thinking. Observing the same social conditions as Spencer, he drew very different conclusions about their origins. Marx declared that the unequal distribution of wealth, power, and other limited resources in society was not the result of "natural laws," but was caused by social forces—specifically, the exploitation of one social class by another. He insisted that social structure and the political and economic institutions that people took for granted were not the result of natural evolution or social consensus, but reflected the opposed interests of different social classes.

Marx believed society consisted of two basic social classes: the "haves" and the "have-nots." According to Marx's viewpoint, the *bourgeoisie* (haves), the powerful ruling class, had assumed power not because they were the "fittest," but because they owned and controlled the means of production. He believed the bourgeoisie used deception, fraud, and violence to usurp the production of the *proletariat* (have-nots), or working class, whose labor created most of society's goods—and hence its profits.

Marx was not a detached social observer, but an outspoken social critic. He concluded that a slow, natural evolutionary process would not bring about necessary social changes. Rather, his analysis called for a major social revolution in which the proletariat would rise up, forcibly overthrow the bourgeoisie, and form a new, classless society. In such a society, Marx wrote, everyone would contribute according to their abilities and receive from society based on need. Marx's contributions to sociological understanding provided the foundation for the *conflict perspective* in sociology. Marx's focus on social conflict was unsettling to many—especially those whom he described as the bourgeoisie. They were relieved when Émile Durkheim's more palatable social analysis emerged and shifted the focus of sociology back to the more conservative approach of *structural functionalism*.

Unlike Marx, who focused on social conflict, French sociologist Émile Durkheim (1858–1917) was primarily concerned with social order. He believed that *social solidarity*, or the social bonds developed by individuals to their society, create social order. Durkheim believed that social solidarity could be categorized into two types: *mechanical solidarity*, the type found in simple rural societies based on tradition and unity, and *organic solidarity*, which was found in urban societies and was based more on a complex division of labor and formal organizations.

One of Durkheim's most important contributions to sociology was his study *Suicide* ([1897] 1951), which demonstrated that abstract sociological theories can be applied to a very real social problem. More important, it showed that suicide, believed to be a private, individualized, and personal act, can best be explained from a sociological viewpoint. By looking at suicide rates instead of individual suicides, Durkheim linked suicide to *social integration*—the extent to which individuals feel they are a meaningful part of society. Those with the strongest social bonds are less likely to commit suicide than those who are less meaningfully integrated and have weaker social bonds. For example, his data demonstrated that married people had lower suicide rates than those who were single or divorced; people in the workforce had lower rates than those who were unemployed; and church members had lower rates than nonmembers. Moreover, those religions that promote the strongest social bonds among their members (e.g., Catholicism and Judaism) had much lower suicide rates than less structured religions (e.g., Protestantism). Today, over a century later, these patterns in suicide, and others discerned by Durkheim's early study, still persist.

Max Weber (1864–1920), a contemporary of Durkheim, was concerned that many sociologists, especially his fellow German Karl Marx, allowed their personal values to influence their theories and research. Weber insisted that sociologists should be *value-free*—analyzing what society is rather than what they think it should be. Weber did not advocate a cold, impersonal approach to sociology, however; he argued that understanding the meaning of social interaction requires *Verstehen*, an empathetic and introspective analysis of the interaction. In other words, Weber believed that researchers should avoid their personal biases and put themselves in the place of those they study, to understand better how they experience the world and society's impact on them.

One of Weber's most important contributions to sociology was his concept of the *ideal type*, a conceptual model or typology constructed from the direct observation of a number of specific cases and representing the essential qualities found in those cases. By ideal type, Weber was referring to a generalization based on many specific examples, not implying that something was necessarily desirable. For example, Weber used bureaucracy as an ideal type to analyze and explain the increasing rationalization and depersonalization that is part of formal organizations. Weber contended that to maximize efficiency, formal organizations such as private businesses, educational institutions, and governmental agencies had become, and would continue to be, increasingly bureaucratic. Although Weber contended that bureaucracy as an ideal type represented the most rational and efficient organizational strategy, he also warned of its depersonalizing and dehumanizing aspects.

As in Europe, the onset of rapid industrialization and urbanization, and the accompanying social problems, gave impetus to the development of sociology in the United States. American sociologists built on and expanded the theories and ideas of the European founders of sociology.

Lester Ward (1841–1913) is often considered the first systematic American sociologist. He attempted to synthesize the major theoretical ideas of Comte and Spencer, and differentiated between what he called *pure sociology*—the study of society in an effort to understand and explain the natural laws that govern its evolution—and *applied sociology*, using sociological principles, social ideals, and ethical considerations to improve society. The distinctions between these two areas of sociology are still made today.

William E. B. Dubois (1868–1963) earned his doctorate from Harvard and pursued postgraduate study in sociology, history, and economics at the University of Berlin, where he studied under Max Weber. After returning to the United States, Dubois applied Weber's methodological technique of *Verstehen* to sociological studies of blacks in the United States. He is considered the founder of "Afro-American sociology." Dubois was also one of the founders of the National Association for the Advancement of Colored People (NAACP), where he applied his theories, empirical research, and sociological imagination to empower African Americans to achieve social justice and equality in the United States.

Sociology came of age in America during the 1920s, 1930s, and 1940s—a period of radical social change that included the Roaring Twenties, the Great Depression, and World War II. During that period, some of the most prominent sociologists and social psychologists of the twentieth century were either faculty members or students in the first sociology department in the United States, at the University of Chicago. They used Chicago as a dynamic sociological laboratory to observe and analyze the social scientific impact of urbanization and industrialization.

The theoretical and methodological contributions of these scholars became known as the *Chicago School*, and provided sociology with symbolic interactionism, one of the major *theoretical perspectives*—a viewpoint or particular way of looking at things—that dominate sociology today. The others are structural functionalism, conflict, and feminist. These overriding perspectives serve as *paradigms*, sets of scientific theories that guide research questions, methods of analysis and interpretation, and the development of theory.

Although science seemed to be on a perpetual ascending trajectory, and is perhaps more important in understanding today's world than ever, there always have been some "bumps in the road" in some social arenas. There has always been some antagonism between science and religion as the one requires observable facts and data while the other demands faith in beliefs. Today, there are some startling examples of distrust in scientific knowledge, as celebrities, politicians, various interest groups, and others weigh in with unscientific opinions on scientific matters such as global climate change, renewable resources, sexual orientation, and reproduction. Shockingly, despite all of the evidence to the contrary, there are still those who insist that the earth is flat!

Science is not dead, however, and despite ideological commitments to the contrary, in the end, scientific facts remain important. Sociology is a social science and as such relies heavily on scientific theories and research. Let's take a closer look at each of the theoretical perspectives introduced earlier and compare their relative strengths and weaknesses.

THE STRUCTURAL FUNCTIONALIST PERSPECTIVE

Heavily influenced by the ideas of Comte, Spencer, and Durkheim, the structural functionalist perspective focuses on a *macro-level analysis*, which examines broader social structures and society as a whole. This perspective emphasizes social structure and order. Often referred to as the functionalist perspective, or functionalism, the *structural functionalist perspective* views society as a system of interdependent and interrelated parts. Within the overall *structure* of the system, each part fulfills a specific *function*, which thereby contributes to the overall functioning of the entire system.

The structural functionalist perspective contends that society has a *structure* consisting of a variety of important components—for example, basic social institutions such as the family, religion, education, politics, and the economy. These institutions are interrelated and interdependent. Each performs an important *function* contributing to the overall structure of society. A problem in one area creates a problem for the entire system, and for society to function properly, all social institutions must fulfill their basic functions. When all aspects of society are functioning properly, they are in a state of *social equilibrium*, or balance. In addition to the emphasis on structure, three basic concepts of the structural functionalist perspective are manifest functions, latent functions, and dysfunctions.

Contemporary sociologists who use the structural functionalist perspective differentiate between *manifest functions*, the anticipated or intended consequences of social institutions, and *latent functions*, or the unintended or unrecognized consequences of social institutions. As an example of the two, let's consider public schools. Their obvious manifest function is to transmit knowledge and prepare students for life in a complex industrial society. They also serve a variety of latent functions. For instance, though usually unacknowledged, America's public school system serves as one of the largest socialized daycare systems in the world.

From the functionalist perspective, some aspects of society are viewed as *dysfunctional* because they threaten to disrupt social stability and order. It is important to note that "functional" and "dysfunctional" do not represent value judgments and are not synonymous with "good" and "bad." Crime can be viewed as dysfunctional in that it threatens social order, hurts people, and costs society a lot of money. But functionalists point out that crime is also functional. For example, laws are reinforced when criminals are caught and punished, and crime creates many jobs in law enforcement and related careers.

An alternative macro-level analysis of society and human behavior is the conflict perspective. Whereas the structural functionalist perspective focuses on balance, harmony, and cooperation, the conflict perspective sees societal structure as much more diverse and characterized by competition and conflict. The turbulent times of the 1960s and early 1970s revived an interest in the ideas of Karl Marx and gave impetus to the conflict perspective in sociology.

THE CONFLICT PERSPECTIVE

The assassinations of President John F. Kennedy, Robert Kennedy, and Dr. Martin Luther King Jr., along with the Civil Rights movement, the women's movement, the Vietnam War, and rising crime and poverty rates in major cities, focused renewed attention on the problems of urban industrial America. The United States was in a state of social upheaval, as were many other countries, and people were seeking answers to sociological questions. Interactionism's emphasis on micro-level issues and functionalism's focus on stability and order seemed inadequate. Problems of racism, poverty, crime, and delinquency threatened the very fabric of the society, and their negative consequences were felt around the world.

The conflict perspective views society as composed of diverse groups with conflicting values and interests. In any society, these groups have differential access to wealth, power, and prestige. The most important aspects of the conflict perspective are the Marxian approach, which focuses on economic determinism and the importance of social class, and the neo-conflict approach, which focuses on differential power and authority.

The theoretical roots of the conflict perspective can be traced to Karl Marx. Often, the values and interests of different groups conflict with one another. According to Marx, these conflicts are determined by economics and are based on social class, and the struggle between the different values and interests of the bourgeoisie and the proletariat is inevitable. When these battles occur, the dominant group attempts to force its values and ideology on less powerful groups. The result is the domination and exploitation of the masses (the proletariat) by the rich and powerful members of society (the bourgeoisie). The conflict perspective is not solely Marxist sociology, however; today, conflict theorists often take a neo-conflict approach.

Social conflict can be viewed as a necessary and even functional social process. From this perspective, conflict necessitates negotiation and compromise; hence, it can produce order and a reaffirmation of the social structure. In a diverse nation such as the United States, conflict between racial, ethnic, religious, age, gender, and political groups is inevitable, but not necessarily destructive. For example, attempts to balance the national budget have typically been thwarted by bickering over which areas of the budget should be increased and which should be cut. Those dependent on Medicare and Social Security resist cuts to those programs and would rather see cuts in, for example, the defense budget or federal aid to tobacco growers. Meanwhile, Pentagon officials and cigarette manufacturers are not about to sit back and allow legislators to balance the budget at their expense. Both sides employ powerful lobbyists to persuade legislators to vote for their relative interests. These political and ideological quarrels are marked by compromises or trade-offs that may not satisfy either group but also do not allow one interest to totally dominate the other. When society is confronted by an external threat, these internal conflicts may decrease, for, as is often said, nothing unites a group like a common enemy. From this perspective, conflict is dysfunctional only if it threatens one or more of society's core values (Coser 1956).

Neo-conflict theorists also contend that class conflict in industrialized countries is not so much a struggle over the means of production (as Marx argued) as a result of the unequal distribution of authority (Dahrendorf 1959). For example, the differing power and prestige of college professors and students sometimes lead to tension and conflict between the two groups that has nothing to do with the ownership of property or the means of production. This version of the conflict perspective focuses on differences in power and authority and the exploitation of some groups by other, more powerful groups. A good example of this approach can be seen in the work of C. Wright Mills.

C. Wright Mills promoted the conflict perspective for analyzing the distribution of power and authority in the United States. In *The Power Elite* (1956), he contended that its post–World War II society was dominated by a powerful military, industrial, and political elite that shaped foreign and domestic policy for the benefit of the wealthy and powerful class. His approach focused on historical and structural analyses of class conflict and the uses of ideology for domination.

THE FEMINIST PERSPECTIVE

Gender experiences define and shape social analysis of a situation; hence the birth of *feminist theory*, which studies, analyzes, and explains social phenomena from a gender-focused perspective. This approach emphasizes the importance of gender for understanding society and social relationships. Feminist theories reflect and synthesize much of the rich diversity among other theoretical perspectives in sociology, especially the conflict perspective (Beasley 1999; Chafetz 1997; Delamont 2003; Kolmar and Bartkowski 2013; Tong 2017). For years before feminist theory was cultivated, males described female life and situations from a male perspective. The importance of gender was overlooked, and universal truths were prescribed to social analysis based on a patriarchal hierarchy. Feminist theory studies the ongoing social meanings of gender and questions commonly accepted definitions and symbols of femininity and masculinity. Sociologists who use feminist theory emphasize that gender is incorporated into the basic social structure of every society. They also study how traditional gender roles and sexism function to maintain the status quo in most societies, yet may be dysfunctional in the way they inhibit some people from achieving their full potential. One of the "hottest" topics among feminist scholars focuses on "the intersection of race, class, and gender" (Chafetz 1997:115). Feminist theory, like the conflict perspective, draws on the historical and contemporary subordination of women and analyzes differential power and authority and the exploitation of one group by another based on gender. Shifting the focus of sociology away from a male-dominated view of the world, feminist theory has emerged as an important theoretical tool for analyzing all aspects of society, but especially in understanding problems of gender inequality, poverty, domestic abuse, pornography, sexual harassment, and violence.

THE SYMBOLIC INTERACTIONIST PERSPECTIVE

The *symbolic interactionist perspective* views social meaning as arising through the process of social interaction. According to Blumer (1969b:2), contemporary symbolic interactionism rests on three basic premises. First, human beings act toward things on the basis of the meanings that they attach to them. Second, these meanings are derived from, or arise out of, social interaction with others. Third, these meanings may be changed or modified through the processes of interaction and interpretation.

Proponents of this perspective engage in *micro-level analysis*, which focuses on the day-to-day interactions of individuals and groups in specific social situations. Three major concepts important for understanding this theoretical approach include meaningful symbols, the definition of the situation, and the looking-glass self. In addition, two important types of theoretical analysis fit within the interactionist perspective: dramaturgical analysis and the labeling approach.

George H. Mead (1863–1931) insisted that the ongoing process of social interaction and the creating, defining, and redefining of meaningful symbols make society possible. *Meaningful symbols* are sounds, objects, colors, and events that represent something other than themselves, and are critical for understanding social interaction. Language is one of the most important and powerful meaningful symbols humans have created, because it allows us to communicate through the shared meaning of words.

Definition of the situation refers to the idea that "if [people] define situations as real, they are real in their consequences" (Thomas and Thomas 1928:572). Simply put, people define social reality through a process of give-and-take interaction. Once a definition is established, it shapes all further interactions. For example, have you ever decided that you were "in love" with someone? If so, how did that change the way you interacted with that person? Conversely, what happens when a married couple decides they are no longer in love? If they define their marriage as meaningless or decide they have irreconcilable differences, how does that affect their relationship? Is a marriage likely to survive if one or both partners have defined it as "over"?

The *looking-glass self* refers to the idea that an individual's self-concept is largely a reflection of how they are perceived by other members of society (Cooley [1902] 1922). Society is used as a mirror to reflect a feeling of self-pride, self-doubt, self-worth, or self-loathing. These important elements of symbolic interactionism contribute to socialization and the process of becoming human as we establish our personal and social identities.

A useful theoretical framework within symbolic interactionism, *dramaturgical analysis* uses the analogy of the theater to analyze social behavior. In this approach, people are viewed as actors occupying roles as they play out life's drama. In real life, people do not passively accept others' definitions of the situation or the social identities assigned to them.

Rather, they take an active part in the drama, manipulating the interaction to present themselves in the most positive light. Thus, people often use *impression management* to communicate favorable impressions of themselves (Goffman 1959). Another theoretical viewpoint within symbolic interactionism is the *labeling approach*, which contends that people attach various labels to certain behaviors, individuals, and groups that become part of their social identity and shape others' attitudes about and responses to them.

SOCIOLOGICAL WISDOM: TAKING AN INTEGRATED APPROACH

In our view, sociological wisdom can be achieved only by taking an integrated approach to sociology that encompasses all of the major theoretical perspectives, as well as drawing on theories and ideas from other academic disciplines. All of the major sociological paradigms are valid ways of analyzing society, and, alone or in combination, they enhance our sociological imaginations and understanding of human social behavior.

Because of different assumptions and approaches, the weaknesses of one perspective are often the strengths of the others. Also, because of their different approaches to society and human behavior, one perspective may be more helpful than another, depending on what you wish to study. For example, structural functionalism is very useful in studying social structure and social institutions such as family, education, religion, politics, and the economy. Yet, its focus on structure, stability, harmony, and equilibrium, along with its emphasis on predictability and "natural laws" that govern society, tends to ignore the importance of diversity and how social variables such as race, ethnicity, gender, and social class may lead to potential tension and conflict among groups. The conflict perspective emphasizes the struggles for power among various classes and groups of people and helps explain social inequality in the social structure. Yet, it tends to ignore the importance of day-to-day and face-to-face interaction—especially the tremendous amount of daily cooperation and harmony among diverse groups and individuals as they interact. These phenomena are the focus of symbolic interactionism, which lends itself to the study of social issues at the micro level. Feminist theory focuses on interpretation of situations based on gender, a status relative to all social interactions.

For the most balanced approach to sociological understanding, and to encourage you to think sociologically, we use all the major theoretical approaches throughout this book. Our goal is to help you develop your *sociological wisdom* and apply it to your everyday life rather than to promote any particular paradigm.

Sociological Wisdom 2

#AnalyzeWithYourBrainNotWithYourHeart

DOING SOCIOLOGY

CLOSE YOUR EYES. Picture a scientist conducting important research. For many, images of people, mostly males, clad in white lab coats, peering into microscopes, surrounded by beakers of bubbling chemical concoctions, come to mind. For some, almost cartoonish characters such as Dr. Frankenstein, or Christopher Lloyd's infamous Dr. Emmet Brown character in *Back to the Future*, or perhaps some of the evil protagonists from the many James Bond movies come to mind. Once again, things are not what they seem, especially if you apply the second wisdom of sociology and *analyze with your brain and not with your heart* or emotions. Contrary to popular belief, research is not something conducted only in sterile laboratories by scientists in white lab coats; sociological research may be conducted anywhere that social interaction takes place. The entire world serves as a laboratory for sociologists, and virtually any time two or more people interact, a sociological research project can be undertaken.

The goal of sociology is to reach a better understanding of the social world in which we live and, ultimately, to make it a better place. Sociologists conduct research in an effort to gain the knowledge that will contribute to achieving that goal. Our focus in this chapter is on *methodology*, the rules and guidelines followed in sociological research, and the way sociologists develop theories and gain knowledge about human behavior, groups, social interaction, and society.

HOW WE KNOW THINGS ARE NOT WHAT THEY SEEM

We have established that sociology tells us that things are not what they seem. This begs the question, "How do we know things are not what they seem?" We know by conducting scientific research. Most of us are curious about our lives and the world around us. We want to know how and why things happen. Often, we analyze our own lives in personal and emotional ways. As we become more aware that we live in a global society comprised of people from diverse racial, ethnic, religious, political, and social backgrounds, this curiosity increases because we discover that although other peoples' daily lives are dramatically different from our own, there still are many social trends and patterns that occur with remarkable regularity and predictability. Around the globe and within any particular culture, people use a variety of types of knowledge, including experience, cultural tradition, faith, authority, and science. Although sociologists use all of these forms of knowledge, science is the primary tool of the discipline.

A common way of gaining knowledge is through *experience*, which is inherently personal and emotional and relies on trial-and-error learning. When his children were young, one of the authors repeatedly told them they were free to play in the fenced-in backyard, but they should not play out in the front because they lived on a fairly busy street, and if they stepped into the street, they might be hit by a car. This warning was repeated over and again, but on occasion one of them would go out unsupervised to pick up the newspaper or get the mail. Despite their motive, they would once again be cautioned of the dangers related to the street out front. One evening the doorbell rang, and the author, accompanied by his four-year-old son, answered the door to find his neighbor standing there, holding the children's dead kitten, Harvey, in his hands. "I'm sorry. I was coming home from work, and your kitten was playing in the front yard when he suddenly darted into the street, and there was nothing I could do." The author immediately looked down at his son, wondering how he was going to explain this horrific event, realizing they had never discussed death. Much to his surprise, his young son, rather nonplussed, looked up at his father and in a matter of fact tone said, "I guess Harvey learned a valuable lesson." Trying not to laugh, the author replied, "Yes, he did," realizing that his son also had gained some valuable knowledge from that experience. Simultaneously, he was overwhelmed with emotion as he realized his neighbor could just as easily have been holding his young son in his arms with the same apology.

An old adage claims, "Experience is the best teacher." If our knowledge is limited to personal experiences, however, then it is limited indeed, for experience is the best teacher only if we cannot also find other paths to knowledge. Because experience is a very personal and individualistic, as well as an often emotional way of gaining knowledge, it is influenced by our social and cultural backgrounds. Experiential knowledge is punctuated by diversity, as people of different racial, ethnic, gender, and socioeconomic backgrounds not only experience vastly different things in life but also, more importantly, often interpret similar experiences quite differently. An individual's perspective shapes their reality, and experience is a key component in shaping one's interpretations.

A second way of gaining knowledge is through *cultural tradition*, whereby an accepted body of "facts" is passed from generation to generation. Farmers and ranchers in the American Midwest, for example, "know" that despite scientific evidence to the contrary, burning their pasturelands early each spring helps remove dead underbrush so that nutritious pasture grasses can get a better start for summer grazing. After all, their fathers did it, as did their fathers before them. Farmers in Iran, however, move their herds into the mountains during the spring and summer months, and then back onto the plains in the fall and winter, allowing nature to kill off undesirable weeds and underbrush and replenish the desirable grasses.

Many cultural traditions have far fewer practical applications. For example, in the United States, cultural tradition dictates that a groom should not see the bride before the ceremony on the day of their wedding. Many people believe that violation of this tradition will lead to bad luck and "doom" the marriage, whereas others see it as a silly superstition. Nevertheless, even those who fall into the latter category often honor the tradition—just in case.

Although cultural traditions and folklore may be modified, or even discarded, as personal experiences require, in most cultures tradition plays an important role in everyday social life. Going against accepted ways of doing things may be tolerated, but questioning or violating important cultural traditions may result in ostracism, punishment, or even death. This is most likely to occur when the cultural tradition is linked to religious beliefs.

Faith—a strong belief in "truths" that cannot be verified by personal experience—serves as an important source of knowledge in almost every culture. The smaller and more homogeneous a society, the more agreement as to what constitutes truth. The larger and more heterogeneous the population, the less agreement and hence many more different *truths, untruths, alternate truths*, and even *heresies*.

Faith goes beyond tradition, however, because it is often supported by intense emotional commitment. The belief in a supernatural being or in life after death, for example, requires faith beyond personal experience. Yet surveys show that the vast majority of Americans (approximately 80%) believe in God, the power of prayer, and an afterlife, although that percentage has declined over the past few decades (Newport 2016). Because of its emotional and moral connotations, faith is a powerful source of knowledge, and those who question it may suffer some of the most serious social consequences a society has to offer. History is replete with religious wars, inquisitions, hangings, burnings at the stake, and other forms of violence motivated by religious convictions and conflicts. In order for people to enforce their beliefs formally, they must have the support of those in positions of power and authority.

Authoritative knowledge is gained by listening to people who are recognized as authorities or experts. Authority is often linked to power; those in leadership positions may be viewed as more knowledgeable than others and can use their power to influence others. Parents usually serve as our first source of authoritative knowledge, and children often are dismayed to discover that their parents do not know everything. Elementary school–aged children often view their teachers as the ultimate source of knowledge, whereas teenagers rely more on their peers for information and advice. Adults have a much wider range of authorities to whom they can turn for answers to their questions.

In modern society, a wide variety of "experts" are considered sources of authority, and many people turn to them as the ultimate source of knowledge and truth. For medical questions, we turn to doctors, nurses,

Snapshots

"I love our lunches out here, but I always get the feeling that we're being watched."

and pharmacists; we get our weather information from certified meteorologists; we consult licensed counselors for emotional problems, and attorneys for legal advice. These experts share a common trait: their training, expertise, and credentials are linked to the rational problem-solving techniques of science and the scientific method. Yet not all who are deemed authorities in a culture have the required credentials and knowledge. In today's popular culture, people often turn to athletes and entertainers or other celebrities as experts on everything from health and wellness to marriage and child rearing. Also, some turn to *pseudo-scientific* explanations for human behavior and social issues, looking for answers through horoscopes, tea leaves, conspiracy theories, stereotypical myths and folklore, and other explanations that are assumed or alleged to be based on some type of so-called "scientific" evidence.

Science bases knowledge on empirical evidence gained through direct, systematic observation. Unlike tradition, faith, authority, and pseudo-science, scientific knowledge requires tangible evidence and *empirical verification* before it is affirmed. Experience, tradition, and faith may also require some type of verification to be widely accepted, but unlike science, they involve subjective interpretations of events that may be highly personal and emotional. Although science may also have subjective elements, the goal of scientists is to observe, measure, and interpret data as systematically and objectively as possible. Thus, science requires that we *analyze with our brain and not with our heart*. Science is built on the logic of *cause-and-effect* explanations for understanding events and an insistence that for every event that occurs (an effect), there is at least one knowable cause that precedes it.

Experience, tradition, faith, authority, and science are not mutually exclusive ways of knowing, and all of us use them at various times. For example, despite the fact that scientific thinking dominates most of the

Western world, it can be argued that scientists rely heavily on *tradition* and *experience*, and that they put a great deal of *faith* in *authority* (especially other reputable scientists). Still, the focus of science is on systematic observation, objectivity, and empirical verification. Sociology, as a science, attempts to adhere to those criteria.

SOCIOLOGY AND SCIENTIFIC KNOWLEDGE

In an effort to demonstrate their scientific credibility, social and behavioral scientists emphasize sophisticated research procedures and statistical techniques for collecting, analyzing, and interpreting data. The goal of science is to gain knowledge about a particular phenomenon in order to more accurately predict and control outcomes in certain situations. Some have argued, however, that because the subjects of sociology are free-willed, thinking human beings, their behavior cannot be predicted, much less controlled. This has led to the claim that sociology and other social and behavioral sciences are somehow inferior to the natural sciences.

Fritz Machlup (1988), former professor of economics at Princeton and New York Universities, addressed this issue by comparing the social sciences with the natural sciences on the basis of seven criteria: (1) invariability of observations, (2) objectivity of observations and explanations, (3) verifiability of hypotheses, (4) exactness of findings, (5) measurability of phenomena, (6) constancy of numerical relationships, and (7) predictability of future events. Machlup pointed out that in each of these areas it is erroneous to conclude that the social sciences are inferior to the natural sciences. Rather, it can be concluded only that the social sciences are *different* from, not inferior to, the natural sciences. And in four of the areas, the two are not even very different. With regard to invariability, verifiability, and numerical constancy, Machlup conceded that the natural sciences may be superior to the social sciences. However, he asserted that saying sociology is inferior to physics in its numerical constancy is like saying "champagne is inferior to rubbing alcohol in alcoholic content" (Machlup 1988:64). This "inferiority" refers to a particular quality, not to overall quality or other specific qualities. Machlup also pointed out that social science disciplines such as sociology may be superior to the natural sciences in predicting the future. He noted that social sciences sometimes predict human behavior accurately over long periods of time (such as Durkheim's findings in 1897 that suicide rates vary by race, marital status, gender, age, and social class, which still holds true today, over 120 years later). By contrast, the natural science of meteorology, despite its state-of-the-art scientific technology, rarely predicts the weather accurately even within a period of 24 hours.

Sociology, which once insisted that *all* human behavior is learned, is today more cognizant of the important relationships among biology, chemistry, physiology, and social behavior. This acknowledgment, along with a vast amount of research linking genetics, diet, chemical imbalances, and other variables to human social behavior, has given rise to the creation of *sociobiology*, a subfield of sociology that explores relationships between biological and environmental influences on humans. Today, most sociologists concede that the only way to understand the limitations of existing knowledge is through more interdisciplinary training and research. As a science, sociology follows many of the same systematic procedures as the natural sciences, to guide its research efforts to develop scientific theories that explain society and human behavior.

THEORY-BUILDING PROCESS

Sociological knowledge is amassed through the process of building, developing, and testing theories that attempt to explain human social behavior. A theory is much more than speculation or a hunch about how or why certain events occur. A *theory* is a set of interrelated propositions, or statements, that attempt to explain some phenomenon. It has been argued that the "acid test of the scientific status of a discipline is the quality of its theory" (Lenski 1988:163). Thus, a major goal of sociological research is to generate theories that explain human social behavior. These theories, then, "give order and insight to research activities" (Denzin 2009:5).

Building theory is a basic part of any scientific process. In sociological analysis, theory building requires critical thinking that involves both *inductive* and *deductive reasoning*. Robert Pirsig (1974:99) described the difference between inductive and deductive reasoning in *Zen and the Art of Motorcycle Maintenance:*

> Inductive reasoning start[s] with observations of the machine and arrive[s] at general conclusions. For example, if the cycle goes over a bump and the engine misfires, and then goes over another bump and the engine misfires . . . and then goes over a long smooth stretch of road and there is no misfiring, and then goes over [another] bump and the engine misfires again, one can logically conclude that the misfiring is caused by the bumps. That is induction: reasoning from particular experiences to general truths.

Fictional detective Sherlock Holmes praised the merits of inductive reasoning when he noted, "It's a capital mistake to theorize before one has data" (Doyle [1892] 1987:13). Much of the theory-building process uses *inductive reasoning*, which puts the sociologist in the role of a detective who pieces together "clues" from specific observations in order to develop a general understanding of the overall puzzle of human behavior, or, as we discussed in Chapter 1, to see the *general* in the *particular*. In other words, inductive reasoning is when someone is looking at the small pieces to understand the larger picture.

Some sociologists believe that sociology relies too heavily on inductive studies; they assert that general theoretical models based on deductive reasoning are also very important (Kiser and Hechter 1991). *Deductive reasoning* is reasoning that begins with a general understanding or theory that is then tested through the observation or study of specific situations. Deductive reasoning is like using the completed picture on the outside of the box to put the puzzle pieces together. Pirsig (1974:99) noted that deductive inferences

> start with general knowledge and predict a specific observation. For example, if, from reading the hierarchy of facts about the machine, the mechanic knows the horn of the cycle is powered exclusively by electricity from the battery, then he can logically infer that if the battery is dead the horn will not work. That is deduction.

Deduction is an important way to test and evaluate existing sociological understandings and theories. Sociological research usually involves a process of interweaving both inductive and deductive reasoning in an effort to increase our knowledge, develop our understanding, and gain insight into the problem and concepts under study.

Theory building begins with the identification of important concepts about what is being studied. A *concept* is an abstract idea or general thought. To conduct meaningful research, sociologists must identify and define concepts, which may be rather vague. For example, sociologists interested in studying suicide must first define the term. The initial process in clarifying concepts is developing a *conceptual definition*—that is, defining a concept through the use of other concepts. A conceptual definition of "suicide" might be "a person intentionally taking their own life." Although this definition helps clarify the concept of suicide, it does not provide a precise enough definition for scientific inquiry and should not be considered the only definition that could be used.

The sociologist's next task involves developing *operational definitions*. An operational definition specifies how a concept is measured. For example, a sociologist studying suicide might operationalize the term to be any death officially ruled as a suicide by a coroner or other official. This definition allows the concept to be measured, but can you think of some problems and limitations with it?

Operational definitions provide specific techniques to measure what is being studied. Two important criteria for sociological measurements are that they must be both valid and reliable. *Validity* refers to the extent to which a technique accurately measures what it purports to measure; *reliability* refers to the consistency of measurement. A measure that is reliable should produce the same results each time it is used. A measure can be reliable without being valid. For example, although measuring suicide as the number of deaths officially reported as such should give consistent results, it is not a valid measurement because we know that a number of suicides may be committed that end up being reported as accidental deaths. For example, when a person dies in a car wreck where they missed a curve and ran off the road at an excess speed, was that an accident, or could they possibly have done it on purpose? Lots of people, including police, family, coroners, insurance adjusters, and others may become involved in determining whether a death is result of suicide, accident, natural causes, or foul play. This is another example of how something that seems pretty straightforward such as suicide—either a person took their own life or didn't—is not what it seems, as classifying a death as a suicide is often a very complex social process involving a lot of people with different viewpoints. Family members, insurance adjusters, law enforcement officers, and others may all have a vested interest in whether a death is ruled a result of accident, homicide, or suicide.

The next step in the theory-building process is to identify variables. A *variable* represents ways in which concepts vary or differ. For example, when studying suicide, a sociologist would want to look at how they vary by age, race/ethnicity, sex/gender, religion, socioeconomic status, and numerous other variables.

When concepts have been defined and operationalized, and variables identified, propositions can be formulated. A *proposition* is a statement that interrelates two or more variables. The statement "Suicide rates are higher among males than among females" states a relationship between two variables: sex and suicide rates. Because a goal of science is to identify cause-and-effect relationships, the linking of variables is an important step in theory building. In linking variables, however, sociologists must be careful not to confuse *correlation* (a measure indicating that two variables are related in such a way that a change in one is accompanied by a change in the other) with *causation*, when a change in one variable creates a change in another variable. To establish causation, (1) the two variables must be related; (2) the *cause* must precede the *effect*; and (3) the relationship between the two variables must persist when all other relevant variables are controlled.

Sometimes an apparent relationship between two variables is meaningless. We call this type of relationship *spurious*. For example, it could be demonstrated that as the deadline for filing income taxes approaches, the sale of swimsuits increases. Despite the strong statistical correlation between the two, it would be ludicrous to assume that filing income taxes causes people to want to wear swimsuits. A much more likely explanation is that because the tax filing deadline falls on April 15, about the same time summer clothing debuts in department stores, people begin to anticipate the oncoming swimming season.

SCIENTIFIC METHOD

Most sociological studies follow the general guidelines outlined in the scientific method, which provides a systematic framework to guide research.

1. *Statement of the Problem.* The first step in sociological research is to formulate a research question.
2. *Review of the Literature.* After stating a research problem or developing a research question, the sociologist seeks out previous studies to determine what is already known about the problem.

3. *Development of Hypotheses or a Statement of Research Objectives.* Based on what is already known about a topic, the researcher develops *hypotheses,* which are propositional statements about the relationships between the concepts or variables under study. These hypotheses are written in such a way that they can be tested and either supported or rejected, according to the research findings. Sometimes, instead of theoretical hypotheses, researchers develop research objectives, which outline specific goals or purposes of their research projects.
4. *Choice of Research Design.* To test theories and hypotheses or to achieve research objectives, sociologists gather data: facts and information. A variety of research methods can be used, including a *secondary analysis* of the available data; experiments; surveys; and field research, such as *ethnographic interviews, participant observation,* and *case studies.*
5. *Data Collection.* In this step, the researcher collects the observations, facts, and information to use in testing the hypotheses or fulfilling the research objectives.
6. *Data Analysis and Interpretation.* At this stage, the researcher considers the study's findings and determines what they mean. Data analysis can be divided into two general categories: quantitative and qualitative. *Quantitative analysis* converts data to numerical form so they can be subjected to a variety of statistical techniques and measurements. Field methods may produce data that cannot be easily translated into numerical form; in that case, the researcher uses *qualitative analysis* to observe and interpret data. In qualitative analysis, the researcher analyzes observations, interviews, and/or behaviors to discover trends, patterns, and other generalizations.
7. *Development of Conclusions.* On the basis of research findings and data analysis, the researcher makes generalizations and draws conclusions regarding the research hypotheses or objectives.
8. *Posing New Research Questions.* Science is a never-ending venture, and a good sociologist realizes that the conclusion of a specific research project does not end the research enterprise. Thus, part of the research process is identifying new problems for future research. In this sense, each of the eight steps of the research process is a building block for the next, and when step 8 is completed, it becomes the foundation for beginning step 1 all over again.

Sociological research is a dynamic process of discovery. It is important to understand that the scientific method is an *ideal type*, designed to serve as a general guideline for scientific research, rather than a recipe to be rigidly followed. We would be wise to remember the comments of Polykarp Kusch and Percy Bridgman when they accepted their Nobel Prize in physics: they declared that there is no such thing as "*the* scientific method" and that scientists must do the utmost with their minds, "*no holds barred*" (Mills 1959:58).

Some of the most significant findings in both the natural and social sciences have developed out of serendipitous observations during research. The discovery of penicillin, for example, occurred quite by accident when scientists became curious about the mold growing in samples they were using in other medical research. Similarly, sociologist Howard Becker (1963) was attempting to explain the use of marijuana among jazz musicians when he realized that virtually all the actions of this group were viewed as deviant by the larger society. Concluding that jazz musicians were considered "outside" the mainstream of conventional society, he wrote *Outsiders*, a significant contribution to the development of the labeling perspective on deviant behavior.

Research procedures fall somewhere between rigid adherence to the scientific method and serendipity. Joel Smith (1991) echoed a recurring theme in contemporary sociology that urges a combination of scientific rigor and methodological flexibility in the quest for knowledge. He asserted that there are five important questions for sociological researchers: (1) What does one want to know and why? (2) What is to be observed? (3) Which and how many objects are to be examined? (4) How are the phenomena to be observed? (5) How are answers to be decided? These questions not only pose methodological issues but also raise ethical issues related to sociological research.

ETHICAL ISSUES IN SOCIOLOGICAL RESEARCH

Because sociologists study people and what they do in the course of their everyday lives, certain ethical considerations apply to every sociological study. Laud Humphreys's study of covert homosexuality in *Tearoom*

Trade (1970) sparked heated debate over the rights and responsibilities of sociological researchers. For example:

1. Do sociologists have the right to study people who do not know they are being studied? (yes)
2. Do sociologists have the right to intentionally deceive the people they are studying? (yes/no)
3. Do sociologists have the right to break the law while conducting sociological research? (no)
4. Do sociologists have the right to collect data under the guise of one type of study when they are actually collecting it for another, clandestine research purpose? (no)

In an attempt to clarify ethical issues and provide ethical guidelines for sociological research, the American Sociological Association (ASA) adopted a comprehensive Code of Ethics for its members. It contains five basic principles:

1. Maintain objectivity, integrity, confidentiality, and social responsibility in research.
2. Respect and protect the privacy, dignity, and safety of research subjects.
3. Do not discriminate or misuse or abuse the research role.
4. Disclose all assistance and support.
5. Disassociate from any research that violates the ASA Code of Ethics. (ASA 2015)

This ethical code is supposed to be applied to all types of sociological research and research designs. Because sociologists conduct research for different purposes, there are different types of research designs: the four most common types in sociology are exploratory, descriptive, explanatory, and evaluative.

TYPES OF RESEARCH

Exploratory research attempts to answer the question *"What?"* The first sociological study of any phenomenon—single parenting, social media, or road rage—is likely to be exploratory, focusing on what takes place. Exploratory research provides a foundation on which future research is built, and although it may not answer all our questions about a topic, it is in some ways the most important type of research in that it involves breaking new ground and asking previously unasked questions.

Descriptive research answers the questions *"What?"* and *"How?"* It describes what takes place and how it happens, as accurately and objectively as possible. Many of the most fascinating studies of religious cults, motorcycle gangs, or teenage Satanists are descriptive in nature.

Explanatory research attempts to explain social phenomena by answering the questions *"What?" "How?"* and *"Why?"* Explanatory studies not only analyze and explain what takes place and how it occurs but also examine why people behave the way they do in given social circumstances. This is the ultimate goal of any science: to understand not only what is happening and how, but also why. This is often difficult in social and behavioral sciences because of the wide variety of possible explanations for human behavior.

Evaluation research measures the effectiveness of a program; it doesn't ask "What?," "How?," or "Why?" Rather, it asks, *"Does it work?"* Is a program accomplishing the specific goals and objectives it set out to achieve?" Evaluation research is used widely in sociology today, and in this era of limited resources and accountability is often more likely to be funded by governmental or private agencies than the more traditional types of sociological research already discussed. For example, the Affordable Care Act is a national program designed to provide low-income individuals with affordable health insurance. Evaluation research can be used to study whether the program has achieved that goal to determine the effectiveness of spending money on it or other programs.

QUANTIFYING SOCIAL LIFE

An important step in the sociological research process is choosing a research design that meets the goals and objectives of the study. *Quantitative research designs* emphasize the use of numbers and statistics to analyze and explain social events and human behavior. Sociologists who use quantitative designs believe that the most objective and systematic way to study and analyze a phenomenon is through quantification of observations and use of statistical techniques. Computer technology and sophisticated mathematical models lead some researchers to argue that the vast possibilities for quantitative research in sociology remain unrealized (Blalock 1989, 2013). Some of the more commonly used quantitative methods in sociology are secondary analysis, experiments, and surveys.

Secondary analysis makes use of existing data and is often used in comparative/historical studies. The population data collected by the U.S. Bureau of the Census every 10 years are some of the most commonly used data for secondary analysis. Because these data have been systematically collected for over 200 years, sociologists can use them to analyze population characteristics and trends. The Federal Bureau of Investigation (FBI) began collecting data in the 1930s on crime in the United States, and subsequently, their annual publication, known as *Uniform Crime Reports*, has become the most widely used source of official crime data. It would be virtually impossible for sociologists or criminologists to independently collect such comprehensive annual and longitudinal crime data.

An advantage of secondary analysis is that it saves the time and expense associated with data collection. With today's technology, millions of pieces of research data are literally at the sociologist's fingertips.

Such convenience has its drawbacks, however. Because the data were collected by somebody else, and for some other purpose, any weaknesses in the data-collection process place limitations on its use by the secondary researcher.

When we think of scientific research, we often think of the experimental method. In practice, ethical considerations and the problem of control severely limit the use of experiments in sociological research. Experimental designs attempt to discover a cause-and-effect relationship between two variables. The standard format for an experiment is to manipulate an *independent variable*—a variable that brings about change in another variable (i.e., the cause)—to measure its effect on a *dependent variable*, which is changed by the independent variable (i.e., the effect). This format requires controlling for *intervening variables,* variables that may come between the independent and dependent variables in an experiment. Because it is difficult to control extraneous variables outside the laboratory, sociologists sometimes use a *quasi-experimental design*, which approximates an experimental design but lacks the rigid control required by laboratory experiments.

Another problem that arises in sociological experiments is that subjects may change their behavior because they know they are being studied. The *Hawthorne effect*, as it is called, was discovered when Western Electric conducted a series of experiments at its Hawthorne factory (Roethlisberger and Dickson 1939). Researchers hypothesized that worker productivity (the dependent variable) would increase if the lighting in the work area (the independent variable) was improved. Sure enough, when the lighting was increased, so was productivity. Then the lighting was decreased. To the researchers' surprise, and contrary to their hypothesis, worker productivity continued to increase. The researchers discovered that the amount of lighting was not causally related to worker productivity. Rather, the fact that they were being studied was an intervening variable that caused the workers to increase their productivity—a phenomenon that continues to appear in later research (Jones 1990).

At one time or another, you probably have participated in *survey research:* research using questionnaires or interviews to obtain data. As a college student, you may have completed a questionnaire for a student or faculty member, or one of the administrative units on campus may have surveyed you on a particular aspect of college life. Many colleges and universities use a standardized form of survey research for students to evaluate courses and instructors.

The two most common survey instruments are questionnaires and interviews. A *questionnaire* is a series of statements or questions to which an individual is asked to respond. Questions may be *closed-ended*, asking the respondent to choose from several standardized responses, or *open-ended*, requiring the respondent to create an answer. Closed-ended questions are much easier to tabulate and analyze because the responses are standardized and need only be counted. Open-ended questions have the advantage of allowing respondents to answer more freely and to explain their answers.

The phrasing of questions and responses is important in survey research. Researchers may influence responses by the way they word questions. For example, when Americans were asked "Do you believe in God?" and were only given the options of "Yes" or "No" as answers, 89 percent said "Yes," but when the third option of "Unsure" was added, the percentage replying "Yes" dropped to 79 percent (Newport 2016).

An interview is a questionnaire administered to respondents by the researcher. Interviews are more expensive and time consuming than self-administered questionnaires, but they offer the advantage of face-to-face contact with respondents. Researchers must be careful, however, not to coach or influence responses by interpreting questions.

An important aspect of sociological research is sampling. In order to make generalizations about a *population*—an entire body of people to which the sociologist would like to generalize research findings—it is important to select a large enough and representative *sample,* or segment of the population.

Suppose you want to survey students at your college or university to determine their attitudes toward capital punishment. It would not be feasible, nor would it be necessary, to survey every student on campus. Although it would be possible to obtain a sample by standing in the student center and asking students to participate in your survey, such a sample would probably not be representative of your school's student population. This is called *availability sampling*; it involves using whoever is readily available as research subjects. Although it is sometimes used for pretesting a questionnaire, it is rarely considered an adequate sampling technique for serious sociological research.

More likely to provide a representative sample is *random sampling*, in which each member of the population has an equal opportunity of being selected. If you obtain a list of all the students enrolled in your school, place their names in a large container, mix them thoroughly, and draw 100 names, then based on the laws of mathematical probability, you are likely to get a representative sample of the student body. Today's computers provide less cumbersome ways of generating a random sample that work on the same principle.

In an attempt to ensure the representativeness of your sample, you might find it necessary to select a *stratified random sample*, which includes proportionate representation of the different categories of people from which a random sample is drawn. For example, you could stratify your sample by race, sex, or classification (seniors, juniors, sophomores, and first-year students) and randomly select from each category so that the right proportions are represented in your sample. There are other methods of sampling, but whatever the strategy, the goal is the same: to choose a sample that accurately represents the population to be studied.

QUALITATIVE STUDIES

Qualitative sociologists contend that numbers and statistics are dehumanizing; some human behaviors cannot be quantified; and that when observations are reduced to numbers, the essence of human social behavior is lost. They embrace the sentiment that "if you can measure it, that ain't it" (Kaplan 1964:206). Qualitative sociologists use an *interpretive paradigm* and use the scientific method as a general guideline for observation and analysis. Rather than stating and testing specific research hypotheses, they usually develop research objectives to guide their studies. *Qualitative research* designs use systematic observation and focus on the meanings people give to their social actions. Despite the subjective interpretation demanded in qualitative research, sociologists remain vigilant in their attempt to analyze and assess their findings objectively and to generate meaningful sociological theories (Corbin and Strauss 2015). They analyze with their brains, not with their hearts.

Earlier, we discussed interviews as a type of survey research in which the researcher reads a questionnaire to respondents. In field research, the ethnographic interview follows quite a different procedure. Rather than *"studying people*, ethnography means *learning from people"* (Spradley 1979:3). An *ethnographic interview* is a qualitative technique where the researcher talks with people in an effort to learn as much as possible about them and their behavior. Ethnographic researchers focus on a particular culture or subculture and attempt to understand what its members do, how they do it, and the meanings they attach to their behaviors.

Ethnographic interviewers rely on locating and interviewing knowledgeable informants. An *informant* is a member of a particular culture or subculture who is willing to share their experiences, knowledge, and understanding with a researcher. Ethnographic interviewers are careful to maintain objectivity in their research and analysis. Because their method requires that they become familiar with people in order to learn more about them, researchers must build trust and empathy with the people they study. But they must not allow this to distort their analyses or allow subjective observations and interpretations to distort their findings.

Participant observation is a qualitative method in which the researcher systematically observes the people being studied while participating with them in their activities. *Nonparticipation* occurs when the researcher observes social action but does not participate in it or interact with participants (Spradley 1980). For example, a sociologist might set up a hidden camera to record the behaviors of people in elevators or, acting as an observant bystander, might watch people at a sporting event.

In *limited participation*, the researcher's participation in the interaction is restricted. *Full participation*, in which the researcher becomes actively and completely involved in the behavior being studied, is the highest level of involvement for the sociologist (Spradley 1980). In *Tearoom Trade* (1970), Laud Humphreys assumed the role of a voyeur who observed covert homosexual behavior between two men in a public restroom while simultaneously being a "lookout," warning the participants when someone approached.

Qualitative field researchers also use *case studies*, qualitative techniques that involve intensive observation of a particular person, group, or event. The researcher gathers as much detailed information as possible. Case studies often use other research methods, including ethnographic interviewing or participant observation. William Foote Whyte took a case study approach when he investigated a Boston slum neighborhood in his classic work *Street Corner Society* (1943). By studying and interacting with a particular group on a personal level, Whyte discovered that, contrary to public assumptions that immigrant slum dwellers had no norms or values, the group of first- and second-generation Italian immigrants who inhabited "Cornerville" had a highly structured set of values, attitudes, beliefs, and norms that governed their daily lives.

KEEPING IT SCIENTIFIC

To overcome methodological weaknesses, whether quantitative or qualitative, sociologists sometimes combine techniques from several different methodologies. *Triangulation* is the use of multiple (usually three) techniques to gather or analyze research data. For example, a common procedure among qualitative researchers is to combine ethnographic interviews with participant observation, or use *team field research*, which involves more than one researcher in order to combine "the cool detachment of the outsider and the committed view of the insider" (Douglas 1976:218).

Researchers employing *content analysis*–research that examines and analyzes communication–may use either qualitative or quantitative methods or a combination. Content analysis can be used to study the content of poetry, literature, newspaper and magazine articles, television programs, commercials, movies, and elements of social media. The analysis may focus on words, themes, or patterns of communication.

One of the ways that sociologists avoid personal bias and keep their work scientific is to wed sociological methods to sociological theory. Sociologist Norman Denzin (2009:56) stated, "Theory guides research while research guides theory." Sociologists' theoretical perspectives influence the topics they study, how they frame their research questions, the methods they use to collect and analyze their data, and how they interpret their findings. Because of the interdependence of theory and method, let's briefly examine how the major theoretical perspectives relate to doing sociology.

The interactionist perspective focuses on analysis at the micro level. Sociologists who use it are most interested in the meanings people attach to human behavior; consequently, they are most likely to use qualitative research methods. Ethnographic interviews, participant observation, and case studies are trademarks of interactionist research.

The interactionist perspective's focus on symbols puts certain demands on its methodologies:

1. Symbols and interactions must be combined before an investigation is complete.
2. The researcher must take the "role of the other" and view the world from the subjects' point of view, but must maintain the distinction between everyday and scientific conceptions of reality.
3. The researcher must link subjects' symbols and definitions with the social relationships and groups that provide those conceptions.
4. The behavior settings of interaction and scientific observation must be recorded.
5. Research methods must be capable of reflecting process or change as well as more stable behavioral forms.
6. Being a sociologist conducting research is best viewed as an act of symbolic interaction. The personal preferences of sociologists shape their activities as investigators (Denzin 2009:19).

Although the interactionist approach is most often linked to qualitative research methods, it does not use them exclusively. The Chicago School, which gave birth to symbolic interactionism, insisted that researchers use introspection and subjective interpretation. In sharp contrast, the Iowa School of symbolic interactionism argues that the theoretical assumptions of symbolic interactionism can be operationalized and used in quantitative, empirical scientific research. Although sharing the basic theoretical assumptions of the Chicago School, the Iowa School favors different research strategies, insisting that even the meanings and understandings of human behavior can be quantified and statistically analyzed.

Functionalists take a macro-level approach to the study of society and human behavior. Their emphasis on structure, social institutions, manifest and latent functions, and entire societies leads them to use quantitative research designs and statistical techniques for data analysis. The most popular method among functionalists is the use of questionnaires in large-scale surveys. Survey data collected from representative samples of large populations (e.g., census data) are especially appealing because they provide a picture of a society as a whole.

The conflict perspective also uses macro-level analysis and traditionally its followers have preferred quantitative research methods designed to gather and analyze data on social institutions over qualitative designs geared more toward studying smaller groups and small-scale interactions. Secondary analyses, surveys, and other methods used by conflict theorists focus on social diversity, conflict, alienation, exploitation, and social change. Conflict theorists attempt to assess the impact of social variables such as age, race, sex, and socioeconomic status on people as they participate in groups and institutions; these theorists want to know how these variables relate to the exploitation of less powerful groups by more powerful ones. Thus, the major differences between research conducted by conflict theorists and research conducted by functionalists are related more to their theoretical analyses than to their particular methodologies.

When it comes to research, there is no single feminist method. The most prominent feature of feminist research is the importance it places on gender in all phases of the research process—from selection of a topic through choice of design, data collection, analysis, and interpretation of findings. Feminist research reconceptualizes knowledge to encompass the female experience. One prominent and influential feminist theory is the *Standpoint Theory*, which contends that people's perspectives are shaped by personal experiences that help form a standpoint from which they see and interpret the world. Dorothy Smith (1989) created this theory because the female experience was lacking in sociological research and theory. She suggests that simply by being women, female sociologists apply their gender bias to research. Standpoint Theory points out that the world of scientific enterprise, historically and cross-culturally, has been viewed as the domain of men. Sexism in scientific research tends to be subtle, and feminists note that the questions scientists choose to ask and the way they ask them often determine the types of answers the investigation will yield (Fisher 2005; Spanier 1997). Consequently, sociological research dominated by men and conducted primarily on men may produce male-biased theories of society and human behavior (Schneider 2000). Perhaps Marjorie DeVault (1996:30) put it most succinctly when she pointed out, "Feminist sociologists are committed to both feminism and social science, and they use the tools of the discipline to 'talk back' to sociology in a spirited critique aimed at improving the ways we know society."

Perhaps one of the most distinguishing features of feminist theory is its unwavering commitment to gender research. Although there is no single paradigm in feminist theory, most agree that research guided by the feminist approach can be summarized as attempting to remedy three major problems that have consistently plagued sociology throughout all but its most recent existence:

1. Most sociological studies were conducted by men who studied men, but then generalized their findings to everybody. Feminists remind us that our experiences, even those guided by the objectivity of science, are shaped in important ways by our gender; consequently, they urge scientific research to "bring women in" (DeVault 1996:32). Although there may be good reason to target one sex or the other in a particular study, it is important in such cases not to generalize the findings to both sexes. The male experience is not equivalent to the female experience. By generalizing to both sexes, a patriarchal bias is created.

2. For many years, gender was considered neither an important topic for research nor a serious subfield of sociology, and women were ignored. Women's activities and contributions are often less visible,

especially in the formal social structure, than are men's. Therefore, it often takes in-depth ethnographic inquiry to bring women's experiences and social activities to light. Moreover, in many cultures, only female researchers are allowed to enter the private, domestic, behind-the-scenes world of women.

3. Often, when women have been studied, their attitudes and behaviors have been analyzed by men and compared with male standards of "normality" and correctness. Although feminists do not argue that only women can study women, they emphasize the importance of gender in choosing a research topic, developing a research design, and shaping our perceptions, analyses, and interpretations (Fisher 2005; Renzetti and Curran 1995). This may make a good case for men and women collaborating, especially in participant observation and ethnographic studies.

Sociologists working from all theoretical perspectives and using a variety of research methods are concerned about how their research findings are used. Over 40 years ago, Mills (1959) warned that sociologists and their research would be used increasingly for bureaucratic and ideological purposes. One of the greatest concerns facing sociologists today is how the mass media and social media present, use, interpret, and often distort sociological findings to support a cause, mobilize people, or otherwise sway public opinion. Increasingly, we seem to live in a world where facts do not seem to matter. In sociology, as in any science, facts do matter. Facts matter a lot, and it is increasingly important to practice the sociological wisdom of *analyzing with our brains and not with our hearts*.

Sociological Wisdom 3

#There'sNoSuchThingAsAnUnculturedPerson

UNDERSTANDING SOCIETY AND CULTURE

MAJOR CITIES, SUCH AS PARIS, London, Istanbul, New Delhi, Los Angeles, and New York City, are often considered to be the cultural centers of the world. Their architectural landmarks, haute cuisine, museums, symphonic orchestras, and people are often held up as role models for other cities to aspire to copy. Conversely, poverty-stricken areas of the world in developing areas of Asia, Africa, and Eastern Europe, as well as Appalachia and the deep Southern part of the United States, are often pitied, ridiculed, and even mocked as being "cultural deserts" full of "uncultured" people suffering through unfulfilled and meaningless lives. The third sociological wisdom tells us, however, that *there is no such thing as an "uncultured" person*. Although we may subjectively judge some cultures as superior or inferior to others, it is important to understand that everyone, everywhere around the world experiences culture.

Have you ever been in a foreign country and become homesick? So homesick that you see the golden arches or a green mermaid and suddenly feel like you're home, even though once you step inside, you find several unfamiliar items on the menu? Perhaps you don't travel outside of the country, but your jet-setting friend just came back from London with a new cookie, or as the British call it, a "biscuit," for you to try. Instead of having to travel halfway around the world, regardless of where you live, you can go online, place your order, and your Hobnob cookie will arrive at your door. These examples not only illustrate the impact of *globalization* on society and culture, but also demonstrate an example of *glocalization*, the interdependence of the global and the local, resulting in standardized values producing unique outcomes in different geographic areas and cultural settings. It also reflects what George Ritzer (2007) calls *grobalization*, or the imperialistic ambitions of nations, corporations, and organizations and their desire to impose themselves on various societies and cultures. Yet it must be remembered that "culture does not make people. People make culture" Adichie (2015).

Because of the media and globalization, few people are unaware of the extraordinary diversity of societies and cultures in the world today. Far-reaching global changes have tremendous local impact (Savage et al. 2005), and today few people have much difficulty comprehending how different cultures and societies affect others. Because culture is so pervasive and taken for granted that it rarely enters into our consciousness, most of us find it hard to understand how our culture and society affect us.

TYPES OF SOCIETIES

All societies were *hunting-gathering societies* until about 10,000 years ago, and they were pretty much alike with respect to size, structural complexity, technology, and other aspects of social and cultural life. In the first great technological revolution, which sociologists refer to as the Agricultural Revolution, *agrarian, or farming societies* emerged and began to supplant them. Farming societies were more complex, more technologically sophisticated, and more densely populated than hunting-gathering societies, and far more competitive.

These trends accelerated in the late eighteenth century as part of the Industrial Revolution, which produced *industrial societies* with much larger populations, many more goods and services, urbanization, militarization, and the erosion and disappearance of thousands of rural communities. Many sociologists believe computers and other advanced technologies have produced a third major revolution—the information revolution—that is generating a very different type of society—the *postindustrial society*. On the one hand, new information technologies encourage greater social consolidation, perhaps the beginning stages of life in a truly "global village," where patterns of social interaction instantaneously crisscross the globe. On the other hand, new technologies encourage a more privatized and individualistic society, where more people may work, socialize, and spend much of their lives at home. They are also creating many more flexible and tentative statuses and identities than in any previous period (Caplow 1991; Kumar 1995; Turkle 2011). Some neurological research even suggests that the continued use of computers from childhood through adulthood may literally "rewire" parts of the brain, affecting the way people process information (Carr 2011).

These great transformations are all part of *sociocultural evolution*, a process in which societies grow more complex in terms of technology, social structure, and cultural knowledge over time. Although there is nothing inevitable about this process, and at any given time a society may decline or collapse, in the course of human history there has been a progressive trend toward more complex and more geographically far-reaching sociocultural arrangements.

Who we are, what we become, what is expected of us, and what we expect from others is determined by the type of society in which we live. Nevertheless, society is taken for granted, and we seldom contemplate it unless forced to do so. Sociologist Charles Lemert (2012) asserted that most of the time people have no reason to think about society, until all of a sudden some unusual occurrence arises out of what is usually considered to be a very ordinary circumstance, causing them to recognize and try to explain the social reality of what has taken place and how it affects their lives.

COMPONENTS OF CULTURE

Culture is the learned set of beliefs, values, norms, and material goods shared by group members. On the surface, the concept of culture is not difficult to understand. Culture consists of everything we learn in groups during the life course—from infancy to old age. Culture includes ideas about what is real and what is not, what we may and may not eat, the clothing we wear, the music we listen to, and the games we play. Culture shapes our understandings of good and evil, health and sickness, and life and death. It lays down rules for serious social concerns as well as guidelines for everyday life. Culture is much more than ideas and rules of behavior, however. It gives our lives meaning, telling us why we should get out of bed each morning, obey the rules, and live from infancy to old age. Culture provides rewards for proper behavior and may promise that these rewards will continue beyond this physical world.

Culture has two major components: material and nonmaterial culture. *Material culture* includes artifacts, art, architecture, and other tangible goods that people create and assign meanings to. Technology, art, architecture, clothing, television sets, and consumer goods at malls and supermarkets are all part of material culture in advanced industrial societies. *Nonmaterial culture* refers to mental blueprints that serve as guidelines for group behavior. They include the collective assumptions, languages, beliefs, values, norms, and attitudes of groups.

Symbols are humans' greatest achievement. The application of symbols to the physical world—specifically, the invention of material culture and technology—follows closely. Material and nonmaterial culture are interrelated in that all societies express their beliefs, values, and understandings in artifacts, architecture, and art. In simple societies, material culture usually supports a consistent view of reality.

For example, the Lakota (Sioux) and other traditional Plains Indians believed that everything that was vitally important in nature—the sun, moon, earth, and stars—was round, and the "sacred circle" represented completeness, wholeness, health, and harmony with nature. Much of their material culture reflected this ideology: their houses (tepees) were circular and were always placed in a circle; battle shields and drums were circular; circular objects were used to process the bison; circular amulets warded off evil spirits; and hoops, rings, and spinning tops were favored for recreation and sport (DeMallie 1984; Geertz 1968; Hand 2010; Wishart 2016).

In modern industrial societies, values and norms are expressed in technology, architecture, and art, although the relationship is more complex than in simple societies. A century ago, Max Weber ([1904–1905] 1958a) demonstrated how values such as thrift, hard work, individuality, and savings, part of what he called the "Protestant ethic," played a central role in the birth and expansion of industrial capitalism. Mass production and the proliferation of objects, gadgets, implements, and devices of every type are a reflection of American values, norms, and "mass society."

If values and beliefs influence material culture, the reverse is equally true. Material culture, especially technological innovations, can have dramatic and often unintended effects on values, beliefs, and social relationships. The invention of the telephone provides a classic example. Some people feared it would be the collapse of communities. The telephone provided people with more opportunities to connect to family and friends, easy access to information, and also helped to provide a sense of security and safety. Even those who thought it might be a negative invention, however, could never have envisioned what the telephone would become. Phones expanded people's social worlds, became new status symbols, and even altered the dating patterns and sex lives of teenagers and adults. In recent years, new technologies and globalization have brought even greater cultural changes and challenges.

A little more than a century ago, biologist Charles Darwin's essay titled *On the Origin of Species* ([1859] 1964) brought about a revolution in scientific thinking about all living things. Borrowing ideas from biology, paleontology, and natural history, Darwin proposed a radical new view of our relationship to animals and the rest of the natural world.

First, Darwin observed that species produce far more offspring than can be supported by the environment. Second, he found that although offspring closely resemble their parents and one another, they differ in some traits. He proposed that it is from this pool of sibling differences that new life is formed; according to the *theory of evolution*, the environment, or "nature," selects those traits that are advantageous and rejects those that are not. This endless process of adaptation and competition and the "survival of the fittest" has generated the great diversity of life on earth, from the simplest bacteria to more complex creatures, including humans.

From the beginning of life on earth, the success of animal species has depended on instincts or genetic programming. Humans are believed to be the only species that combine genes and culture to solve the problems of living. For example, higher primates, such as chimpanzees, our closest relatives in the animal world, sometimes use stones to process food or defend themselves, but these rudimentary forms of culture are not essential for species survival. For humans, both material and nonmaterial culture clearly are necessary.

The first clear evidence of culture is from about 2 million years ago on the plains of Africa. Crude stone tools found at several sites show that our early ancestors gradually adapted to the environment with tools and traditions that were passed on from generation to generation. In this sense, technology helped transform human biology, with each small technological advance altering both the structure and size of the brain, until learning and cultural solutions became the primary way that all humans adapt to the world.

Is a smile universally recognized as a sign of friendly intentions? Sociologists caution that, like most human behaviors, smiles are complex, and groups may interpret them in various ways. For example, think of the possibilities of a smile in interactions with your friends. When you smile, it may reflect friendliness, but it may also express uncertainty, derision, or even contempt. And, of course, your friends may or may not agree with your interpretation. Add to that the ways various groups from around the world may interpret a smile, and you have some idea of the complexity of what is popularly assumed to be a "universal behavior."

Beauty is often described as universal as well—especially by the media. For example, *Newsweek* reported that research had shown that "body symmetry and a .7 waist-hip ratio" were universally recognized as "beautiful" (Cowley and Hager 1996). Are they indeed essential to *every group's* standard of beauty? Knowing the extraordinary variation in people's ideas of beauty around the world and even in the United States, where ethnicity, sex, and other factors influence people's ideas of beauty, beauty treatments, and cosmetic surgery, most sociologists doubt it. In some cultures, women are seen as beautiful; in others, it is men. Some associate ideal beauty with facial and body scarification. Others—including Americans 100 years ago—consider plumpness and obesity marks of beauty. Today, models are mostly tall, thin, and athletic looking, and in the United States, the "multiracial look" has become increasingly popular; it is becoming a popular standard of beauty in the United States and worldwide (Halter 2000). Nevertheless, research indicates that standards of attractiveness and beauty vary across cultures (Sugiyama 2004).

Although different groups and societies around the world may have very different cultural understandings, all create worlds of meaning with the same basic components: symbols, language, beliefs, values, norms, and material culture. Humans use signs to express emotions, but somewhere in antiquity we began to convert them to symbols to communicate messages about emotional states and everything else. A *symbol* is anything to which group members assign meaning. It may be an object, color, sound, gesture, person, or anything else. The important difference between signals and symbols is that the latter are purely arbitrary. For example, water has real physical properties, but as a symbol the same water may be defined as pure water, dirty water, holy water, or spring water with curative powers. With only a slight chemical change, the same water may also be transformed into an expensive beverage that may be used to express one's social standing.

Colors also may be interpreted in diverse and even opposite ways because of symbolic behavior. In the United States and other Western cultures, white is a symbol of life, purity, and goodness. Black can symbolize something serious and solemn. For example, black is worn at graduation ceremonies and in courts of law by judges. But black in Western culture more generally symbolizes evil and death: people wear black at funerals, and football teams with black uniforms have menacing reputations. In China and many other parts of Asia, many of these meanings are reversed. White is a symbol of mourning and death, and people wear white, not black, to funerals (Rosman 2017). Wearing a green baseball cap, a symbol of a sports team in the West, might cause embarrassment in China, because there it mocks a man's masculinity and is a symbol for a cuckold (Smith 2002).

Clothing is symbolic, although most of the time we hardly notice what classmates, professors, and our friends wear. But look more carefully at the symbolic messages people convey through clothing. Some T-shirts carry obvious messages, but every item of apparel makes some kind of statement. Of course, symbols may change over time. Today, blue jeans are so common on campus that few people notice them. Had you worn jeans to church or a college classroom a century ago, however, you would have shocked and angered almost everyone, because they were "working-class" apparel. And only a few decades ago, jeans were considered appropriate for males, but not females.

Harley-Davidson motorcycles were once significant symbols as well—of deviance and "outlaw bikers." Today, most Americans consider them socially acceptable because in the past few decades, stockbrokers, attorneys, dentists, and other Harley enthusiasts have redefined the term "Harley-Davidson" to mean "mainstream." And because they are as expensive as some luxury automobiles, they now are status symbols to the rich and successful (Thompson 2012). Of all the symbols that people use, language is by far the most important in preserving and transmitting the cultural heritage of groups.

A *language* is a complex system of symbols with conventional meanings that people use for communication. Language is often thought to include only the spoken word, but in its broadest sense language contains verbal, nonverbal, and written symbols. There are estimated to be 3,000–5,000 languages worldwide today, and within these languages there is often linguistic variation based on regional, class, ethnic, and other subcultural differences. Most spoken languages make use of 15–60 distinct sounds to communicate messages. English, for example, uses 44 distinct sounds. These few sounds and the rules for combining them into words, sentences, and more complex structures are the primary basis of all social traditions (Howard and Dunaif-Hattis 1992).

Humans are biologically predisposed to learning language. Infants are born with the ability to produce many sounds, hear subtle differences among these sounds, and process this information in the brain. As with all symbols, sounds chosen by a culture and how they are arranged to produce meaning is decided by social convention.

Not all language is spoken. To be an effective speaker in any society or group, it is not enough to know the sounds and arrangement of its words and sentences. We also must learn the nonverbal symbols—the proper uses and the meanings of gestures, eyes, posture, and space. *Body language* is often used to reinforce spoken messages, but at times it may be used independently. For example, many Americans shake their head from side to side when they mean "no," whereas Greeks express "no" with a sudden upward jerk of the head. Likewise, whereas raised eyebrows is an appropriate way to greet another in American culture, it is considered "indecent" in Japan and is rarely used except as an insult (Haviland et al. 2016). Moreover, every culture has clear rules about touching—some are deemed high-touch cultures, others low-touch (Ferraro and Andreatta 2018).

Language, thought, and culture are interrelated (Kottak 2015). Without language, there would be no culture, for language enables groups to store meanings, communicate with one another, and transmit knowledge between generations. Moreover, language plays an important role in how various cultures think about their "worlds." According to the *Sapir–Whorf hypothesis*, the language of each culture does not merely influence how people understand the world; it shapes perceptions and leads people to think in particular ways (Mandelbaum 1949; Sapir 1929; Whorf 1956). From this perspective, people who speak different languages live in different sensory worlds, for the structure of their languages and the words highlight some things and ignore others. This theory has generated much controversy among scholars, but research suggests that languages do facilitate particular ways of thinking because they make it easier to code or symbolize some events and objects, which as a result are easier to remember (DeLamater, Myers, and Collett 2015).

Although each language shapes reality, it does not imprison its speakers in a narrow and changeless world. This is because all languages are flexible and acutely sensitive to change. New words and ideas are regularly adopted by speakers of any language to fill various cultural needs. For example, computers and other technology have influenced our speech and thoughts noticeably. More and more people are using "text speech" in everyday conversations. It is not uncommon to hear a person speak the letters, "OMG" or "LOL" when conversing. In fact, "googling" has become a verb used when people are talking about looking up information on the internet.

Beliefs are assertions about the nature of reality. They provide groups with a fundamental orientation to the world and answer questions about proper relations among people, good and evil, and the destiny of humans and the universe. Unlike scientific knowledge, which is based on empirical understandings, many beliefs may be seen as "truths" by group members; they are based not on objective reality, but on social agreement. Moreover, yesterday's beliefs and the common sense of the moment are the falsehoods and "myths" of tomorrow. For example, the word "lunatic" is derived from the popular nineteenth-century belief that a full moon caused madness, a belief that had folk origins in European farming and hunting societies. Today, such thinking is derisively labeled "superstition"—although police officers, mental health professionals, and emergency room personnel tell of bizarre happenings during full moons. Many elementary teachers can tell you when it's a full moon without even referring to a calendar.

Belief systems in complex societies—particularly advanced industrial and postindustrial societies—include multiple and competing belief systems that often contain many contradictions. Scientific knowledge and religious beliefs present very different approaches to reality. One demands that we consider only what is empirical and observable in the "natural world." The other stresses a world beyond nature, and how the "supernatural" affects our lives. Cultural contradictions often require that people rationalize one set of beliefs in order to accommodate others. Likewise, beliefs typically change at a rapid rate. So do values.

Values are shared ideas about what is socially desirable. For all groups, values define what is desirable by ranking behaviors, people, events, objects, and social arrangements. These rankings define what is good or bad, beautiful or ugly, moral or immoral, just or unjust, and desirable or undesirable. In modern pluralistic societies, such as the United States, with its many ethnic, religious, and other groups, value orientations are complex. Some values may be widely shared, but others may be hotly disputed by various groups. Sociologist Robin Williams (1970) charted several core values that he maintained exert a particularly strong influence on the national culture and are especially prominent in the popular media.

In all complex societies, there are many inconsistencies and conflicts in cultural values. In addition to conflicting ideas based on ethnicity, religion, and other social divisions, there are conflicts in core values themselves. Some U.S. values—for example, freedom, achievement, progress, and individuality—may be logically consistent. Many others, however, are inconsistent and may even be contradictory. For example, although most Americans value work, they also value leisure; consequently, people may simultaneously resent *and* admire lottery winners and people with inherited wealth.

Conflicts in core values are but one aspect of value conflict in complex modern societies. According to the conflict perspective, social class, age, occupation, gender, race, and ethnicity all influence a person's value orientation. Because each of us is a member of many social categories, at any given moment our values may or may not all be in agreement. For example, the same elderly farmer who is opposed to "welfare handouts" may expect and demand federal farm subsidies and protest even the slightest changes in Social Security policy. We also regularly choose among alternative values in the course of our daily lives. In some social situations, total honesty may be required. In others—for example, when acquaintances casually ask how you are doing and you are in a terrible mood—they neither expect nor desire the "truth."

Often, social situations demand that we choose a particular value over others, and there are many ways to justify our decisions. At times we may rank certain values, believing that in a particular context one value is more appropriate than another. We may rationalize why we have chosen one value or another, or even deny that our values conflict. Sometimes powerful groups decide issues for us, or in some cases public opinion may resolve difficult issues. If the issue is sufficiently important, the vague abstractions and guidelines that are the basis of all values may be converted into specific rules, or norms.

Norms are expectations and rules for proper conduct that

guide the behavior of group members. Among all groups, norms provide guidelines that tell members how they should think and act in any given social situation. There are four major kinds of norms: folkways, mores, laws, and taboos.

The most common norms are *folkways*, informal rules and expectations that guide people's everyday behavior. They include such things as etiquette, table manners, proper appearance, and many other simple, everyday behaviors that in American culture are indicators of "self-control." Although people find violations of folkways annoying, they typically tolerate them. Moreover, when *sanctions*, penalties or rewards society uses to encourage conformity and punish deviance, are applied, they are usually *informal sanctions* that are loosely defined and applied by individuals rather than by an authorized social body. When a child holds a fork in the proper hand, a parent may sanction the behavior with praise. Conversely, if the child spreads butter on bread using fingers instead of an appropriate utensil, negative sanctions may be applied; the child may be ridiculed, threatened, or sent away from the table.

A breach of folkways is not ordinarily considered a threat to society, nor is the individual who occasionally violates them subjected to serious penalties. Nevertheless, the persistent violation of folkways may be interpreted by others as evidence of social deviance, and this could have serious consequences. The cumulative effect of many violations may be recognized as sufficient grounds for divorce, termination of employment, incarceration, or even confinement to a mental institution.

Norms are basic to every social situation; yet because they are so tightly woven into the fabric of social life, we often take them for granted. Typically, we conform to norms, and in most social situations we expect others to do the same. Some norms tell us what we should *not* do—for example, that students should not cheat on exams; these are called *proscriptive norms*. Others spell out what we *should do*—for example, take and pass exams; these are *prescriptive norms*.

Mores (pronounced "more-ays") are salient norms that people consider essential to the proper working of society. Mores have considerable moral (and sometimes religious) significance and are closely tied to values. People believe that mores protect what is right and good. *Formal sanctions*, which are clearly defined rewards or punishments administered by specialized agents of society, are often employed to ensure conformity to mores. Medals and awards may be given in recognition of heroic acts and special contributions to society. Conversely, people who commit serious violations of mores may be imprisoned, tortured, and executed.

A large number of mores have their roots in ancient religious traditions, and these include many proscriptive norms that have near-universal application. The "Thou shalt nots"—steal, commit adultery, or commit murder—and other "sacred commandments" are serious mores, and their violation brings strong and immediate public response. The desecration of important public symbols, such as burning the American flag, elicits similar responses. Unethical conduct may sometimes be recognized as a breach of mores as well. If an auto body shop does a sloppy paint job, the owner of the vehicle may become upset, but it is unlikely others would feel offended. If a mechanic is careless while adjusting an automobile's brakes, however, and a family is seriously injured or killed, most people would consider the lapse morally reprehensible and demand punishment.

Conformity is ensured partly by public understandings that mores are important to everyone and that detection and punishment for wrongdoers is almost a certainty. No society relies on coercion alone, however, to get people to conform to and uphold its most serious norms. During childhood, individuals are taught the rules of proper conduct. People internalize the rules and in effect become society's police—society's standards become "our" standards, and adherence to norms strongly influences how we view ourselves. When we conform to societal norms, we feel good knowing that we have done the "right thing"; when we violate norms, we feel bad, even if we are certain our offenses will never be known.

Important mores typically become encoded into *laws*, formal rules enacted and enforced by the power of the state, which apply to members of society. Laws that codify mores are usually recognized as vital to society, and most people believe that without them public order would be impossible. The relationship between laws and mores is complex, however. Sometimes laws and mores correspond closely; for example, it is both immoral and illegal to steal another's property. In other cases, laws may reflect the power of one group or segment of society relative to another, and their legitimacy may be challenged by opposition interests or groups. For example, prior to 1972 and *Roe v. Wade*, abortion was illegal in the United States. After the landmark Supreme Court decision that year, women gained the legal right to have an abortion. Although this law is supported by a large segment of American society, another portion has challenged it because, according to their views of morality, it violates the societal norm that we do not take another's life.

Sometimes laws may not correspond to a society's mores, and these laws are the most difficult to enforce and most subject to change. For example, in the United States, there is little public consensus regarding the morality of gambling. In some states gambling is illegal, but in others, state-sponsored lotteries and horse racing not only are legal but also contribute important revenues to the state. Thus, a police officer may make a gambling arrest in Utah on Friday, then cross the border into Nevada, go to Las Vegas, and gamble all weekend without seeing the slightest inconsistency in the two behaviors.

Taboos are prohibitions against behaviors that most members of a group consider to be so repugnant they are unthinkable. Eating human flesh, for example, is considered to be such a heinous act that in most societies neither sanctions nor laws are needed for compliance with the taboo against this behavior. Another taboo is the incest taboo, especially parent–child and sibling sex, that is widely shared around the world; incest is also a serious breach of the law in most nations. Their definition as "unthinkable," however, does not mean that people are not fascinated by taboos, as the *National Geographic* channel airs a series by that title featuring various taboo practices around the world.

Norms are enforced by the use of sanctions. For example, parents are expected to feed, clothe, and care for their children. If they do not, they may not only be punished for their neglect, but they may also lose custody of the children. Some norms apply in certain situations, but not in others. In the United States, for example, people should not spit on the floor of a home, nor should they spit on a crowded street. During baseball games, however, spitting is so common among the players that people who do not know the sport might think it was an essential part of the game.

ETHNOCENTRISM AND CULTURAL RELATIVISM

Small children are acute observers of human behavior, and for a few years they are receptive to every cultural tradition on earth. Children learn languages—even 10 or 15 languages in some parts of the world—and are able to imitate hundreds of gestures with ease. Young children willingly sample foods, wear different clothing styles, and accept as fact an extraordinary variety of beliefs. For example, children learn that only some plants and animals can be eaten and that some are better than others. Children also learn to distinguish and rank houses, clothing apparel, automobiles, people, and virtually everything else.

Sociologists call this kind of thinking *ethnocentrism*—the tendency to evaluate the customs of other groups according to one's own cultural standards. Ethnocentrism is such a strong tendency that when social scientists encounter particularly exotic cultures, even they are not always able to restrain their cultural biases.

Ethnocentrism has a positive side. It can enhance group stability by providing members with roots and a strong sense of meaning and purpose. The tendency to view one's culture as "the best" also has provided humans with many different solutions to the problems of living. If groups had taken their cultures lightly or even pragmatically, cultural homogeneity rather than cultural diversity would now be the norm. But most people are attached to their religious beliefs, foods, clothing, and other customs, and are unwilling to give them up except under extreme conditions. Even social researchers may experience difficulty identifying their own cultural assumptions and biases—especially when there are strong emotional responses to people, groups, and places (Cylwik 2001).

Throughout history, ethnocentrism's negative side has been equally pronounced. Viewing one's values and customs as natural and right, and those of others as inferior and wrong, often contributes to prejudice and discrimination, interethnic conflict, exploitation, and even ethnic cleansing and genocide.

Multiculturalism recognizes cultural diversity as a national asset rather than a liability. Further, it recognizes that in different regions of the country much of the population is considered "multicultural." The movement emerged in the 1980s, on campuses and in other social arenas, during the second-largest wave of immigration in American history. *Multiculturalism* encourages respect and appreciation for cultural difference. In many ways, the multicultural movement seeks to reverse centuries of cultural intolerance and oppression of minority groups in the United States, Canada, and Europe. The majority historically has taken an *assimilationist approach* to immigrant groups, demanding that they abandon their cultural heritages and adopt the traditions of the host group. In the United States, this meant adopting the English language and the foods, dress, religion, and other cultural practices of the dominant European (Anglo-Saxon) groups, which established the early colonies and dominated American institutions (Gitlin 1996).

Some call this one-sided approach to minority groups and their cultures *Eurocentrism*, the belief that European cultures have contributed the most to human knowledge and are superior to all others. This perspective is especially pronounced in the U.S. educational system, where European accomplishments, interests, and perspectives have dominated history, literature, and all other subjects from grade school through college. In recent years, some minority groups have sought to balance these views with educational programs that emphasize their unique perspectives and accomplishments. *Afrocentrism*, for example, emphasizes the preeminence of African and African American culture in human development. Like Eurocentrism, however, it suffers from a unidimensional view of history, literature, and art by placing African culture above all others (Schlesinger 1998).

Multiculturalism has brought fundamental changes to American education, and "developing the ability to adapt to different cultural contexts may be one of the key learning areas of the curriculum of the future" (Campbell 2000:31). The shift toward the appreciation of cultural diversity is reflected in a new emphasis on global languages in most school curricula and in efforts to bring the literatures and perspectives of many ethnic groups to human understanding, especially those that have been ignored in history and education, such as Native American cultures. Multiculturalism also has raised people's consciousness about the importance of gender, disability, sexual orientation, and other cultural differences that were previously neglected. The movement has also led to ethnic revival in many cities and in the nation as a whole, as evidenced by the celebrations of ethnic foods and folk customs and by the holiday parades that celebrate ethnicity. Nowhere is this celebration more apparent than in popular culture and media celebrations of global diversity, from Disney World to the Olympics, that are now beamed to billions of people worldwide.

The introduction of multiculturalism has not been without controversy, and there has been a strong backlash against the movement in politics and education. For some, "affirmative action," "welfare," and "multicultural" have become "code words" that license more subtle forms of racial and ethnic exclusion (Macedo and Bartolomé 1999). Some conservative politicians have called multiculturalism misguided and even dangerous to the nation's future. Supreme Court nominee Robert Bork (1996:120–123), for example, called challenges to Eurocentrism "ignorant and perverse," noting that "European American culture is the best the world has to offer." More tangible effects of the conservative backlash have been anti-immigrant legislation and efforts in many states to legislate "English only" in schools and government offices. At the national level, several bills have been introduced in Congress to make English the "official language" of the United States, and in 2006, Congress passed a law stating that English was the "common language" that unites the United States. President Trump's oft-repeated phrase "America First" seemingly takes this even a step further, discounting diversity in favor of nationalism, or "Americentrism," ignoring even the European influence on American culture.

One important way in which we can guard against ethnocentric biases is by adopting *cultural relativism*, a perspective that asks that we evaluate other cultures according to their standards, not ours. For example, a highly unusual custom to most Americans is the extension of lips that once marked ideal beauty in Central Africa. Circular plugs were inserted into the lips and then gradually enlarged until the lips were stretched 4 inches or more. On the surface, this custom seems to make little sense, but let's examine it more carefully.

First, sociologists have found that most cultures modify the face and lips in some way to achieve beauty. For example, many American women use lipstick; some have enhanced their lips surgically. But why did so many villages in Central Africa take what may seem to Americans a more extreme approach to beauty? Some functionalist scholars attribute the custom of placing large circular objects in the lips to intense slave raiding a century ago. They contend that villages that practiced lip extension were often avoided by slave raiders, and this may have encouraged villagers to exaggerate lip extension as a symbol of beauty.

IDEAL VERSUS REAL CULTURE

Another important source of cultural variation in every contemporary society is contradictions and disagreements between *ideal culture*, what people should do, according to group norms and values, and *real culture*, what people do in everyday social interaction. Value conflicts create strains and tensions in society, social problems, and sometimes even wars. Ideally, the United States is a land of opportunity where everyone is given an equal chance to succeed. In fact, social barriers such as age, gender, class, and race inhibit the chances of some and enhance the chances of others. Parents are expected to love and care for their children, yet it is estimated that as many as a million children each year are victims of abuse, and another million and a half suffer from neglect (Gelles 1997; Straus et al. 2006; National Children's Alliance 2014).

Contradictions between ideal and real culture can be an important source of social change. For example, for many years police tolerated drunk-driving violations. Conforming to the public view that occasional excessive drinking was not socially harmful, police may have ignored violations or subverted the law by taking drunk drivers to their homes. The efforts of some individuals and the social movement Mothers Against Drunk Driving (MADD) led to changes in public opinion on this issue, resulting in much stricter enforcement of the law.

Almost 100 years ago, well before television, computers, and cell phones, William Ogburn (1922, 1964) noted that material culture tends to change more rapidly than nonmaterial culture and that this can cause cultural strains and even contradictions. This may result in *cultural lag*, inconsistencies in a cultural system, especially in the relationship between technology and nonmaterial culture. Recent advances in medical technology have had precisely the effects Ogburn proposed. We now have the ability to keep terminally ill patients alive indefinitely, using heart pumps, human and animal organ transplants, and artificial respirators. Cultural lag is obvious in such cases, for neither doctors nor family members are entirely sure of their responsibilities to the patient. Laws vary widely as well, for medical innovations have so redefined the fundamental nature of human existence that judges and juries regularly decide these issues. Recent experiments with genetic engineering and cloning have raised even more complicated questions that will provide new challenges in the future.

SUBCULTURES AND COUNTERCULTURES

Subcultures are groups that share many elements of mainstream culture but maintain their own distinctive customs, values, norms, and lifestyles. There are subcultures based on age, gender, wealth, sexual orientation, education, and occupation, to name only a few. Within organizations, management and workers maintain their own symbols, specialized languages, and material culture, as do subcultures in rural and urban areas. Even within a 10-block area in most cities, there may be hundreds or thousands of subcultures, including jazz musicians, street people, inner-city gangs, investment bankers, garment workers, motorcyclists, and topless dancers.

Every region of the United States is a mosaic of ethnic and religious subcultures as well. For example, although Lowell, Massachusetts, is famous as the birthplace of the Industrial Revolution, from its beginnings it has also been the crucible for an important and continuing multicultural experiment. The town, founded in 1826, was initially the home of Boston-based English gentry who financed and built the textile mills that attracted immigrants from all over the world. Jewish, Greek, Polish, and Portuguese people arrived first, along with over 30,000 Irish Catholic immigrants who moved to Lowell during the Irish potato famine of the 1840s (Kiang 1994). French Canadians arrived next and created the Little Canada community. In the 1950s, large numbers of Puerto Ricans and Dominicans relocated to Lowell to work in the garment industry. The most dramatic and rapid growth in Lowell, however, occurred in the 1980s. At that time, more than 25,000 Cambodians and several thousand Vietnamese and Laotians moved from other states to work as entry-level assemblers in new high-tech industries, bringing with them Buddhism, Confucianism, and many other forms of ethnic and religious diversity (Kiang 1994).

Countercultures reject the conventional wisdom and standards of behavior of the majority and provide alternatives to mainstream culture. For these reasons, they are considered threats to society, their members are labeled "deviant," and they are subjected to a variety of negative sanctions. Inequalities of class, race, age, gender, and other forms of social differentiation in contemporary postindustrial societies provide fertile ground for the development of countercultures. For example, political and social protests in the 1960s spawned dozens of countercultures, including the Black Panthers and the hippie movement. More recently, skinheads, the Aryan Brotherhood, the Christian Identity Movement, and the so-called alt-right have emerged to challenge multiculturalism, nonwhite immigration, and racial harmony, with calls for a return to white domination and "racial purity."

A number of sociologists suggest that the marginal status of adolescence has contributed to the proliferation of youth subcultures and even countercultures. This theory of *marginality* was first used to explain the predicament of second-generation immigrants (Park 1928; Stonequist 1937) who, while trying to assimilate and emulate the dominant cultural group, also attempt to retain some visibility as minorities, and consequently are not fully acculturated. Nor are they fully accepted members of either cultural system. This has encouraged the formation of adolescent subcultures and sometimes countercultures in the United States and worldwide (Thompson and Bynum 2017). Throughout the twentieth century, numerous youth countercultural movements, from heavy metal in the 1970s and 1980s to gangster rap and grunge in the 1990s, to rave subcultures with their drug use, all-night "rave" dance parties, and computer-generated music (Wilson 2003) have attacked traditional adult norms and values. Some sociologists believe that traditional ways of distinguishing between subculture and countercultures may be confusing and even ethnocentric where some "countercultures" are involved. According to James and Laura Dowd (2003:34), "Rather than continuing to think of countercultures as constituting an altogether different entity from the more common and less deviant subcultures, . . . [we] would emphasize the key distinction of a group's likelihood of assimilating into the surrounding culture. That is, countercultures publically and actively resist assimilation, whereas other types of subcultures are far less likely to do so" (Dowd and Dowd 2003:34).

POPULAR CULTURE

Popular culture comprises tastes and creations that appeal to the masses. Because popular culture consists of products and creations designed for leisure, entertainment, and mass consumption, it includes a bewildering assortment of things that critics say favor "vulgarity," "the commonplace," and the "lowest common denominator" (Bogart 1991:63). Examples of popular culture include prime-time television, Elvis statues, live concerts by popular artists, tractor-pulling contests, UFC, baseball cards, NASCAR, and the mall Easter Bunny and Santa Claus. Some people argue that those who indulge in these elements of culture are "uncultured," implying or even outright saying that they have no culture. But the third wisdom of sociology teaches us that *there's no such thing as an "uncultured" person.*

Some sociologists contend that globalization and new information technologies have blurred "taste cultures." Anthropologist Terry Eagleton (2000:125) believes that traditional high culture has been supplanted by new media combinations and that there is "almost no popular culture outside commercial forms." At least one scholar argues that the Disney model has had such a profound effect on social structure and culture that it has created a *Disneyization* of global society (Bryman 2004). Technology, from cell phones and tablets to interactive videos and the World Wide Web, has given anyone access to virtually all of the arts, from the great books to comic books and graffiti. One study suggests that members of the upper class (highbrows) no longer limit themselves to the fine arts to distinguish themselves from other classes (lowbrows), as they did in previous periods. Instead, upper- and upper-middle-class professionals have become "cultural omnivores," who appreciate a great variety of art, music, and dance from around the world. Cultural eclecticism, of course, is highly functional in a global economy and can be used to express such things as a broad-based education, international experience, and cultural tolerance and understanding (Peterson and Kern 1996).

This is not to say that every kind of cultural production has become equal, however. One researcher found that art, music, dance, and other leisure activities that are considered highbrow culture in nations such as the United States, Israel, and Sweden may be considered "popular culture" in nations such as Germany and Italy, where they receive considerable funding by the state, cities, and even towns. Further, in pluralistic societies today, class divisions and cultural consumption are differentiated by national context, but "there are significant linkages between race, religion, and gender" (Katz-Gerro 2002:224). Moreover, "taste," now in the guise of a broad knowledge of global music and fine arts, continues to be useful in class ranking. For example, corporate employers may use evidence of "cultural eclecticism" as one important measure of managerial competence. Cultural tolerance, however, has its limits, and this, too, may reinforce class and other social boundaries.

Culture is such an integral part of our lives that we take it for granted. We tend to assume that values, norms, and beliefs are inherent. People are not born with culture, and it cannot be genetically transmitted. Culture must be acquired and is transmitted from one generation to the next through the process of socialization.

Sociological Wisdom 4

#WhenYouWereBornYouWereNotYetYou

BECOMING YOU: A SOCIAL BEING

HAVE YOU EVER HEARD OR PERHAPS said yourself that you "rely on your instincts?" Scientists have discovered that they can take a baby wren's egg from the nest, incubate it, and after the bird is hatched, when it becomes nesting time, it will instinctively build a wren's nest. The same holds true for robins, sparrows, or virtually any other species of bird. Likewise, many animals seem to be "hardwired" to instinctively build their nests, hives, dens, and other domains in a particular design and fashion. Conversely, if a newborn human is taken from its parents shortly after birth, even though it has all of its biological and physiological needs met, they are not likely to grow up and know how to build a four-bedroom, three-bath home with a two-car garage on a cul-de-sac. In fact, if a developing child's emotional and social needs are not met, they likely will never learn to walk, speak, or display any other attributes that we typically refer to as being "human," and may in fact die at a very early age. Legends about feral children, such as infants Romulus and Remus being raised by wolves and growing up to found the city of Rome, or Tarzan being raised by apes, are very popular and make wonderful stories and movies. In these stories, the characters not only learn to walk, speak, and perform all other human activities, but they also tend to be more honest, noble, and trustworthy than the rest of us, who seemingly have been corrupted by civilization. These popular legends are entertaining, but they also are emblematic that *things are not what they seem*. Not only are these legends based on pure fiction, but they also should make us realize that becoming who we are is a complex process that goes well beyond our biology and physiology. Thus, illustrating the fourth wisdom of sociology: *when you were born, you were not yet you.*

We know that babies are born with very few, if any, instinctive behaviors and cannot survive without the care, nurturance, and guidance of other humans. It is through the process of *socialization*, in interacting with others, that we become human beings. Socialization is a process in which we learn and *internalize* the attitudes, values, beliefs, and norms of our culture, and develop a sense of self. This lifelong procedure begins at birth and continues until death. Socialization provides a vital link between an individual and society. And by the way, research indicates that although birds instinctively build certain types of nests, their nest-building skills are also partially learned and improved by watching and participating with other birds in the process (Walsh 2016).

NATURE AND NURTURE

Scientists have debated the influence of nature (*heredity*) versus nurture (*environment*) in *personality* development for many years. During the late nineteenth and early twentieth centuries, the argument was dominated by those on the side of heredity. In *On the Origin of Species*, Charles Darwin ([1859] 1964) contended that all organisms are in a constant struggle, and that to survive, species must make continuous biological and physiological adaptations to their environments. Some social scientists used Darwin's ideas to argue that human organisms are driven by biology and physiology. By the 1920s, several thousand so-called human instincts that determine human behavior had been identified (Bernard 1924).

During the twentieth century, the pendulum swung in the opposite direction; the influence of environment and learning was viewed as paramount in human development. Many behaviorists went so far as to declare that humans are totally devoid of instincts, and *all* behavior is learned (Watson 1924).

As organisms, we have certain genetic, biological, and physiological attributes that establish behavioral constraints and boundaries. At the same time, as social beings with the ability to think, learn, rationalize, and interpret our behavior, we have the ability to develop countless unique characteristics within our biological and physiological makeup.

Since the mid-1970s, a more balanced approach to personality and social development has emerged, with social scientists acknowledging that the nature versus nurture debate has been futile and unproductive. Today, there is much agreement that both nature and nurture are

"So, how do you want to play this? Nature, nurture, or a bit of both?"

important and that, as humans, we are products of both our heredity and our environment. The nature versus nurture debate is over, and both sides lost (Bradshaw and Ellison 2009), or as Matt Ridley (2003) put it, it is no longer nature versus nurture, but nature *via* nurture.

A controversial approach that has gained popularity by combining the influences of nature and nurture is *sociobiology*, a field that integrates theories and research from biology and sociology in an effort to better understand human behavior. Much of the sociobiological literature concludes that genetics, biology, and physiology set parameters on a wide range of human characteristics, traits, and even temperament; environment, socialization, and experience then shape the final product (Tabery 2014; Wilson 2000). Clearly, all of us are affected by our biology and physiology, but our personalities and behavior are largely shaped by social and cultural variables. Consequently, it can be stated with confidence that who we are and what we do represent a dynamic interplay among (1) genetic traits and characteristics, (2) the environment, and (3) what we learn in interaction with others (Cherry 1994; Ridley 2003).

The interplay between heredity and environment is important, and nowhere is this better demonstrated than in the process of early childhood socialization. At conception and during prenatal development, we are genetically programmed for characteristics such as sex, race, skin color, and hair and eye color, as well as height and weight. In addition, neurobiological research indicates that, contrary to previous beliefs that infants' brains are fully developed at birth, during the first two to three years of life a baby's brain is literally being "wired" for skills and activities such as thinking; mathematics; music; and, most importantly, language. These studies show that the brains of institutionalized children and infants who are ignored or not spoken to often are less active and hence do not physically develop in the same ways as the brains of children whose parents talk to them a great deal, play music for them, and otherwise stimulate brain activity (Begley 1997; Kantrowitz 1997; Cowley 2000).

From birth, people are bombarded with cultural and social experiences that shape their development. Since newborn infants are totally dependent on others and seemingly totally malleable, the earliest stages of socialization are critical in the development of personality and the process of becoming human. Because we must learn the distinctive behaviors associated with being human (especially the use of language), early childhood socialization takes on compelling significance.

DEVELOPING A SOCIAL SELF

The process of becoming human involves the development of what psychologists call a *personality*—a dominant pattern of attitudes, feelings, and behaviors—or what sociologists call a *concept of self*. Sigmund Freud ([1923] 1947), noted physician and psychologist, contended that there are three important components of personality: the *id*, the *superego*, and the *ego*. George Herbert Mead, a contemporary of Freud, also saw personality as being multidimensional, but he viewed its development as a social process. Mead (1934) contended that an individual's mind and conception of *self* are inseparable from society and social interaction. Research indicates that almost half of all parents (43%) think that children's personalities are genetically determined, but that same research demonstrates that how parents and others treat children has dramatic impact on personality development and shaping a sense of self (Hayden 2000). These studies emphasize the importance of the socialization process on personality development and the powerful influence of society on the individual. According to Mead, the *self*, a person's conscious recognition that they are a distinct individual who is part of a larger society, emerges through social experience. Using the symbolic interactionist perspective, Mead divorced the self from biological components and viewed people's ability to think of themselves as social objects in relation to others as the characteristic that distinguishes human beings from other animals. Behaviorists such as John B. Watson (1924) and Ivan Pavlov ([1926] 2013) had demonstrated that animals could be trained to react to certain stimuli; Mead insisted that humans not only react to stimuli in their environment but also, more importantly, *interpret* them. Human actions are, then, based on the meanings that humans impute to stimuli.

Mead contended that the self is composed of two related and interdependent components: the "I" and the "me." The *I* is the unsocialized self as subject. More spontaneous, creative, and uninhibited than the "me," the "I" is the initiator of social action. Young children tend to be "I-dominated," in that they usually see themselves as the center of the social universe. In other words, they view the world as revolving around them. Correspondingly, much of their conversation is punctuated with the word "I": "I'm hungry," "I want a drink," "I want a toy," and so forth.

Through socialization, as the sense of self develops more fully, the *me* component, or the socialized self as object, develops. The sense of "me" represents people's ability to realize that they are members of a social world and that, although they have the ability to act in a way that has an impact on others, others can also act in ways that have an impact on them. Although the "I" is spontaneous and creative, the "me" is reactive; it is based on our perception of how others will respond to our actions. The "I" and the "me" are the basis of thought and allow the individual to experience social interaction, even in the absence of others. Through effective socialization, the "I" and the "Me" work in harmony to allow us to act, react, and interact while taking others into account.

Mead's conception of the self was influenced by his colleague Charles Horton Cooley, who coined the term *looking-glass self* to describe the process in which individuals use others like mirrors and base their conceptions of themselves on what is reflected back to them during social interaction. Also working from the interactionist perspective, Cooley ([1902] 1922) described three successive steps in the process:

1. The imagination of our appearance to others
2. The imagination of their judgment of that appearance
3. The development of feelings about and responses to these judgments

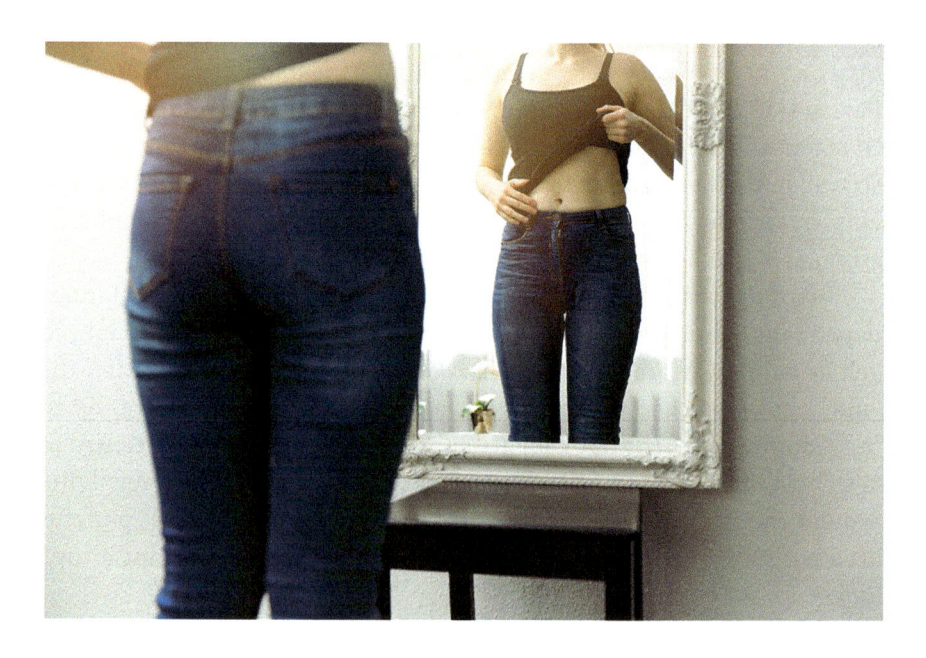

For example, if you approach a group of people, you are immediately aware that you are giving off an impression. Generally you want that impression to be as favorable as possible, and you may view yourself as being friendly, witty, and charming. As you interact with members of the group, you "read" both their verbal and nonverbal reactions to assess whether they view you in the way you imagine you appear to them. If their feedback is positive and they include you in the group, you will have your positive concept of self reaffirmed. On the other hand, if they suddenly stop talking, seem to feel ill at ease, look away, or make a hasty retreat, you might reassess your feelings about yourself and wonder if maybe you are less friendly, witty, and charming than you thought.

It is possible to misinterpret the feedback we receive from others. We have all experienced the uneasy feeling of not being quite sure how people were responding to us as we interacted with them. Did their laughter mean they enjoyed my joke? Or were they laughing at me in ridicule? How a person answers those questions relates to their conception of *self* based on past social experiences and particular social situations.

Because our most important identities lend continuity and unity to our behavior, we tend to think of our "selves" as fixed and changeless. In fact, social interaction requires that the selves we present to others vary from situation to situation; that is, we all have multiple selves. *Situated self* describes the self that emerges in a particular situation. For example, being African American and being a woman are both important identities. Nevertheless, when an African American woman interacts with African American men, she is most likely to think of herself as a woman; when she interacts with white women, she is more likely to activate her African American identity (DeLamater et al. 2015).

How does a social self develop? It is taught and learned through the process of socialization by the major *agents of socialization*: family, school, church, peers, and in many cases, the mass media.

AGENTS OF SOCIALIZATION

Socialization is considered too important to leave to chance, so every society has institutionalized ways of carrying out the process. Agents of socialization are those groups and institutions that both informally and formally take on the task of socialization.

In all societies, the first major agent of socialization for most individuals is the family. From birth, or at the time of adoption, parents and siblings influence the social development of the newborn infant, or young child, helping him or her to internalize culture and develop a social identity. Much of the family's impact on socialization is intentional and carefully designed, but some of it is inadvertent and unrealized. Parents have been known to admonish a child to "do as I say, and not as I do," but in many cases another old adage comes into play in the form of "actions speak louder than words."

Parents and older siblings play a key part in early sex-role socialization. In the United States, often the infant's bedroom is decorated according to whether the baby is a boy or a girl, and clothing and toys deemed appropriate to the child's gender are chosen. As the child develops a sense of self, parents and siblings serve as important role models for gender identity (Marshall 2003; Robinson-Wood 2017).

Socialization within the family is not a one-way street. As parents and older siblings are socializing younger family members, they are simultaneously being socialized themselves. Harriet Rheingold (1969) contended that human infants are social by nature and that socialization is always a mutual process. She believes that during the first months of life, babies socialize others more than they are socialized. She pointed out that the birth of a baby affects all other family members, who must learn to modify their routines and needs to fit those of the baby. Rheingold suggested that an infant's cry is an important social signal. It is the first way the child learns to communicate with others and to exert some control over the environment. Parents learn to distinguish cries of hunger from cries of pain and discomfort. The child also learns that crying is a way to manipulate others. Similarly, a baby uses a smile as a social signal to indicate recognition, comfort, or pleasure. Babies soon discover that through crying and smiling they can significantly control the behavior of others.

As the demands of work and careers increase, as family structure changes and more women enter the workforce, families are increasingly abdicating their role in their children's socialization to other social groups, agencies, and institutions. Robin Leavitt and Martha Power (1989) opened an important avenue for future research with their study of the impact of day-care centers on children's emotional development. Subsequent studies suggest that day-care centers are just as important as the family and, more importantly, just as capable of providing primary socialization, teaching verbal skills, and teaching young children to think (*Washington Post* 1997). Past sociological research on early childhood socialization concentrated on the family; future research must include day-care centers, preschools, and other surrogate family settings (Grusec and Hastings 2008; Berns 2015).

The second major agent of socialization encountered by most children is the school. All societies have an institutionalized process for teaching important knowledge to new generations. It may involve youngsters sitting at the feet of the eldest and wisest tribal member while the elder provides them with an oral history of their cultural traditions, or it may involve a complex bureaucracy that includes preschools, kindergartens, elementary and secondary schools, community colleges, universities, and graduate and professional schools.

The school's primary charge in the socialization process is the transmission of the cognitive aspects of culture (i.e., knowledge and ideas) from one generation to another, and preparation for assuming future roles. In a postindustrial society like the United States, education is formalized and highly structured. Language and mathematical skills as well as scientific and technological knowledge are taught. The culture's art, music, literature, and history are also usually considered essential.

Teaching cognitive culture is widely accepted, but the teaching of the normative aspects of culture can be controversial. Some resent the "hidden curriculum" of the school and believe that the school should limit its socialization efforts to teaching academic skills and knowledge, leaving the teaching of values and beliefs to the family and church. Others argue that the school has an obligation to socialize young people into the roles of "good and productive citizens," believing that intellectual knowledge should be supplemented with teaching values, ethics, and morality.

Beyond teaching culture, the school also plays an important role in the development of social identity. Whether a student is viewed as "gifted" or "dumb," "good" or "bad," "cooperative" or "a troublemaker" influences their sense of self. Jonathan Kozol (1967) described what he called "the destruction of the hearts and minds" of black children who were subjected to the racial prejudice and discrimination of teachers and administrators in the Boston public schools during the 1960s. The children were labeled "dumb," "dirty," and "failures"; their self-esteem was crushed; and they followed a self-fulfilling prophecy of illiteracy, truancy, and vandalism, eventually dropping out of school in large numbers.

Schools have become increasingly dependent on mass media, social media, and technology for educational purposes. Almost all forms of media and technology are standard features in many schools today and will become even more commonplace in the future. Schools also have become dependent on computers, which supplement instruction by teachers in many school systems. In the future, computers and other forms of technology may become the primary means of instruction and hence major agents of socialization.

A third agent of socialization is religion. Not all societies have organized churches, but all have institutionalized religious practices. Functionalists point out that an important role of religion is to contribute to the socialization of societal members by instilling in them a sense of purpose in life and providing them with moral instruction. This function is so important that according to anthropologists, over the past 100,000 years no group of people anywhere on earth have been found that did not practice some form of religion (Haviland et al. 2016).

One outcome of religious socialization is the development of a *life theme*, an overriding way of viewing and interpreting the world (McNeil 1969). The teachings of the church may influence eating habits, dating practices, mate selection, birth control practices, funeral customs, and many other elements of lifestyle. For example, the powerful influence of religious socialization on developing a *life theme* can be found among the Old Order Amish. Although the family serves as the primary socialization agent in Amish communities, their religious beliefs permeate every aspect of everyday life.

Peers are also important agents of socialization. A child's first peer group is made up of children of roughly the same age who live in the same village or neighborhood or attend the same day-care center. Parents and older siblings, teachers and school administrators, and church officials and religious leaders all have more power than those they are attempting to socialize. Peers, however, are relatively equal in social status and have no recognized authority to sanction behavior. Also, the peer group is a voluntary association, usually the first one experienced by children. Thus, youths have the option of leaving their peer group, but not their family or their school, at any time. Nevertheless, in the United States, peers, especially during adolescence, often emerge as the most powerful among the major agents of socialization. Fear of losing friends is a strong element of social control because people tend to evaluate themselves on the basis of the number of friends they have (Feld 1991; McKay and Fanning 2016).

There are times when parents, teachers, and the church come into direct conflict with peers in the socialization process. For example, these different agents of socialization often disagree on values and attitudes toward truancy, drinking, taking drugs, music, and sexual activity. Adults generally view these activities as serious norm violations, but peers often see them as harmless and may encourage participation in them. Research indicates that much of what constitutes delinquency among middle-class adolescents may be largely attributable to the importance of belonging to and identifying with the youth subculture (Thompson and Bynum 2017).

The workplace provides an important agent for the socialization of adults. This is especially true in the United States, where a person's occupation becomes an integral part of their personal and social identity. In the United States, much of our *anticipatory socialization* as children and young adults is oriented toward preparing us to assume work and occupational roles. Once we enter the workplace, a more specific socialization into occupational roles occurs. The socialization process usually follows two lines. First, formal socialization by supervisors teaches us the policies, rules and regulations, and perhaps the technical skills needed to complete the assigned work successfully; second, informal socialization by coworkers teaches us the "unofficial rules" we must abide by to be accepted by our peers on the job (Hughes 1958; Ritzer 1977).

Socialization into a work role may take place at a college or training program; however, when individuals enter the workplace they experience additional socialization by those with whom they work. Most employers realize that the socialization of employees as they enter the workplace is important, and research indicates that employees may view training and socialization as being even more important than their employers do (Jacobs, Lukens, and Useem 1996). Sometimes this necessitates shedding former attitudes, values, beliefs, and behaviors, as well as acquiring socialization into almost an entirely new identity.

Assuming a work role is an important part of one's social identity; it is thus a continuation of the process of developing a self. Work experiences during adolescence have been linked to self-esteem (Steitz and Owen 1992). There is mounting evidence that socialization experienced in the workplace is important and "has diverse psychological consequences, including effects on intellectual flexibility, self-concept, worldview, and affective states" (Miller 1988:350).

One of the important goals of socialization is the transmission of culture from one generation to the next. This involves communication, and communication is what media and technology are all about. Media help tell us who we are and help shape our identities; they give us aspirations and provide us with a means of escape. They also promote traditional cultural values and serve to maintain the status quo. Meanwhile, technology can reinforce traditional values or shatter them almost overnight.

We are only beginning to understand the influence of media and technology on the socialization process. *Social learning theory* contends that much human behavior is learned from modeling others (Bandura 1977, 2015), and studies show that when children identify strongly with media characters, they are influenced by them (Patterson 2004; Stephens 1994; Williams, LaRose, and Frost 1981). Moreover, research indicates that media should not be underestimated as a source of racial, ethnic, and sex-role stereotypes (Evra 1990; Milkie 2007; Stephens 1994; Williams et al. 1981). In short, media penetrate our daily lives and shape our consciousness.

Popular celebrities and entertainers often serve as role models for children and adults, especially in the areas of grooming and dress. Parents are often concerned about their children emulating some celebrities whom they view as negative role models.

Stereotypes are often learned through socialization, and media play a powerful role in this capacity. The media promote age, race, and gender stereotypes and socialize people in how to see and act toward the elderly, racial and ethnic minorities, and women. Moreover, they tend to provide a dichotomous view of society that simplifies complex issues into conflicts between right and wrong, good and bad, moral and immoral. In most media scenarios, the side of right, good, and moral eventually prevails. Not coincidentally, the conflict theorists point out, these are almost always represented by those viewed as having legitimate power and authority over others: the government, the police, the rich, and the powerful. Criminals, drug addicts, lunatics, and others who pose a threat to the existing order are often portrayed in the media as coming from the lower social strata, foreign evil empires, or other planets (Parenti 1992).

Whether the media establish cultural norms and values or merely reflect them can be debated *ad infinitum*. Probably, media do both. We are socialized by all forms of media, and at the same time, through our power as consumers and by interacting with them, we influence what appears in and on them. Today, powerful new forms of social media not only have changed our ability to communicate but also have transformed the way we think and recreate who we are (Langmia and Tyree 2017). It is virtually impossible to overemphasize the power of social media in regard to socialization and social interaction.

Sociologist Sherry Turkle (2005, 2009, 2011, 2016, 2017) noted that the computer is much more than a tool. It becomes a part of our identity, what she calls the *second self*. In the world of cyberspace, people create new identities that may be part reality, part fiction, or total fantasy. The impact of media, especially the effect of new technologies on socialization throughout the entire *life course*, certainly warrants more sociological investigation.

SOCIALIZATION OVER THE LIFE COURSE

Socialization is a lifelong process. Early childhood socialization involves a complex process through which children form important attachments, or bonds, with their parents, while simultaneously developing a concept of self that is separate and apart from them. The first two to three years of a child's life are critical for both physical and social development. Despite over 100 years of so-called expert advice on raising children, little of the anxiety and unpredictability of childhood socialization has been relieved (Hulbert 2011, 2018).

The works of Mead and Cooley focused on *primary socialization*. Beginning at birth and extending through childhood, primary socialization is important because it provides the foundation for our personality and the development of our social selves, which influence our behavior throughout our lives. It also teaches us some of the basic norms, values, and behavioral expectations of our culture.

Mead believed that the most important outcome of socialization was *role taking*, the ability to anticipate what others expect of us and to act accordingly. According to Mead, role taking develops in stages over a period of time. These stages are not based on biology or physical maturity as much as they are related to the extent of one's social experience. During childhood, because our social interaction is limited, we first learn to respond to *significant others*, specific people with whom we interact and whose response has meaning for us, such as parents, siblings, and perhaps a few close playmates. As our social world expands, we learn to anticipate and internalize the expectations of *generalized others*, the dominant attitudes and expectations of most members of society. It does not matter that we have not interacted with all of these people, for that is no longer necessary. Rather, we have conceptualized our place in the social world and base our actions on how we think they will be received by others.

Mead outlined three developmental stages involved in the process of learning roles. Stage 1, the *imitative stage*, is a period when children mimic the behaviors of others. During this stage, little children often imitate their parents or older siblings. Stage 2 is the *play stage*, in which children begin to play at the roles of specific other people. Elementary school–age children often come home and line up their dolls and stuffed animals, assume the role of teacher, and "teach" the toys how to say the alphabet or how to count to 10. The play stage is the beginning of anticipatory socialization, which involves learning designed to prepare an individual for the fulfillment of future statuses and roles. Stage 3, which Mead called the *game stage*, involves the assumption of different roles (often as part of an organized game). For example, a child who plays on a soccer team not only must understand their position as forward but also must understand the role expectations of halfbacks, fullbacks, the goalie, and other players. The game also demands an understanding of the rules and the roles played by coaches, officials, and others connected with it.

Mead divorced his stages from physiology and biology. He did not suggest at what age an individual might move from the imitative stage to the play stage, or from the play stage to the game (role-taking) stage, because he believed age was irrelevant to the process. Rather, Mead viewed the developmental process as purely *social*. By interacting with others, an individual develops a self; then, as a result of further social experience, they learn to see the world through the eyes of others.

Socialization in childhood and adolescence varies from one culture to another. For example, although parents in the United States traditionally encourage children to become independent and "stand on their own two feet," Japanese parents emphasize dependence on parents and the family throughout childhood and adolescence. These two contrasting views reflect and reinforce the different cultural values of the two countries. In every culture, the socialization process is not confined to childhood and adolescence, but continues throughout the life course.

Until the beginning of the twenty-first century, 18- to 30-year-olds were ignored by social and behavioral scientists studying socialization. If addressed at all, they were simply considered young adults and were lumped in with other adult populations. As the new millennium dawned, however, a social phenomenon arose in American society and in other parts of the postindustrial world. More and more millennials were graduating high school and refusing to leave home, enjoying the lack of responsibility and stress associated with living with parents in a lifestyle they could never afford out on their own. Many went off to college and graduated, only to return home to live with their parents. Sociologists coined terms such as "twixters," "tweens," and "kidults" to describe millennials who had entered a new life stage sometimes referred to as "youthhood" or "adultescence"—a period between adolescence and adulthood (Grossman 2005).

Differing explanations have arisen for this ever-increasing phenomenon. Many concerned, stunned, and even embarrassed parents attribute it to laziness. Researchers suggest the trend may be far more complex than that. Sociologists, psychologists, and economists who study millennials contend that twixters are not growing up because the social and cultural mechanisms that used to turn children into adults have broken down or no longer exist. They argue that growing up is much harder than it used to be and that society no longer provides the social and moral background or the financial wherewithal for young adults to take a meaningful place in the adult world. In short, the socialization process, for whatever reasons, has failed (Grossman 2005; Harris 2017; Twenge 2007).

Works on adult socialization point out that we spend a great deal of our research and socialization efforts studying children and preparing them for their developmental stages so that they can make successful transitions to adulthood. An important criticism of theories of socialization that outline stages of development through childhood, adolescence, and adulthood is that they are based on research conducted almost exclusively by males on males.

An exception was Gail Sheehy (1976, 2006), who outlined a set of adult developmental stages for both men and women in *Passages*. Sheehy described the "trying twenties" as a time of making a break from parents, selecting mates, and starting careers—a time of high expectations, hopes, and dreams. The "catch thirties" are the years when bubbles often burst, and people realize their mates and jobs are not exactly perfect. This difficult period is characterized by high divorce rates and sudden career changes. The "forlorn forties" follow, when adults enter their midlife crises. Sheehy described these as dangerous years during which the dreams of youth must be reassessed. It is common for men to become dissatisfied with their jobs and to want to stay home; it is a time when women who have not worked outside the home become dissatisfied and want to take jobs. Sheehy focused more on this development stage—especially the social and psychological effects of menopause—in *The Silent Passage* (1993). Next come the "refreshed" (or "resigned") "fifties." Sheehy contended that for those who free themselves from their old roles and embrace life with a renewed sense of purpose, this can be the best stage of life. It may also be a time when people face the fact that they have not accomplished their youthful ambitions and simply resign themselves to the status quo. Sheehy (1996) also identified developmental stages beyond the fifties, all the way up to people in their eighties.

Although from a young age we are socialized to follow the same norms and American traditions, males and females, as well as members of different social classes, are socialized very differently from one another. Traditional roles filled by men and women are called gender roles. These gender roles are idealized behaviors we are taught from a young age. The feminist perspective suggests these gender roles are taught to maintain the patriarchal society in which Americans live. The socialization of our gender roles can be seen in the toys children are guided to play with and prefer. Young boys are led toward trucks and army men while young girls are encouraged to play with dolls and pretend to be princesses. Even earlier, we begin socializing traditional gender roles with nurseries and clothing in certain colors. Boys are often steered toward blues and greens, whereas girls are dressed in pinks and purples. Feminists feel this is a form of indoctrinating children into the desired gender roles of society. Today, many families are more aware of this indoctrination and make conscious efforts to be more neutral and less gender specific as they socialize their children.

Sociologists whose research is guided by feminist theory argue that gender is an important but often overlooked variable in the socialization process because it affects not only personality traits but also how people think (Gilligan 2016; Gilligan, Ward, and Taylor 1989; Marshall 2003; Thorne 1993). They contend that the stages of social and psychological development—especially moral development—differ in important ways for males and females. Carol Gilligan's research, for example, shows that males tend to rely on rules and abstract ideals when determining right from wrong—what she called a "justice perspective on morality." Females develop more of a care and responsibility perspective, preferring to use personal experience and social relationships as important criteria in developing moral judgments about social situations.

Socialization is one of the most powerful and effective tools used by those in power to maintain the status quo and legitimize existing social inequalities. At a very fundamental level, socialization prepares people for class-related roles they will fill throughout their lives. For example, even as children, members of the upper class are socialized for positions of authority and leadership roles. They are trained how to interact among members of the same class as well as how to deal with servants, staff, and members of the lower classes. Similarly, members of the lower class may be socialized from childhood to show deference to those above them in the social hierarchy and may be trained in skills that will increase their opportunities for serving those who are higher on the social ladder.

The conflict perspective also points out that socialization is not a unidimensional process. Throughout the life course, especially during adolescence, people are bombarded with contradictory and conflicting attitudes, values, beliefs, and behaviors. Most of us remember at some time being told "Do as I say, and not as I do" by someone in authority whom we may have caught violating one of the rules they taught us. We probably all remember being told by our parents, teachers, and religious leaders that certain behaviors were wrong, and perhaps forbidden, only to find that our peer group insisted they were not only okay but also mandatory. Most adolescent boys, for example, are taught that fighting is improper, but they are considered cowards by their peers if they walk away from a fight. Similarly, although teenage girls may be taught that premarital sex is immoral and will ruin their reputation, they realize boys are not held to the same standard and may feel tremendous pressure from both male and female peers to be sexually active in order to be "normal" or enter "adulthood." This intersection between social class and gender expectations emphasizes the need for *developmental socialization*, learning better to fulfill the roles we already occupy, and possibly even *desocialization*, the "unlearning" of previous normative expectations and roles, and *resocialization*, learning a radically different set of norms, attitudes, values, beliefs, and behaviors.

DESOCIALIZATION AND RESOCIALIZATION

Sometimes people must be desocialized from one set of values and concept of self and resocialized to another that may be totally different. From a functionalist's perspective, socialization serves the important function of reinforcing the social structure, perpetuating society, and transmitting culture from one generation to the next. The socialization process is viewed much like inoculation: members of society are injected with the attitudes, values, beliefs, and norms that will allow them to assume and successfully fulfill the roles of full and productive citizens. Functionalists identify motivation and ability to perform role expectations as one of the basic prerequisites for survival of the social system, and these motivations and abilities are acquired through socialization (Parsons 1951).

A breakdown in socialization leads to a breakdown in the social system. Hence, functionalists attribute various forms of deviant behavior to inadequate socialization and failure to internalize society's norms.

Resocialization is important from the functionalist perspective because it serves the critical function of helping an individual abandon a previous role in order to fulfill a new one. This process is viewed as essential in order to make successful transitions from home to school, school to work, civilian to military life, the "free world" to prison, and so on.

The most dramatic examples of desocialization and resocialization take place in the context of *total institutions*, places where people carry out virtually all of their activities. Total institutions are cut off from the wider society and hence become a society unto themselves (Goffman 1961a; Wallace 2017). Prisons; hospitals; mental hospitals; monasteries; military bases (especially during boot camp); and, to some extent, private boarding schools are all examples of total institutions.

Total institutions are unique social settings; it is unusual for us to work, play, eat, sleep, and carry out all routine daily behaviors within the context of one social institution. For example, most college students leave their homes to live in residence halls or apartments and then leave these to attend classes in different social environments, and may take part-time jobs. If students go out in the evening, they go to places other than the classrooms or workplaces they inhabit during the day. In other words, their different life activities take place in a variety of social spheres. An inmate in a maximum security prison, however, does not have this flexibility. Inmates live within the confines of the institution and works, eats, sleeps, and plays there—in short, carries out all day-to-day activities there.

Recognizing the unusual nature of total institutions and the perceived need for total conformity, administrators and staff emphasize the necessity to desocialize individuals from the identities they have developed outside the institution and to resocialize them to the appropriate role identity within the institution. Often, the first step in this process is what sociologists call a *degradation ceremony*, in which an individual is stripped of their former self, publicly stigmatized, and assigned a new identity (Garfinkel 1956). An example of the degradation ceremony is the criminal trial, in which accused criminals are publicly charged and convicted, and their identities changed from "law-abiding citizens" to "criminals." This is an important step preceding their induction into a correctional facility, which then further strips them of their previous social identities in order to prepare them for socialization into the inmate role. Military boot camps, mental hospitals, some isolated private schools, and other total institutions use similar techniques in their resocialization efforts. Sociologists who use the conflict perspective view resocialization as an example of how those in power attempt to coerce and exploit others and attempt to perpetuate their own authority. Resocialization in total institutions such as the military, prisons, and mental hospitals reaffirms the importance of status hierarchies and obedience to the rules established by those in power. Moreover, they legitimate the status quo by rewarding unquestioned conformity and punishing those who challenge existing authority structures, question social inequalities, or even dare to be different.

Total resocialization seldom occurs. Despite the adverse circumstances of total institutions, people still play an active role in shaping their identities through interaction with others (Paterniti 2000; Wallace 2017). Even prisoners of war who are subjected to systematic brainwashing often resist its effects and maintain a sense of their former identities. Research indicates that people confined in total institutions form an assortment of subcultures that provide alternative social roles. For example, John Irwin (1970) described the social world of convicts in maximum security prisons, indicating that they undergo two resocialization processes simultaneously. They are formally socialized into the inmate role as it is defined by the warden, staff, and guards; at the same time, they are informally socialized into the inmate subculture as it is defined by the other inmates. Not surprisingly, many of the expectations are at odds with one another. For example, in the inmate world some may become "merchants" of contraband on the black market, whereas others become "enforcers" of the inmate codes, both roles that violate official rules and expectations of the prison. Goffman (1961a) described a remarkably similar "inmate subculture" among patients in a mental hospital.

Although they provide the most dramatic examples, total institutions are not the only places where desocialization and resocialization occur. As people change their social statuses, switch roles, or otherwise assume new or different identities, there is almost always some need for "unlearning" old ideas and behaviors and learning the new. For example, when young children leave the family to attend school for the first time, a certain amount of desocialization and resocialization must occur for them to make the transition successfully from the role of son or daughter to that of student (Gracey 1977; Thompson and Thompson 2016).

Likewise, when students leave school and enter the world of work, they must make another important social transition, discarding the role of student to assume the role of employee. Almost all professions contain elements of a subculture and require a certain amount of desocialization and resocialization at the entry level. For example, research shows that medical students must overcome much of their previous socialization about the human body if they are to assume the role of physician successfully (Smith and Kleinman 1989). A particular problem for medical students is removing any sexual connotation from physical contact with intimate body parts. This is done by desocializing students from thinking of breasts and genitals as sex organs and resocializing them to think of these body parts as distinct parts of an organism, totally devoid of any sexual implication.

Finally, it might be argued that in the United States and many other modern nations, the changing attitudes toward gender roles over the past several decades may require a certain amount of desocialization and resocialization for those who grew up during the immediate post–World War II era, the 1950s, and the 1960s. Traditional notions about what is appropriate for little girls and boys as well as for grown women and men have changed dramatically and require different attitudes, values, beliefs, and behaviors from those which millions of people may have been taught as they were growing up.

These examples illustrate how life experiences within any particular culture may necessitate desocialization and resocialization. But what are the chances that people are going to live their entire lives within the culture in which they were born and socialized? In today's global society, people are far more likely than not to travel, work, and live in countries with cultures different from those in which they were socialized. Those who make the most successful adjustment to their new social environments are those who most readily learn and adopt the new customs and norms. This may require discarding some of the attitudes, beliefs, and norms they were originally taught.

Even if people live their entire lives in the same country, state, and city, they are very likely to interact with people from other parts of the world, whose socialization experiences are as diverse as the people themselves. This, too, requires some desocialization and resocialization to attitudes, values, beliefs, and norms if people hope to interact with one another successfully.

Globalization and cultural diversity require a certain amount of desocialization and resocialization as "we" become more like "them," and "they" become more like "us" through the process of social interaction—no matter who "we" and "they" are. The acquisition of additional languages is an example of desocialization and resocialization, as it involves far more than simply learning new words and vocabularies. Understanding a language, especially thinking in another language, requires an understanding and appreciation of the culture that produced it. This is one reason why it is generally easier for young children to learn and speak languages than it is for adults, who are often more culture-bound and hence reluctant to change long-held attitudes, beliefs, customs, and ways of thinking. With the growing popularity of Americans adopting children from other nations, unless the child is an infant, desocialization and resocialization is almost inevitable on the part of both the adoptive parents and the child (Thomas 2007).

Human beings are thinking creatures actively involved in their own socialization and that of others. Thus through the lifelong process of socialization, people are constantly evolving, changing, learning and relearning culture, and continually in a process of becoming. This illustrates and reinforces the fourth wisdom of sociology: *when you were born, you were not yet you.*

Sociological Wisdom 5

#TheWorldRevolvesAroundTheSunAndNotYou

INTERACTING IN EVERYDAY LIFE

WHEN YOU WAKE UP IN THE MORNING and prepare for the day, you perform many acts—solitary behaviors that seemingly affect no one but yourself. You might stretch and yawn, scratch yourself in a place that you would never touch in front of another person, burp out loud, look out the window, and eat a bowl of cereal. In everyday life, such behaviors are common. But if we could examine everything we do in the course of a day, we would discover that *social acts*, which are behaviors influenced or shaped by the presence of others, are far more numerous and important. This simple process of taking into account other people before acting illustrates the fifth wisdom of sociology, the awareness that you are not the center of the universe and that *the world revolves around the sun and not you.*

When people enter our presence, we alter our behavior based on their expectations and demands, or at least on what we think they will consider appropriate. This is what makes an act *social*. Social acts include countless daily behaviors that are usually taken for granted—such behaviors as walking across campus, shopping at a mall, or merely standing in a crowded elevator. Whether we feel that an elevator is crowded or not is also socially and culturally determined, based on our attitudes and values regarding personal space.

PERSONAL SPACE AND NONVERBAL COMMUNICATION

When people from different cultures interact with one another, or when people of different ages, sexes, races, or social classes interact, what they view as appropriate interaction varies greatly. Each of us surrounds ourselves with an invisible "bubble" that constitutes what we consider our *personal space*, an area around our body that we reserve for ourselves, intimate acquaintances, and close friends. On occasion we must allow others to "invade" this personal space, for example, when a doctor examines us, or perhaps when we are standing on line or in a crowded elevator. These situations often make us uncomfortable, however, and may call for "defensive strategies" such as folding our arms across our chest, placing an obstacle (an umbrella, a briefcase, or a backpack) between us and the other person, or at the very least, avoiding eye contact and verbal communication.

Anthropologist Edward Hall (1959, 1990) discovered that Americans surround themselves not with one, but four "invisible bubbles," and identified four different zones of comfort regarding social interaction:

1. *Intimate Distance.* For most Americans, this distance extends from the body outward approximately 18 inches. Generally, we protect this space fiercely and allow it to be penetrated only by loved ones, very close friends, and our family pets. In the course of our daily interactions, this intimate zone is reserved for hugging, kissing, lovemaking, or comforting. Occasionally, medical professionals such as doctors, nurses, and dentists must invade this intimate space, sometimes making us feel rather uncomfortable. When strangers invade this space, we defend the space and our bodies by either retreating to a safer and more comfortable distance or striking out in defense. Criminologists and law enforcement officials, for example, know that deaths by stabbing and strangulation are more often committed by family members or friends than by total strangers, because of the nature of intimacy involved in the crime.
2. *Personal Distance.* This zone extends from approximately 18 inches from the body out to about 4 or 5 feet. Although this space is not

reserved for intimates, we tend to feel most comfortable allowing friends and acquaintances within it for any length of time. Generally, when we are being introduced to people for the first time, we like to maintain somewhere from 2 to 4 feet between our bodies and theirs, not coincidentally the most comfortable distance for two people to shake hands. Again, criminologists and police figure that if a person is shot from this distance, the perpetrator was probably an acquaintance, friend, or family member.

3. *Social Distance.* A distance of 4 or 5 feet out to approximately 12 feet is commonly used for impersonal and formal interactions. This is a common distance used in job interviews, for example. It also is the distance at which podiums are usually set from the front row to separate speakers and audience. Shootings from this distance are as likely to have been committed by casual acquaintances or total strangers as friends or family members.

4. *Public Distance.* This distance, beyond 12 feet, is open to just about anybody, and rarely do we feel threatened when somebody is 12 or more feet away from us. We can walk past total strangers, acknowledging them only with a glance or a nod, or ignoring them altogether if we choose to do so. Secret Service agents and bodyguards like to keep this much distance between dignitaries and the general public. Killings that take place from this distance often involve total strangers, as in the case of drive-by shootings, or random sniper shootings.

As we mentioned earlier, these "comfort zones" vary from one culture to another and within cultures when people of different ages, races, sexes, and social classes interact. Middle Easterners, for example, have much smaller distance requirements for casual interaction, and men often embrace or kiss on the cheek when introduced for the first time—something that makes American men very uncomfortable. Despite living in a densely populated country, the Japanese often maintain a larger social space when interacting with strangers. When two Japanese men are introduced, they bow toward one another, an act that requires a distance of about 6 feet to prevent bumping heads.

In the United States, women are generally far more comfortable touching, hugging, or kissing one another than are men, and women will allow other women within their intimate distance, something a man rarely allows from another man, even if they are blood related. Also, not all men are comfortable with the same amount of personal and social distance. For example, cowboys out on the Great Plains have a much larger "invisible bubble" surrounding them, and although they will allow others closer to them on their side, they generally keep 5 to 6 feet (coincidentally, about the length of a horse) between them and others during face-to-face interaction (Hickey and Thompson 1988).

The difference in attitudes toward personal space between the sexes can cause some awkward situations. For example, if a woman touches a man, he often misreads this gesture as a sexual overture because she has invaded his intimate space; hence, he considers it an intimate gesture—something she may not have intended at all. Similarly, older people often feel comfortable touching younger people, but children often feel uncomfortable approaching adults they do not know. While members of the lower socioeconomic classes often hug one another, embrace upon meeting, and feel comfortable in close proximity, members of the upper class usually maintain a "proper" distance between themselves and others, especially when interacting with members of lower social classes. All of these examples involve *nonverbal communication*—the body movements, gestures, and facial expressions that we

"HE'S NOT GOOD AT READING BODY LANGUAGE."

use to communicate with others. Smiles, nods, winks, eye contact, hand gestures, and other forms of nonverbal communication can be just as important as, if not more so than, words in shaping our interactions with others. They are especially important in helping social actors to define social situations and give meaning to everyday interactions.

When we interact with others, we constantly define and redefine the social situation in order to provide meaning to our actions and theirs. William I. Thomas (Thomas and Thomas 1928) contended that a critical element of everyday social interaction involves creating a *definition of the situation*, the idea that when people define situations as real, they become real in their consequences. For example, when people anticipate going to a party and look forward to it being fun, it usually is. Conversely when people dread going somewhere, like to the dentist, it usually is not a fun experience. Of course, not everybody defines situations in the same way. So, an activity that is fun and pleasant to some is not to others, and vice versa.

Also, because we constantly define and redefine social situations in ways that are meaningful to us, we always run the risk of misinterpreting other people's actions, especially their nonverbal forms of communications. The meanings imputed to actions and gestures become critical in shaping the meaning of our present and future interactions with others. How we define social situations becomes an important part of our presentation of ourselves to others and how we attempt to manage their impressions of us. In that sense, to paraphrase Shakespeare, life becomes much like a drama, with each of us performing various roles on the stage of life.

We all have been encouraged to "put our best foot forward" when meeting somebody for the first time. Similarly, we have all heard that "you only get one chance to make a first impression." These admonitions acknowledge that much of our day-to-day interaction constitutes a performance—one that is judged by others and, as a result, has tremendous impact on how we are viewed by others and how we view ourselves. Erving Goffman introduced the theoretical framework of *dramaturgical analysis*, which uses the analogy of the theater to analyze social behavior as a way of understanding these social performances. Dramaturgical analysis focuses on the ways we present ourselves to others and our attempts to manage their impressions of us in a favorable light.

In everyday life, some interactions are simple and direct, and people's behaviors are fairly predictable. Casual greetings are a good example. Most other face-to-face interactions, however, require more of participants, and people's responses may be highly variable. According to symbolic interactionists, who study how symbols, language, and gestures shape social behavior, we do not respond directly to individuals, events, acts, and objects, but to our images of them (McCall and Simmons 1979:66). As Herbert Blumer (1969a) wrote, in social interaction the key to a person's response is how he organizes, defines, and interprets another's behaviors. William Swann (1998:399) noted that people's identities and self-views are not like bowling balls that are unaffected by either people or objects they encounter in their travels. For people, the exact opposite is true; we are acutely sensitive to those with whom we share ongoing relationships. This may explain the remarkable consistency of "self" over time—even over a lifetime. People usually cling to their self-views because dramatic changes would disrupt relationships with those we deem important—in some cases, even relationships with others that may sustain negative self-views and behaviors (Apter 2018; Swann 1998).

Many everyday interactions appear as if they were scripted mini-dramas, in which people encounter one another, assess one another's personal and social characteristics, assume identities, and behave in appropriate ways. Given the complexity of most social situations and the fact that spontaneity and surprise are integral features of virtually all social interactions, however, improvisation is usually required (Apter 2018).

Using the analogy of the theater, *dramaturgy* analyzes social interaction as though participants were actors in an ongoing drama.

Dramaturgy, however, emphasizes that in real life "actors" passively accept neither the definition of the situation nor the identities granted by others. Instead, people take an active part in social interaction, manipulating it to their perceived advantage. Erving Goffman (1959) called this *impression management*, ways that people use revelation and concealment to make a favorable impression on others.

Dramaturgists note that people not only have an interest in presenting their best "selves" to others but also tacitly agree to support one another's performances and help one another maintain face. Teamwork requires that people overlook or ignore poor performances (a professor who stutters), embarrassing acts (a growling stomach), and deceits (excuses for being late). Also, we may sometimes be called on to do remedial work or help out by agreeing with others, even though we may totally disagree with their definition of the situation. Why we do these things should be obvious. When a "bad actor's" performance is called into question, the entire social interaction may be threatened. Few cultures are more aware of this fact than the group-oriented Japanese, who recognize that when emotional outbursts occur, those present must realign their behaviors to suit the individual's goals rather than those of the group.

The self that we present in one social situation may be inappropriate in another. This discrepancy is illustrated in a series of experiments conducted by Harold Garfinkel ([1967] 1991), who introduced *ethnomethodology*, which literally means *people's methods*, or is more generally described as a way of analyzing the "taken-for-granted" aspects that give meaning to social interaction. Ethnomethodologists contend that much of what transpires when we interact with others relies on unspoken and commonly understood assumptions about the meanings of our words and actions. For example, when you pass somebody on the street who may nod and say, "How's it going?," you probably nod in response and say, "Fine," and go on about your business. What really transpired in that brief conversation? Basically, two people just acknowledged one another in an informal greeting and response. What would have happened, however, if you had no understanding of the taken-for-granted aspects of the other person's question? What if you had stopped and replied with a lengthy, personal response about all the things going on in your life at the time? No doubt your fellow actor would not want to hear all that, and you probably would be ignored to avoid such an awkward situation happening again. Occasionally, these types of interactional miscues occur when people from other cultures or with language barriers interact with one another—a situation that requires what Goffman called *remedial work*, an explanation that clarifies the situation and puts the actors at ease.

To illustrate the taken-for-granted aspects of everyday interaction, Garfinkel had his students act as though they were boarders when they returned home from college during a visit, instead of behaving as sons or daughters. Pretending to be strangers in their own homes, the experiments tended to last only a few minutes because parents could not comprehend why their children were behaving so courteously and formally, and so "out of character." In some cases, tempers flared, and parental responses included, "What's the matter? Are you sick? Are you out of your mind, or are you just stupid?" (Garfinkel [1967] 1991:47).

Despite the extraordinary complexity of social life in all contemporary societies, social relations are not random. Everyone's life has certain patterns of social interaction that are repeated over and over again. Sociologists call this *social structure*—the ordered relationships and patterned expectations that guide social interaction—and it is fundamental to life in all societies.

STATUSES AND ROLES

People often use the word "status" to refer to high social standing or prestige (one has high status or possesses status symbols, such as a Mercedes Benz or a Rolex watch). Sociologists define *status* as a socially defined position in a social structure. A status is not an individual possession, but rather a *relationship* to others. For example, the status of mother is socially meaningful only in relationship to the statuses of child or father. Statuses define a multitude of other relationships as well, including those of father–son, doctor–patient, teacher–student, and shopper–merchant. These and other statuses affect the expectations and behaviors of others, a person's social identities, and even one's sense of self.

Statuses, which may be ranked high or low, determine where a person fits in society. Moreover, every person occupies a variety of statuses, and each status has an appropriate social context. Sociologists call all of the statuses a person has at a given time that person's *status set*. In the course of a day, a woman may occupy the statuses of spouse, mother, Hispanic, friend, shopper, and attorney. The statuses that people occupy change not only according to social context but over the life course as well. As a young person, a child may occupy the statuses of daughter, Girl Scout, soccer player, ballet student, and 4-H leader. In college, she may assume statuses such as college student, roommate, and part-time worker.

Usually a person's statuses are more or less consistent, but occasionally a person occupies two or more statuses that society deems contradictory. This is called *status inconsistency*. For example, students pursuing degrees in education typically must complete an internship in which they do their student teaching. During that semester they are simultaneously a student earning a grade, and a teacher assigning grades to other students. This *marginal status* creates a situation in which a person is fulfilling two statuses at the same time without being fully accepted into either. Teenagers often experience a similar type of marginality when they realize they are torn between two statuses: no longer a child, but not fully an adult.

Every society limits access to statuses. *Ascribed statuses* are statuses assigned to individuals without reference to their abilities or efforts, such as age, sex, race, ethnicity, and family background. Although these statuses influence how a person is defined, they allow the individual few options or choices. Being born a member of the British Royal Family entitles one to a number of highly ranked social positions should one desire to claim them. On the other hand, being born poor and a member of a racial or ethnic minority often places limits on one's chances of securing many valued statuses.

Some societies allocate a great many statuses on the basis of ascription. For example, in the traditional Indian caste system, family background determined one's occupation, marriage choice, neighborhood, political affiliation, and most statuses a person could claim during life. By contrast, modern industrial and postindustrial societies favor more competitive access to social positions.

Achieved statuses are statuses secured through effort and ability. College professor, church member, spouse, janitor, priest, juvenile delinquent, fashion model, and college student are all examples of achieved statuses—statuses usually gained by education and training or by going through a particular process performing certain acts.

In all societies, a person's ascribed statuses influence those statuses he might achieve. For example, sex, gender, age, race, and ethnicity have either restricted or boosted a person's opportunities of gaining entry to a college, a country club, a job, or the position of president of the United States.

Often, a particular status in an individual's status set dominates the thinking of others. This status is called a *master status*, a status that dominates all other statuses. It defines who that person is and his limitations and opportunities. Sometimes a person's master status is revealed by self-definition. For example, if you ask a young boy who he is, he will usually respond by noting his age and sex ("I am a six-year-old boy"). Most people in college describe themselves as students, and the master status of most adult Americans is their occupation. Occupation is so important that many years after retirement, people often continue to define themselves and others in terms of their former occupations—professor emeritus, ex-nurse, ex–auto worker, or retired Navy. Likewise, students often identify themselves by their academic major—which identifies their future occupation. Many proud parents tell their friends that their son or daughter is a pre-med major, clearly implying that their offspring soon will be a doctor.

Because rather strong expectations are attached to a person's master status, they may have either positive or negative consequences. For example, the master status of judge is highly regarded. A judge convicted of or even accused of child molestation, however, is a child molester, a master status with severe social limitations. Likewise, no matter what other statuses they may occupy, people who have been in prison are usually labeled ex-convicts—ex-con painters, ex-con fathers, and ex-con neighbors—a master status that denies them many opportunities. Registered sex offenders, regardless of other statuses, are always going to be known as sex offenders. This is not always the case with all deviant identities, however. In contemporary societies, deviant identities, such as "former substance abuser," have been transformed into what J. David Brown (1991:219) called "professional ex-s," who capitalize on a deviant past by transforming it from a liability to an occupational asset—in this case, for example, substance abuse counselors.

A status is a social category and as such is somewhat fixed. Roles, which are dynamic, bring statuses to life. As Ralph Linton (1936) put it, we *occupy* statuses, but we *play* roles. In a sense, statuses indicate *who we are*, and roles denote *what we do*. A *role* is a set of expectations, rights, and duties that are attached to a particular status. Some sociologists use the metaphor of the theater to describe how roles influence social life. Like actors on a stage, all of us play roles in our daily lives—sons, daughters, friends, pizza deliverers, students, sorority sisters, and a multitude of other roles. Attached to each role is a script that tells us how we should behave toward others and how they should act toward us. But, as noted earlier, social life is far more complex than any stage, and in most roles people are allowed considerable latitude in how they interpret their "scripts."

Without roles, human social life would be almost impossible, for roles guide our interactions in virtually every social situation. Roles simplify the process of interaction because we do not have to base our actions on the unique personality of each individual with whom we interact. Rather, we respond to their roles, and they respond to ours.

Although expectations are attached to roles, the *role performance*, or how each occupant of a status fulfills their role, may vary widely. One reason is that people's emotional commitment to and identification with roles may vary. A college athlete, for example, may never miss football or basketball practice, but cut classes because they view the student role to be of minor importance. Another reason role performance varies is that role expectations are usually flexible enough for individual interpretation. Some roles, for example the role of Buckingham Palace guard, allow a narrow range of individual expression. By contrast, artists and musicians are expected to be creative and as a result are given great latitude in how they behave. This too is restrictive, however, in that artists and musicians must be creative and talented to be judged competent in their roles.

Most roles constrain certain behaviors but allow freedom of expression in others. Although fast-food chains make an effort to standardize employee roles and minimize elements of personality as well as regional, class, and ethnic influences on role performances, they have not been entirely successful. This is because during interaction people evaluate their performances by imagining how others view them, and adjust their behavior accordingly. This process, called *role taking*, gives the individual some influence in how a role is defined.

Some roles are entered into or discarded with little effort or commitment. At other times, in cases of *role distance*, people play a role but remain detached from it to avoid any negative aspects of the role. Erving Goffman used the example of adults riding a merry-go-round with their children to describe role distance. According to Goffman (1961b), because their adult role might be threatened if they appeared to enjoy the ride, adults express their detachment by exaggerating the performance of merry-go-round rider or by acting bored and disinterested.

Role embracement occurs when a person's sense of identity is partially influenced by a role. Sometimes *role merger* occurs when a role becomes central to a person's identity and the person literally becomes the role they are playing.

People try to fulfill their roles as they understand them, but role performances also are influenced by the multiple roles that are attached to almost every status, which sociologists call a *role set*. The student role, for example, includes all of the patterned expectations of all people with whom the student interacts. The role set of a student includes rights and duties toward professors, classmates, roommates, friends, parents, employers, and many others in reciprocal roles. In everyday interaction, we play many roles simultaneously. Sometimes we move from role to role with relative ease. Not all roles, however, are logically consistent.

In cases of *role strain*, there are contradictory expectations and demands attached to a single role, which is quite common in everyday life. The student role offers a good example, for it includes numerous expectations that pull students in opposite directions. Professors expect students to study, but friends who visit expect students to put away their books and talk or go out for fun. Roommates may expect each other to remain on campus during the weekend, whereas their parents demand that they return home, or their employers expect them to work. In the course of our everyday interactions, all of us must make such difficult choices.

Role conflict occurs when a person cannot fulfill the roles of one status without violating those of another. Television dramas probably could not exist without role conflicts—such as the cop show favorite where a police officer responds to a burglary only to discover that the thief is a child, sibling, or close friend. Both authors of this book ride motorcycles. In doing so, we often interact with people very much like us, who may be doctors, dentists, attorneys, teachers, or other professional people who ride motorcycles for fun. We also, however, sometimes come in contact with bikers who may be members of outlaw motorcycle clubs, live a deviant lifestyle, may be blatant racists and sexists, and may openly use illegal drugs and/or participate in a wide variety of other illegal activities. When attending motorcycle rallies and other organized events, it is not uncommon for liberal feminists who ride motorcycles to walk past wet T-shirt contests or bikini bike washes; for Jewish attorneys to interact with fellow riders sporting black vests with swastikas; and for African American college professors to find themselves side by side with Southern bikers decked out in apparel adorned with Confederate flags. Reconciling the shared status of motorcyclists with the conflicting role expectations associated with hardcore bikers often requires a certain amount of mental gymnastics.

Role strain, conflict, and the choices they demand are important forces in social change. In everyday interaction, people must tiptoe through a minefield of role conflicts and strains, and make choices they may or may not wish to make. That people play their roles so well, and adhere so strongly to them despite the costs, tells us much about the power and necessity of roles. They provide the vital framework of social interaction that links individuals to others in reciprocal roles, patterned relationships, and social networks.

SOCIAL NETWORKS

All of us fulfill many social roles, and a large part of our lives is spent developing a *social network*, which includes the total web of an individual's relationships and group memberships. Social networks include our families, friends, and neighbors as well as all other people and groups with whom we have ongoing relationships. People often create and maintain social networks for functional reasons such as advancing their careers, for social support, and to promote a host of other interests and needs.

Social networks do not have clear boundaries, and their members may or may not interact on a regular basis. Moreover, people in social networks do not always have a sense that they belong together, nor do they necessarily have common aims and goals, as do members of a group. Nevertheless, social networks are a vital part of social structure and are extremely important in our everyday lives. Social networks radiate out from individuals and groups, and through them groups, organizations, and nations are bound together. Social networks also provide linkages between one individual and another, and then through other people's social networks to still others, until, in theory, people everywhere are linked together.

Every person's social network is unique. The social networks of husbands and wives differ, as do those of brothers and sisters. For example, a husband's social network might include family members, neighbors, his carpool, coworkers, and members of his bowling league. A wife's network overlaps with her husband's to some extent; she and her husband share ties with some family members, neighbors, and friends. But her network may also include members of her carpool, her coworkers, and friends and acquaintances with whom she alone maintains a relationship.

Each person's social network also includes two kinds of relationships. One kind, which is characterized by *strong ties*, is a relationship that is intimate, enduring, and defined by people of special importance. A person typically has strong ties to family members, some neighbors, and a small circle of intimate friends. People in this kind of network usually exert considerable influence on one another; they share information and resources and usually can be counted on if needed.

A person's network also includes *weak ties* to distant kin, coworkers, acquaintances, and people who they have only interacted with through cyberspace on the internet (Warschauer 2003). Social media may increase a person's social network exponentially. Although social media are more tenuous and impersonal, they provide the individual with many contacts, beyond family and friends, that offer a wide range of information and services that would not be available otherwise.

Social networks are useful to individuals and of critical importance in most societies. Contrary to popular thought, social networks are just as important to city dwellers as they are to rural folks. Although urbanites are likely to have fewer family members in their social networks, they are nevertheless just as likely to use networks for procuring goods and services and finding jobs (Borgatti, Everett, and Johnson 2018; Greeley 2002). It is through social networks that information, knowledge, and resources are shared among individuals and groups. For example, many companies prefer these networks in hiring, and they pay bonuses to employees for recruiting friends and acquaintances, believing social networks produce savings in screening costs (Fernandez, Castilla, and Moore 2000). In both small-scale and complex societies, social networks can be very useful for such things as getting a promotion, mobilizing political support, gaining entry to a club, getting a date, or finding a marriage partner.

In addition to serving the needs of ordinary people, conflict theorists see social networks as being particularly useful to those at the top of the social hierarchy. What might conflict theorists say about President Trump appointing his daughter Ivanka; her husband, Jared Kushner; and his son Donald Jr. to high-level positions in the government? Personal networks are influenced by age, race, sex, social class, and a variety of other social factors that can serve to expand or limit one's access to information, resources, and power.

In many societies, networks composed exclusively of men who are members of dominant class, racial, and ethnic backgrounds routinely exclude women and minorities from becoming members of their clubs and associations, thereby denying them access to information and other resources. And as John Scott (1991) noted for the larger political economy, "informal social networks of social connection" are becoming an increasingly important means through which corporate decision makers (and the capitalist class as a whole) maintain and reproduce their power and influence not only nationally but also globally.

Beyond social networks, even encountering total strangers has an impact on our behavior. Imagine that you are strolling down the street, absorbed in thought. What happens when you suddenly realize somebody is walking behind you? Does your behavior change in any way? Unless you are totally engrossed in thought, the answer is probably yes. There is a basic change as you and the other person acknowledge and respond to each other's presence. This is but one of countless forms of *social interaction*—the mutual influence of two or more people on one another's behavior—that profoundly affect our lives. Social interaction is the building block of the entire social order.

PATTERNS OF SOCIAL INTERACTION

Sociologists recognize that among individuals, groups, organizations, and societies there are five fundamental patterns of social interaction: exchange, cooperation, competition, conflict, and coercion. Robert Nisbet (1970:50) described these elements as the "molecular cement" that binds people, groups, and societies together.

1. *Exchange* is perhaps the most basic form of social interaction (Blau 1963, 1964). Social exchange theorists maintain that our interactions with others are guided by the "profit motive"—that is, we seek to maximize rewards and minimize costs (Homans 1961). Social exchange is based on the *norm of reciprocity*—that we help and do not harm those who have helped us (Gouldner 1960). This norm establishes the expectation that gifts, recognition, love, and other favors will be returned. In the course of a day, people exchange smiles, waves, and other simple courtesies. Exchanges of this kind are most often taken for granted—at least until people fail to meet our expectations. The norm of reciprocity, of course, has a negative side, which includes the expectation that hostilities, threats, social slights, and other acts meant to harm will be reciprocated.

2. *Cooperation* is a pattern of interaction in which individuals, groups, and societies work together to achieve shared goals. Cooperation is fundamental to human survival; without it, social life would be impossible. Cooperation sustains routine, face-to-face encounters. It is also necessary if people are to raise children, protect themselves, and make a living. Some societies place greater emphasis on cooperation than others. For example, the Japanese, whose norms and values promote sharing and "selflessness," have altered the American version of baseball, which stresses individualism and encourages "stars" to stand out from the group. In Japan, people expect all players to exhibit *wa*, a sense of team spirit that obligates the individual to subordinate everything to the group (Whiting 2009).

3. *Competition* is much like cooperation in that both individuals and groups strive to achieve a shared goal. It differs from cooperation, however, in that instead of joining with others to achieve valued goals, people or groups in competition contest for them, recognizing that society's prizes are in limited supply and only one person or group can attain them.

Competitive relationships are especially common to capitalist economies and pervade almost all aspects of people's lives. For example, corporations compete for customers; professional athletes vie for trophies and championships; students compete for grades; political rivals contest for votes; and even pastors must win converts from competitors.

4. *Conflict* is a pattern of interaction in which people or groups struggle to achieve a commonly prized object or goal. Conflict is especially common when competitors violate rules and seek to gain their objective by any means available. We most often consider conflict to be opposed to human interests, harmful to the social order, and something to be avoided or resolved as quickly as possible. Yet, as conflict theorists emphasize, conflict has a positive side. It may enhance social solidarity, for nothing reduces conflicts and strains within a relationship (whether marital or between nations) better than an external threat (Coser 1956; Nisbet 1970; Simmel [1908] 1955). As Robert Nisbet (1970) observed, it also may serve as a vehicle for social change in which stagnant beliefs and values are dissolved, old tyrannies loosened, and individuals released to achieve new and higher goals.

5. When people or groups are compelled to interact with one another, *coercion* is the glue that binds them together. Coercion is the threat of force that those with power sometimes use to achieve their objectives. For example, in the United States, education is compulsory; children must attend school whether they want to or not. The relative strength of coercion as a cohesive force lies not so much in blatant expressions of power and authority as in the myriad expressions it may assume in everyday life. Ridicule, gossip, the silent treatment, and withdrawal of affection are but a handful of coercive devices people use in their daily interactions with others. Coercion involves an individual or group that dominates another, the *superordinate*, and a person or group that is dominated, the *subordinate*.

These five patterns of social interaction are neither distinctive nor mutually exclusive. In everyday life, there is a fine line between competition and conflict, coercion and exchange, and the same is true concerning other patterns of social interaction. Certainly, power influences whether it is one or the other, but this may not be the only factor involved; people's definitions, too, may influence the nature of the interaction—what is exchange to one may be coercion to another. Married couples may experience all five patterns of social interaction in a single day, not to mention over a long-term relationship. Because people's perceptions of interaction vary, much of our social interaction is guided by social perception and stereotypes.

In addition to defining a situation, we must decide whom we have encountered before we activate what we believe to be the appropriate self. We attempt to answer this question through *social perception*, which is the process by which we form impressions of others and of ourselves. In everyday life, we both give off and receive cues about the kinds of persons we are. We do this in almost every situation: when we enter a room, during a stroll in the park, while shopping at the mall, or when trying to flag down a taxi. How we perceive others and how we are perceived by them depend on such symbolic elements as physical appearance, clothing, gestures, tone of voice, facial expressions, posture, and other elements that reveal our various statuses, attitudes, and expectations.

Social perception depends in part on our impressions of other people's personal characteristics, such as whether we perceive them to be attractive or ugly, good or bad, strong or weak. At the beginning of an encounter, people appear to devote considerable energy to discovering with whom they are dealing. Once people feel they have enough information, their attention to this assessment wanes, and early impressions continue to dominate their thinking and behavior (Dreben, Fiske, and Hastie 1979; Todorov 2017).

Our initial impressions of others also depend on our perceptions of people's social identities. When we encounter others, we mentally make a checklist of their various statuses, such as age, sex, and race, as well as search for clues to their less obvious identities. We scan clothing, hairstyle, and body posture, as well as hand and eye behaviors, for clues to occupational identity, social class, group membership, and other social statuses. Because we cannot know everything about everyone we meet, we cut corners by fitting people into ready-made categories.

In everyday life, we use a variety of *stereotypes*, which are static and oversimplified ideas about a group or social category that influence our expectations and behaviors. In American society, there are stereotypes of women, men, athletes, the elderly, racial and ethnic minorities, college students, professors, and countless other groups and social categories.

When people are identified as belonging to a particular category, we assume they possess particular traits, and we act accordingly.

Many generalized perceptions and stereotypes of other groups and individuals are formed spontaneously as we interact in specific social situations. Yet that experience alone cannot account for some of the powerful perceptions and stereotypes that many people hold toward certain groups and categories of people—some of whom they have never encountered personally. Many of these assumptions have been taught and learned through the process of socialization, and help shape and influence our social acts.

MEDIA AND TECHNOLOGY: REDEFINING SOCIAL INTERACTION

In today's world, the presentation of self, impression management, and the taken-for-granted aspects of interaction now involve using technology and interacting through cyberspace. Media and technology have had tremendous influence in shaping social interaction in our everyday lives and redefining social interaction. Our social perceptions and stereotypes have been influenced by portrayals of institutions (i.e., family, education, religion, the economy, and government) and various categories of people on television.

Today, perhaps no genre of television programming is more popular than the so-called "reality" shows. Every night of the week, at least one if not all of the major networks and several cable stations offer some type of "reality" programming. A host of programs put noncelebrities in both conventional and unconventional social situations while viewers watch their every move and sometimes become involved in these programs by calling in or logging on to specialized websites. Program participants live together, date, have sex, argue, fight, and compete for prizes sometimes worth over a million dollars. Viewers "interact" with the people on these programs by helping to select their mates or determining whether they remain in the competition or are "voted off" the show. For many Americans and other people around the world, participants in these programs vicariously become friends, enemies, partners, and adversaries. Social attitudes, values, beliefs, norms, and stereotypes are simultaneously reinforced, challenged, questioned, redefined, and shattered. From a sociological perspective, however, the question looms as to whose reality this is. What lasting impact do these programs have on our values, attitudes, beliefs, and norms? This question was somewhat answered in 2016 when reality-show celebrity Donald Trump was elected president of the United States with virtually no political qualifications. Further questions include these: To what extent is the so-called reality displayed in these programs shaped and altered by television producers, directors, film editors, and corporate sponsors? More importantly, how do these programs affect our social interactions with others in our everyday lives? And remember, television is but one form of the media and technology that influence our day-to-day interactions with others.

Technologies, especially the internet and social media, have expanded our daily social interactions and social networks, from personal face-to-face encounters to the realm of cyberspace and interaction in virtual communities. Toddlers (at least with the help of their parents) interact online (Tenore 2008), and adolescents make friends, fall in and out of love, and may even be prompted to commit suicide on social media (CBS News 2007; Subrahmanyam and Greenfield 2008). Research shows that 90 percent of Americans have used the internet by age nine, and more than a third of all 11- to 12-year-olds have their own profile on

Facebook (Cox News Service 2008). Moreover, 39 percent of three- and four-year-olds and 54 percent of children between ages 5 and 10 have used the internet (National Center for Education Statistics 2017).

College students expand their social networks and evaluate their teachers online. Campus police have found media sites to be valuable tools to discover parties and functions that might include underage drinking and use of illegal drugs, and city police use them to find out about a wide array of criminal activities (Hass 2006). Corporate executives and human resource officers use social media sites to conduct background checks on future employees, looking for risqué or provocative photographs or comments about drinking, drug use, and sexual exploits (Finder 2006). Journalists and other professionals have found it beneficial to join social media, and as one Harvard sociologist boasted, "Our predecessors could only dream of the kind of data we now have" as Facebook has become a "petri dish" for social science researchers (Rosenbloom 2007:6A). In 2007, MySpace overthrew Google as the most visited website by U.S. users, to be surpassed only a year later by Facebook (Thelwall 2008). Worldwide, there are over 2.1 billion daily Facebook users, with five new profiles being created each second; about 50 percent of college-age adults (18–24 years of age) check Facebook the first thing upon waking, but 25- to 34-year-olds comprise the most common demographic (Zephoria 2018). Although the thousands of "friends" teens and young adults brag about having on Facebook may be an exaggerated number and stretch the definition of "friend," there is no question that social networks have grown exponentially by virtue of access to the World Wide Web and cyberspace.

Online shopping allows people to browse and shop from the comfort of their own homes without the need to interact with salespeople or other customers. Although rumors that online shopping is driving retail merchants out of business may be exaggerated, e-commerce has dramatically altered the way people shop and forced retail chains to compete with popular online venues such as Amazon and others (Thau 2017). In 2018, retail giant Sears filed for bankruptcy and closed hundreds of stores nationwide (Jones and Bomey 2018). Texting, snap-chatting, email, chat rooms, virtual communities, and other forms of communication through cyberspace have made letter writing almost a lost art, and the widespread use of cell phones, along with widespread computer access, has led to households increasingly no longer using landlines

(Luckerson 2014). Moreover, on the World Wide Web people can be anybody they want to be. Thus, influential variables and potential barriers to social interaction, such as age, race, ethnicity, sex, gender, social class, and others, are at least temporarily suspended as people interact with one another through cyberspace.

The future of social interaction in our everyday lives promises some fascinating possibilities. As society changes rapidly, new statuses and roles emerge on a daily basis, and our constantly increasing status and role sets provide more potential for role strain and role conflicts than ever before. Perhaps no single aspect of society has more dramatically influenced and changed social interaction in our daily lives than the new technologies associated with the internet and social media (Langmia and Tyree 2017). Manuel Castells (2002:xx) noted that the new "Internet Society" is

> a social structure built on networks. But not any kinds of networks, since social networks have been an important dimension of social life since the origins of humankind. The networks that characterize contemporary social organization are information networks powered by microelectronics-based information technology. . . . The emerging pattern is one of self-directed networking . . . it does not substitute for face-to-face sociability or for social participation. It adds to it.

The impact of media and technology on social interaction will increase in the future as more technological developments alter our ability to communicate with one another locally, nationally, and around the globe. In 2007, after 19-year-old Facebook founder Mark Zuckerberg turned down a billion-dollar offer from Yahoo to purchase Facebook, one of Facebook's board members proclaimed, "In five years, we'll have everybody on the planet on Facebook" (Levy 2007:42). Although that prediction did not come true, by 2015, it was estimated that Facebook had approximately 1.44 billion monthly users (Statistica 2015), and by 2017, that number had jumped to over 2.1 billion, with new profiles being created every second of the day (Zephoria 2018).

Today, parents can monitor their baby's every activity, whether in the next room, at work across town, or on vacation on another continent, by the use of two-way radios, video cameras, computer programs, or via satellite. Elementary school children as well as university students carry smartphones and other electronic devices that keep them in contact with babysitters, parents, friends, drug dealers, parole officers, and anybody else with whom they feel the need to communicate locally or around the world. Computers and the internet have revolutionized contemporary education, and the use of texting, email, online chat rooms, and the creation of virtual communities have permanently altered our abilities to communicate and interact with others in our everyday lives. In the future, these and other technological advancements will create more, not fewer, changes and complexities in our interaction capabilities.

Is a person sitting all alone in front of a computer engaged in social interaction? What about people living and interacting in virtual communities? If so, how does this type of interaction differ from face-to-face interaction? What happens to those ever-important variables such as age, race, ethnicity, sex, gender, and social class that traditionally have had such powerful influence on social interaction in our daily lives? Howard Rheingold (2002:xxviii) posed some additional questions that will be of increasing interest to sociologists in the future:

- Does using the internet make people happier or unhappier?
- Is the internet empowering, or is it a tool of social control?
- Is the internet addicting?
- Does virtual community erode face-to-face community?

As interaction on the internet increases and more virtual communities emerge, Anne Hornsby (2008:95–96) posed some additional sociological questions based on the theoretical foundations of Émile Durkheim:

> In addition to mechanical and organic solidarity, has a new form of social solidarity emerged that might be called cyborg social solidarity?
>
> - How does one treat machines that perform roles previously reserved for humans?
> - Will we create new social rituals whose participants are humans, computers, and other forms of artificial life?
> - Will we enter an era in which we talk about the "human" rights of androids?
> - What will be the impact on interaction in the future as we increasingly find ourselves in a world of secure network communications (SNCs), vlogs (video blogs), spogs (spam blogs), wikis, blikis (wiki+blog), Wi-Fi, Really Simple Syndication (RSS), podcasting, and mashups?

Some in the popular media lend strong support to the idea that technological advances eventually will solve all social problems and ultimately produce utopian societies. Others believe dystopian societies are more likely and that unbridled technological change will eventually lead to environmental destruction and global terrorism and war. Visions of the future, however, are never passive reflections of historical reality, but are often self-fulfilling prophecies that influence and shape the future. Regardless of future predictions, it is important to embrace the fifth sociological wisdom and understand *the world revolves around the sun and not you.*

Sociological Wisdom 6

#TheWorldIsAMessyPlace

ORGANIZING OUR SOCIAL WORLD

LIFE IS SOMETIMES CHAOTIC, and our sixth sociological wisdom tells us that *the world is a messy place*. We like to pretend that we live in a nice, orderly, predictable world, and the fifth sociological wisdom discussed the importance of predictability for our everyday lives. A fundamental task assigned to elementary school children is learning to sort things. They learn to put round things together while separating them from square and triangular things, which similarly are placed with their like objects. Boys and girls often stand in separate lines; photographers tell the tall children to stand in the back while the shorter ones stand in front; and before long, everybody in a class pretty well knows who are the "smart" ones and who aren't, as well as which students are well behaved and which ones tend to defy the teacher's instructions or disrupt the class. All of these examples are ways that we place things, or in this case, people, into *categories* based on some common characteristic. Putting people into categories based on age, race, ethnicity, sex, gender, social class, and a host of other characteristics makes life simpler and helps us to predict how people will respond when we interact on them. This process, however, can lead to overgeneralizations and even dangerous stereotypes that interfere with social interaction in our everyday lives.

Nevertheless, categorizing is a common social phenomenon and occurs any time people gather in the same place at the same time, creating what sociologists call a social *aggregate*. *The world is a messy place*, so when people interact with one another, they organize what otherwise might be random and unpredictable acts by using elements of social structure, including statuses, roles, and social networks. To make the world even less messy, as we interact with one another, it is common to form social groups based on common characteristics and common interests.

SOCIAL GROUPS

Most human activity occurs in a *social group*, which consists of two or more people who interact in patterned ways, have a feeling of unity, and share interests and expectations. Group interactions are fundamental to human existence. We spend most of our lives in groups. We typically are born in the presence of a group; we work and play in groups; and in large and complex societies such as the United States, a multitude of groups, including hospital employees, funeral directors and their staffs, church congregations, and insurance workers ensure that we make a proper exit.

Because human activities of every kind are embedded in social groups, they are highly variable. Social groups may be large or small, temporary or long lasting, intimate or impersonal, loosely organized or tightly knit. Some groups have a strong influence on people's behaviors, and their members are deeply committed to the group. Others have little influence, and people do not much care whether they continue or disband. If we combine group dimensions of every kind, all groups can be classified into two major categories: *primary* and *secondary* groups.

A *primary group* consists of people who regularly interact and have close and enduring relationships. When he coined the term, Charles Horton Cooley (1909:23) used the word "primary" because he believed small, intimate groups were "fundamental in forming the social nature and ideas of the individual."

In primary groups, people interact with one another on an informal basis, and relationships are flexible and enduring. Moreover, people are treated as total social persons, not just in terms of particular statuses or roles. In primary groups, relationships are valued not for what they can do for members, but for the relationships themselves. These *expressive*

relationships usually have deep emotional significance and meaning for people. People develop strong attachments to primary groups and often use the word "we" when referring to them (Cooley 1909). Two lovers, a family, close friends, and neighbors who see one another regularly and who care about one another's welfare are good examples of primary groups.

A *secondary group* consists of two or more people who interact on a formal and impersonal basis to accomplish a specific objective. Sociologists call these activities *instrumental behavior*, because people interact with others not as an end in itself, but to achieve specific goals. In most secondary relationships, interactions are limited and often brief; rules are important; and people relate to one another in terms of specific roles. For example, professors and students may get to know each other pretty well during a semester, but primarily in terms of their reciprocal roles. Secondary groups may be small or large, but all large groups in which regular face-to-face interaction is impossible are secondary groups.

If you examine your daily routines, you will discover that whereas a few hours each day may be devoted to your family and friends, much of the day's activities are embedded in secondary groups. When you visit a restaurant, shop at the mall, go to church, have a doctor's appointment, participate in a club meeting, or have a brief chat with the mail carrier, you are engaging in secondary group activities. The distinction between primary and secondary groups, however, is not always clear-cut, and in everyday life, groups may include elements of each *ideal type*.

Even groups that we are not members of may have a strong influence on our behavior. This is because all groups distinguish and maintain their boundaries with the help of outside groups. An *in-group* is a group with which people identify and have a sense of belonging. By contrast, an *out-group* is a group that people do not identify with and consider less worthy and less desirable than their own. In-group boundaries are commonly maintained by challenges and threats—either real or imagined—from out-groups. Likewise, the "we-ness" or cohesiveness of a group is often proportional to the nature and intensity of these threats (Lamont and Fournier 1992; Sumner 1906).

At the heart of the in-group–out-group distinction is the concept of *social boundaries*, material or symbolic devices that identify who is inside or outside a group. In some cases, groups are distinguished and interactions regulated by means of actual physical barriers, such as the Great Wall of China. In others, territories such as neighborhoods, regions, and nation-states may contain fences, gates, and other physical barriers to keep some people in and others out.

Social distinctions and symbolic barriers are equally effective in boundary maintenance. High schools, athletic teams, fraternities and sororities, and youth gangs use colors, language, emblems, mascots, insignias, and other symbols to set themselves apart from others as well.

Are you attractive? Are you a good person? Are you rich or poor? There is no objective answer to any of these questions. Rather, the answer depends on the groups that people refer to when evaluating their personal qualities, circumstances, attitudes, values, and behaviors. Sociologists call these *reference groups*, and they may serve both positive and negative functions. For example, when Little League players choose Major League Baseball players as their reference group, they may copy their best behaviors and become cooperative, honest, and fair. Of course, the Little Leaguers may also learn to curse, chew tobacco, spit, throw temper tantrums, argue with the umpire, and exhibit other socially disapproved behaviors.

Some reference groups give us a sense of *relative gratification* (Singer 1981). For example, people of average income may judge themselves rich if they use people on welfare or the homeless as reference groups. On the other hand, most people would experience a sense of *relative*

deprivation—feelings of dissatisfaction based on the gap between what they have and what they would like to have—if they used billionaires Bill Gates or Warren Buffet as their reference group. In much the same way, if we judge our looks by how well we compare with top fashion models on the covers of *Vogue* and *GQ*, we are unlikely to feel very good about our appearance.

Many people boost their self-esteem and social standing by associating with successful groups (Felson and Reed 1986). A good example is some people's strong identification with winning athletic teams. Many fans proudly display the banners, flags, coffee mugs, and license plates of these teams—not only to declare their allegiance but also to make a public statement about themselves: that they, too, are winners.

In modern, complex societies, people may choose from among a multitude of reference groups, and these groups may conflict with or reinforce one another. Corporate marketers depend on trendsetters as well as peer group influence "to encourage" teenagers and preteens to purchase and display luxury brands—brands that they aim "to register so strongly in kids' minds that the appeal will remain for life" (Holstein 2003:1). Because there are so many choices, people also can be creative when it comes to selecting a reference group. For example, a student who received a C on an exam may choose as his reference group students who got an F—at least for parental consumption (Pike 2011). Parents, on the other hand, rarely accept the worst students as their children's reference group; instead, they almost always choose A students.

Although groups may range in size from two friends to a giant corporation with thousands of workers all over the globe, most people conduct their day-to-day lives in *small groups* in which members have regular face-to-face interactions. Because of the importance of small groups, researchers—beginning with George Homans in his classic work *The Human Group* (1950)—have conducted a number of studies of *small group dynamics*. Three factors—group size, group leadership, and group decision making—have received the most scholarly attention.

Georg Simmel was one of the first sociologists to examine the impact of group size on the nature of social interaction ([1908] 1955). If you threw a party, would it matter to you whether 2 people or 200 showed up? For most people the answer is yes, because numbers can have a dramatic impact on our thoughts and actions. Lab studies and our everyday experiences tell us that the smaller the group, the more direct, personally satisfying, and emotionally intense is the interaction. Research indicates that learning occurs best in small groups, and whether face-to-face or even in cyberspace and on social media, small groups tend to have more influence on people than larger, less personal groups (Adams 2011; Barnier et al. 2018; Bolinger and Stanton 2014).

The smallest possible group is a *dyad*—a two-person group. In the dyad, the individual must take account of no one but the other person; thus, individuals can totally focus on each other. However, because the relationship is totally dependent on the continued participation of both parties, it is also the most fragile, demanding, tension-filled, and precarious of all relationships. Should either party even temporarily ignore the other, the relationship may be threatened; if one withdraws, the dyad ceases to exist.

When another person is added, and a *triad* or a three-member group, emerges, the nature of the interaction becomes less intimate but more flexible. In a triad, one member may temporarily withdraw, daydream, or become silent without harming the group. Moreover, within the triad, various coalitions are possible that cannot be found in a dyad. A third person may mediate conflicts, join with one member to gang up on the third, or take power by manipulating the other two. Even small increases in group size can have a dramatic impact on social interaction.

In a dyad, there is only one relationship, but with each added member the number of relationships increases dramatically. For example, if a group expands to four, there are 6 possible relationships; with the addition of only one more member—a group of five—there are 10 possible relationships.

A number of studies suggest that five members make the ideal discussion or work group. When a group exceeds seven, direct interaction among members becomes difficult, and as any observant person knows who has attended a party, the group begins to fragment into smaller groups. If the group exceeds 12, it becomes impossible for people to interact with all members of the group, and usually someone is chosen to direct group activities. At the same time, members' participation decreases, and people begin to treat others in a more formal and rigid way, addressing the group as a whole rather than as individual members (Beebe and Masterson 2016; Levine and Moreland 1998).

As group size increases, there is also an increased chance for a specialized division of labor. With more individuals and more talent and specialized skills available, proportionately greater results can be achieved in many social spheres. Studies have shown that this is not always the case, however. As groups grow, people often reduce their efforts, a phenomenon sociologists call *social loafing*. People seem to do this because they think their efforts cannot be monitored or appreciated, or because they expect that others will loaf, and they do not want to carry more than their share of the load or be exploited. Experiments also have shown that in the presence of large public groups, people are less willing to assist someone in need than they would be if they were the only one available to help. In large groups, witnesses often assume that someone else will help out, so they shift responsibility to others (Beebe and Masterson 2016; Jackson and Harkins 1985; Latané and Nida 1981; Levine and Moreland 1998).

LEADERS AND LEADERSHIP STYLES

Most groups have leaders. It is often assumed that leaders possess special traits that distinguish them from followers, but this may not always be the case. This is because leadership is situational and task-specific, and leadership qualities and skills that are appropriate in one situation may be inappropriate in another. Moreover, leadership is a two-way street. Any understanding of leadership must include knowledge of how followers perceive their leaders, as well as how this affects group processes and the behavior of leaders.

Leaders often vary according to their leadership style, and although several specific leadership styles have been identified, sociologists tend to categorize them in one of three basic forms: authoritarian, democratic, and laissez-faire (Chestnut 2017; Lippitt and White 1958). *Authoritarian* leaders give orders and direct activities with minimal input from followers. In extreme cases, they may be said to rule with an iron fist that crushes all dissent. In egalitarian societies, authoritarian leaders may be tolerated, but members of small groups typically prefer individuals with a *democratic* leadership style, who attempt to involve others in decision making. Laissez-faire–style leaders take a "hands-off" approach; they neither set the agenda nor try to direct followers in any obvious way. Instead, they allow group members the freedom to choose whatever direction the group thinks is best.

No single leadership style is effective in every social situation. Because they require neither agreement nor support, authoritarian leaders often fail to recognize conflicts and strains within the group that may reduce its effectiveness. But when a situation is unclear, authoritarian leaders can provide structure and, in emergencies, immediate action. Democratic leaders operate well under ordinary circumstances, where there is time for leaders to gain input from all group members and then take action. Laissez-faire leadership seems to be the least effective of the three styles, at least in lab experiments with American youngsters. Laissez-faire leadership can be productive if group members are highly motivated, but without direction, group members eventually work at cross-purposes, and interpersonal tensions and conflicts may threaten the group.

To function properly, group members must cooperate to accomplish a task. Leaders can help define and coordinate group activities, but something more is required if groups are to achieve their goals: individuals must conform to the group's opinions and expectations. One of the most important discoveries in the area of small group dynamics is that there are intense pressures on individuals to conform, sometimes called the *social influence effect*.

In an early study of conformity, Muzafer Sherif (1936) asked subjects to stare at a stationary point of light that, because of the autokinetic effect, appeared to be moving. First, individuals were asked how far they thought the light had moved, and their estimates were plotted. Next, groups of two or three people were asked to do the same thing. Sherif found that when subjects were uncertain about their own judgments, they relied on the opinions of others, and that estimates in groups converged on a common judgment.

The classic experiment on group conformity is the Asch experiment. Asch (1952) created an experiment in which groups of various sizes were selected and coached to give the wrong answer about the length of lines on various cards. He found that these groups of perfect strangers were able to pressure individuals into agreeing with their distorted view of reality. The pressure to conform was so intense that more than one-third of the subjects, though convinced their judgments were correct, changed them to accommodate to the majority opinion. Though Asch was a psychologist, and the experiment was conducted in the 1950s, the results of his experiment resonate with sociologists today because they emphasize the nature and power of social forces and norms in our everyday lives. The behavior and expectations of others shape how we think and act on a daily basis and help determine how we define social issues and social problems (Crossman 2017).

If individuals can be persuaded by strangers, there should be much more intense pressure to conform within primary groups, in which individuals are committed to others. Irving Janis (1972) found that in tightly knit groups the pressures to conform are indeed strong because they are reinforced by intense feelings of loyalty. According to Janis (1972), this can result in *groupthink*, decision making that ignores alternative solutions in order to maintain group harmony. Janis wrote that groupthink can have disastrous results. Some journalists argue that groupthink may have been an important factor in several NASA space shuttle disasters—including the loss of the *Challenger* in 1986 and the *Columbia* disaster in 2003. For example, the journalists claim that once engineers and important decision makers in the *Columbia* case reached a consensus that the falling foam insulation did not endanger the shuttle, the missions were allowed to proceed, although "other engineers who had been consulted became increasingly concerned and frustrated" (Schwartz and Wald 2003:1). One nuclear engineer contends that similar problems may characterize nuclear power plants as well: "As you go up the chain, you're asked harder and harder questions by people who have more and more control. The group answering the questions then tend to agree on a single answer, and to be reluctant to admit it when they don't have an answer" (Schwartz and Wald 2003:2).

Experiments have shown that during the decision-making process, group members often shift toward extreme positions—either conservative or high-risk—a tendency that is called the *group polarization phenomenon* (Myers and Lamm 1978). But, as in social life in general, the opinions of group members are not all equal. Any model of social influence must allow for inequalities of interpersonal influence for situations where there is no initial consensus and where no group members' opinions are fixed (Bond 2014; Friedkin 1999).

FORMAL ORGANIZATIONS

In some parts of the world, small primary groups of kin, neighbors, and friends continue to play a central role in people's lives, not only providing emotional support but also fulfilling most of their members' basic needs. In modern societies, though, primary groups often form the backdrop rather than center stage in people's day-to-day lives.

In modern societies, people's lives are largely shaped by *formal organizations*, which are secondary groups that are formally organized to achieve specific goals. Such organizations are the fundamental building blocks of the contemporary social order—they produce and distribute goods and services, maintain order, and fulfill our spiritual and physical needs. If you are injured, you would appreciate the help of a group of bystanders. However, your survival depends on formal organizations—the telephone company that enables people to notify an emergency crew, hospital workers to assist in your recovery, and insurance companies to help you pay hospital and emergency care bills.

Moreover, since the beginning of the nineteenth century, large organizations have played the key role in shaping stratification systems across the globe. Today, more than half of the working population works for highly stratified organizations, and those organizations also exist within a system of highly stratified organizations (Perrow 2000, 2014).

Formal organizations may be classified into three major types: voluntary, coercive, and utilitarian (Etzioni 1975). Organizations that people join freely to accomplish goals are called *voluntary organizations*. They typically contain like-minded people who pursue shared goals because they find them personally and socially rewarding. *Coercive organizations* are those that people are forced to join. Prisons; mental institutions; elementary schools; and, where military service is compulsory, the armed forces are examples of coercive organizations. People join *utilitarian organizations* for practical reasons. For example, we may join a company to earn income or attend college to increase our knowledge and skills.

BUREAUCRACIES AND US

Large-scale formal organizations came into being at least 6,000 years ago in Egypt and Mesopotamia, when cities and trade networks became so complex that regional centers developed. Religious elites began to coordinate the activities of many villages, and more complex organizations appeared in order to regulate water and maintain irrigation canals. Still others emerged to defend city-states against a growing list of enemies. Over the millennia, as organizations increased in size and complexity, a special kind of organization developed, which sociologists call a *bureaucracy*, a large-scale organization that uses rules, hierarchical ranking, and a rational worldview to achieve maximum efficiency.

For many of us, the word "bureaucracy" evokes images of long lines and delays and petty officials adhering to rules at the expense of reason. In the late nineteenth century, when Max Weber began his sociological investigation of bureaucratic organizations, he recognized that they had limitations. He warned that bureaucracy could become an *iron cage* "that shrinks a person's moral capacity into a mere duty to obey" (Weber 1947:129). At the same time, however, Weber and his contemporaries were most impressed with bureaucracy's ability to coordinate the activities of large groups of people—especially in business, medicine, and the military—and to outperform and outproduce all other forms of organization.

Weber analyzed bureaucracy as an ideal type, which isolated for study only the essential characteristics of this form of organization. That is, instead of describing the various kinds of bureaucracies in government, education, business, and religion, Weber abstracted from them certain features that were common to all. To Weber (1978), bureaucracies owed their technical superiority to other forms of organization because of five basic characteristics:

1. *Specialization and Division of Labor.* There is a clear-cut division of labor among workers, with each person held responsible for a small portion of the total operation.
2. *Hierarchical Structure.* Positions are arranged in a hierarchical fashion. Rank and authority increase as one moves from the bottom to the top of the bureaucracy, and authority is clearly defined at every level.
3. *Formal Rules, Regulations, and Procedures.* Written rules and regulations specify the goals of the organization, the work to be performed, and what workers can and cannot do.
4. *Impersonality.* Interactions with clients and coworkers are guided by rules, not personal feelings.
5. *Merit and Careers.* Positions in the bureaucracy are based on qualifications and performance, which benefits the organization and gives people a sense of continuity and security; a "meritocracy" enables people to plan for careers, which ideally ensures a stronger worker identification and a greater commitment to the organization and its goals.

SOCIAL INSTITUTIONS

No society can ever take its survival for granted. To this end, all societies create *social institutions*—relatively enduring clusters of values, norms, social statuses, roles, and groups that address fundamental social needs.

Sociologists generally identify five major social institutions that exist in every society: family, education, religion, government, and the economy. These institutions serve as powerful social forces that shape and alter our social structure and impact social interaction in our everyday lives.

Family. Because the family is the only institution with origins in biology, people tend to believe that families are pretty much the same everywhere—or at least that families should suit their ideal images. But everywhere, societies are highly selective in terms of which aspects of biology and "human nature" they emphasize, ignore, or downplay; hence the controversial nature of the family and the great diversity of families in the United States and around the world (Schultz and Lavenda 2017).

The U.S. Bureau of the Census defines the family as two or more persons (one of whom is the householder), related by blood, marriage, or adoption, who share a common residence. But this definition ignores current living arrangements and the preferences of many people. Although there may have been some consensus about the family several decades ago, what constitutes a family today is a matter of public debate. To account for the extraordinary diversity of families in contemporary society, sociologists define *family* as two or more people who are related by blood, marriage, or adoption or who are part of a relationship in which there is commitment, mutual aid and support, and often a shared residence.

As in the past, most families today are formed through *marriage*, a legally recognized economic and sexual relationship between two or more persons that includes mutual rights and obligations and is assumed to be permanent. This definition highlights three important aspects of marriage. First, marriage includes not only the marrying parties but also the members of society, who must approve of the union. Second, marriage provides for the regulation of sex and childbearing, and in most societies marriage and the family are the primary—and in many cases the only legitimate—contexts for both activities. Third, although Americans often emphasize romantic love and downplay the economic aspects of marriage, most societies acknowledge that economic exchanges are basic to the relationship (Schultz and Lavenda 2017).

Sociologists distinguish two kinds of families, each with its own norms, roles, and relationships. During the life course, most Americans are members of both the *family of orientation*, which is the family into which an individual is born or adopted, and the *family of marriage*, the family that a person forms at marriage. The family is typically the first socializing agent in a person's life, but soon thereafter it is joined by another important social institution: education.

Education. Ask almost any adult in any country around the world why they send their children to school, and they are likely to respond, "To learn." When sociologists speak of education, however, they are not referring simply to learning, which is an ongoing process that includes every facet of the human experience. Instead, *education* is the institutionalized process of systematically teaching certain cognitive skills and knowledge and transmitting them from one generation to the next. Institutionalized education exists in every culture, from the simplest to the most complex, because it is vital to the survival of any society. In preliterate societies, education may be as simple as the adults in a tribe teaching traditional roles and basic hunting and domestic skills to younger tribal members. In industrial and postindustrial societies, education may include a complex myriad of preschools, kindergartens, elementary and secondary schools, postsecondary vocational schools and technical institutes, two-year and four-year colleges, universities, graduate schools, and postdoctoral institutions. From a sociological viewpoint, education, like other social institutions, reflects a society's historical development and cultural values.

The first public school established in the United States, in 1634, was in Boston. Over the past three and a half centuries, America's public schools have undergone tremendous change. Once dominated by one-room schoolhouses with children in grades one to eight, ranging in age from 5 to 15 years, today's public schools in the United States include massive school districts with separate buildings, faculty, and curricula for schools limited to pre-K through second grade; another for second grade through fourth grade; and yet another for fifth- and sixth-graders. Teachers must have special certification to teach in middle schools that are specially designed for preteen students in grades seven and eight. After completing middle school, students progress to an intermediate high school for ninth and tenth grades, and ultimately they graduate from a senior high school comprised solely of students in the 11th and 12th grades. Students' public school experiences may include vocational and occupational training, online courses, participation in virtual educational communities in cyberspace, service-learning, paid and unpaid internships, advanced placement in classes for college credit, and concurrent enrollment in courses taught by university faculty for university credit; and in some cases, students may receive an associate's degree from a two-year college at the same time as they receive their high school diploma (Ballantine et al. 2017).

Today, many speak of the educational system of the United States as if it were some large, homogeneous structure in which students have similar academic experiences regardless of where they attend school or what type of school they attend. Yet students in the United States may undergo a wide range of educational experiences, including homeschooling, a vast array of religious and secular private schools, and public schools that range from decrepit and dangerous racially and socioeconomically segregated buildings to highly diverse magnet schools in state-of-the art facilities—and everything in between. Whatever the configuration and process, education is primarily responsible for transmitting cognitive culture (knowledge) from one generation to the next. And although education is also influential in teaching moral values and giving people a sense of purpose, the institution of religion exists in every society as the fundamental inculcator of morality and supernatural explanations for life.

Religion. On the surface, worldwide religious ideas and institutions seem to have little in common. In many preliterate societies, people consider almost everything sacred. The ancient Greeks and Romans believed in a pantheon of gods, whereas Jews, Muslims, and Christians recognize only one supreme deity. The word *Christian* also has many meanings, and there are hundreds of Christian organizations. For some, Christianity consists of worship services, Bible classes, and intellectual discussions; for others, it is more emotional, personal, and even ecstatic (Chalfant, Beckley, and Palmer 1994; Johnstone 2015; McGuire 2008).

Early in his career, sociologist Émile Durkheim sorted through this maze of religious beliefs and practices—exploring both historical and diverse cultural examples—searching for something that was common to them all. His findings provide the basis for defining *religion* as a system of socially shared symbols, beliefs, and rituals that address the sacred and the ultimate meaning of human existence.

One of Durkheim's ([1912] 1965) initial findings, which remains basic to the sociological understanding of religion today, is that people everywhere make a distinction between the *sacred* and the *profane*. According to Durkheim, religion pertains to the sacred, which represents uncommon and extraordinary aspects of social life that inspire in believers feelings of awe, reverence, and respect. He contrasted this with the profane, which represents ordinary, commonly understood, and routine activities that people take for granted as they go about their daily lives.

Durkheim emphasized that an object, person, place, or event is not inherently sacred. Rather, "sacredness"

is bestowed by a community of believers. Because the supernatural is beyond this sensory world, all religions include *religious symbols* that represent the sacred. They include such things as icons—holy pictures, statues, masks, and relics—as well as sacred words, places, food, clothing, people, and other tangible things that facilitate contact with the sacred.

All religions also include beliefs that guide people's perceptions and thinking about the natural and supernatural domains and serve as plans for action (Davie 2013; Johnstone 2015; McGuire 2008). For example, most of us usually ignore strange sounds, interpreting them as being caused by wind or other natural forces. By contrast, many Native Americans pay particular attention to them because they believe it is through such sounds that spirits communicate important messages to the living.

In Western societies, much emphasis is placed on intellectual and formal beliefs that are fashioned into elaborate doctrines and creeds, and most historical religions also provide a general theory of the universe—or *cosmology*—which explains creation, how the world works relative to humans, and a vision of the future. Religion also includes many informal beliefs, including religious myths, legends, proverbs, and folktales (Davie 2013; Johnstone 2015; McGuire 2008).

As belief and myth express the sacred order in words and images, ritual dramatizes them in performance. *Rituals* are formal, stylized enactments of beliefs that, in the case of religious rituals, detach people from the "ordinary" and focus their attention on the sacred. Prayers, chants, dances, fasting, and sacrifice are but a few of the many ritual expressions that enable people to make contact with the sacred and experience a deeper, more profound reality. Religious rituals may be brief and private or involve great collective celebrations, such as seasonal festivals or *rites of passage* of birth, puberty, marriage, and death that effect a permanent change in a person's position in society (Johnstone 2015; Paden 1995).

Rodney Stark and William Bainbridge (1985) contend that religious groups and organizations owe their existence to the fact that in all societies many of the population have far less of some rewards than they would like. And some intensely desired rewards, such as immortality, do not appear to be available at all. In response to these universal conditions, people everywhere create religious organizations to provide themselves with *compensators*, which are "beliefs that a reward will be obtained in the distant future or in some other context that cannot be immediately verified" (Stark and Bainbridge 1985:6). Most religions also provide *theodicies*, which are emotionally satisfying explanations for meaning-threatening experiences. For example, throughout history, it has been common for leaders to promise soldiers that if they were "martyred" in combat, they would go directly to heaven (Johnstone 2015; McGuire 2008). As this indicates, the institution of religion must coincide alongside another powerful institution: government.

Government. The desire for freedom and autonomy seem to be almost universal, yet sociologists have long contended that whether living in a simple hunting-and-gathering society or a highly complex postindustrial one, a fundamental social institution necessary for survival is some form of government, consisting of people and organizations that formulate and implement public policy. As the poet John Donne ([1624] 1988) so eloquently noted, "No man is an island . . ." and as such, as tribes, nations and other forms of societies are created, people must grapple with living with others and determining how much individual and personal freedom can be maintained while acknowledging the rights and freedoms of others. Consequently, since the time of Ancient Greece, philosophers have alluded to the development of what became known during the Age of Enlightenment as the *social contract*, in which people individually and collectively agree for the common good to relinquish some of their individual autonomy and freedom to a government that is tasked with protecting their remaining rights. How much of that individual autonomy and freedom should be relinquished is the subject of debate that has contributed to the formation of anarchists, libertarians, political parties, and a wide range of political movements focused on power, politics, and authority.

Power and authority are fundamental to politics, and politicians use both to affect the actions of others. Those with power can compel obedience and force people to do what they may not wish to do. When people have authority, others follow their commands not because they have to, but because they want to or believe it is their duty.

Max Weber (1947:328–29) identified three major types of legitimate power, which he termed *traditional, legal-rational*, and *charismatic* authority. Because it has become increasingly important, we add *expertise* as the fourth major source of authority.

Traditional authority is a form of authority based on custom and habit, which has its roots in the distant past and often is religiously sanctioned. Traditional authority is usually hereditary and based on ascribed statuses (age, race, sex, religion), and people typically obey those who have it because they always have done so—not because their leadership is especially good, just, or wise.

Legal-rational authority is authority based on explicit rules, regulations, and procedures that define who holds power and how power is to be exercised and distributed. Legal-rational authority is legitimated by law rather than custom, and stresses qualifications, credentials, and other achievements that entitle a person to occupy a position of authority.

Charismatic authority is based on unique personal qualities, which include the ability to excite and inspire followers. When a person has it, he or she invariably becomes the center of attention wherever people are gathered.

Expertise is a form of authority derived from the possession of specialized knowledge. Today, almost all of us defer to the authority of experts, not only because they produce vaccines and send rockets into outer space but also because they define problems and offer solutions to important concerns of modern life. The relative influence and power of experts is further enhanced by collective organizations such as the American Bar Association and the American Medical Association, which not only restrict membership to those with proper credentials and monitor members' activities but also attempt to codetermine major developments in government and industry (Roy 2011).

Even a cursory examination of the fortunes and careers of political leaders demonstrates that the various ideal types of authority are by no means mutually exclusive. In real life, skilled politicians often employ them in various combinations to enhance their power. For example,

Presidents Kennedy, Reagan, and Clinton combined charismatic and legal-rational authority to achieve many of their political objectives, and members of the Bush and Kennedy families can even draw on traditional authority by emphasizing their family's long history of service to the nation. Although political leaders' authority often comes from personal characteristics, history shows that their political "success" or "failure" is often linked to the economy.

Economy. The *economy* is one of the basic social institutions that exist in every society. Consequently, sociologists are interested in the economy and how it affects society and social life around the globe, believing that "the relations of 'economic' life are too important to be left to economists" (Centeno and Cohen 2010; Frieden 2017; Ross and Trachte 1990:4).

Sociology has always shared many important concepts and theories with economics. For example, Karl Marx and the conflict perspective were influenced by economic studies, and much of the conflict analysis of human social behavior is based on economic determinism—that is, social class is of paramount importance in shaping people's values, behavior, and life chances. The structural functionalist perspective also was influenced by economics; Talcott Parsons studied at the London School of Economics. Exchange theory, developed by George Homans and Peter Blau, uses rational choice theory and incorporates many of the tenets of utilitarian economics in an effort to explain human behavior. In fact, it would be almost impossible for any sociologist, regardless of specific interests or theoretical orientation, to ignore the economy and its powerful impact on human social life.

The *economy* consists of the systematic production, distribution, and consumption of goods and services in a society. *Production* is the process by which goods and services are brought into existence. *Distribution* is the allocation of goods and services to societal members. *Consumption* is the process of accumulating and using goods and services. Every society's economy depends on consumers who want, need, and use goods and services. The basic staples of an economy—food, clothing, and shelter—have inherent value, as people cannot survive without them. By contrast, most objects produced in industrial and postindustrial societies are valued not because they are needed, but because they are wanted. Over a century ago, sociologist Thorstein Veblen (1899) coined the term *conspicuous consumption* to describe consumers' desire to express their social standing by acquiring goods and services simply for the purposes of having, displaying, and consuming them (Stillerman 2015).

Because production, distribution, and consumption are vital to all societies, they are institutionalized into an *economic system* that includes the ideology, values, norms, and activities that regulate an economy. The economic system holds the same interest for sociologists as other major institutions—the family, education, religion, and politics—because it is part of the social fabric that shapes and defines human social interaction. Economic systems can be placed on a continuum ranging from the ideal type of capitalism at one end to that of socialism at the other. Those that fall somewhere in between, which includes most countries, are referred to as mixed economies (McConnell, Brue, and Flynn 2014).

Capitalism is an economic system in which the means of production are privately owned, and goods and services are distributed competitively for profit. Three key elements of capitalistic ideology are private ownership, competition, and profit.

Socialism is an economic system in which the means of production are owned and controlled by the state, and goods and services are distributed as a cooperative enterprise without regard to personal profit. Under socialism, the state restricts private ownership to only a few personal items and thus limits social stratification based on wealth.

Through state ownership of factories and service agencies, revenue generated from production is put back into the economic system for the benefit of all citizens. This does not mean that socialist countries are without stratification, however, as party membership, the region of the country, and urban versus rural residence create important economic differences (Gerber 2002; Schumpeter 2014).

A *mixed economy* combines central elements of capitalism and socialism and allows private ownership and free enterprise to compete with businesses, industries, and services owned and operated by the state. Some scholars argue that economic and political circumstances have changed so much that the socialism-versus-capitalism debate may be obsolete (Lanz 2008). Yet the strong, conflicting ideologies behind capitalism and socialism do not die easily, and many government leaders and citizens still argue that one system or the other is inherently superior (Schumpeter 2014).

There can be no question that we live in a global economy. Many of the major corporations with which Americans are familiar, which once manufactured and sold products exclusively in the United States, are now enjoying the benefits of worldwide production, marketing, and sales. Consider the following facts: two-thirds of all sales of the Colgate-Palmolive Company and Coca-Cola are outside the United States; Procter

& Gamble leads the market among all shampoos, soaps, and detergents sold in China; Pepsi-Cola is the dominant soft drink in Jamaica; MTV has regional production centers in Brazil, Europe, Japan, and India; the National Football League, the National Basketball Association, and the National Hockey League are all pursuing franchise teams outside of North America; Pringles potato chips are shipped to more than 40 countries around the globe; Kentucky Fried Chicken is sold in Paris, London, and Beijing; McDonald's can be found in almost every major city in the world; and hundreds of other companies that once operated solely in the United States have expanded their markets into a worldwide global economy, which has increased U.S. exports by almost 30 percent since 1990 and promises to continue to grow (Ritzer 2018).

Although everyone is affected by transnational corporations and the global economy, most people's economic concerns are more local and personal in nature. This reflects the wisdom that *the world is a messy place*. Part of trying to organize the "messy" world causes people to focus on controlling the actions and behaviors of others around them, the focus of our next sociological wisdom.

Sociological Wisdom 7

#SomeRulesAreMadeToBeBrokenButSomeAren't

CONTROLLING SOCIAL BEHAVIOR

FROM THE FIRST DAY OF KINDERGARTEN, you were taught several rules of the classroom that could not be broken under any circumstances. You were never to shove, hit, bite, or otherwise inflict any harm on another student. In fact, you were taught to always keep your hands to yourself. Unlike at home, if you needed to go to the bathroom, you were taught to always raise your hand and ask permission first. There also were rules about putting away supplies, not talking while the teacher was speaking, and so many others too numerous to mention. The first several weeks, if not the entire school year of kindergarten, are spent learning the rules of how to be a successful student. The rules about not hurting others are nonnegotiable, and most schools have instituted "zero tolerance" policies regarding them. But what about the rule that you should always raise your hand and ask permission to go to the restroom? Most kindergartners are five years old, and some are only a couple of years past the process of toilet training, and many, if involved in an interesting activity, fail to anticipate needing to "go" in time to raise their hand, get permission, and then make it to the restroom before an accident occurs. Consequently, kindergarten teachers often keep a change of underwear and dry clothes in their room for those incidents. In order to avoid such embarrassing episodes, many kindergarten teachers tell their students that if they feel the need to "go" come on urgently, to just go, and then come back and explain the circumstances later. This is especially true when children suddenly feel sick to their stomachs and may urgently need to leave the room to avoid catastrophe. These simple but common examples illustrate the seventh wisdom of sociology, that *some rules are made to be broken, but some aren't.*

Deviance and *conformity* are powerful yet elusive concepts on which there is no unanimous agreement. Nevertheless, the extent to which people conform to or deviate from the rules of society is one of the criteria by which we set them apart for differential and unequal treatment. In reality, everybody is both a deviant and a conformist, as on almost a daily basis we violate some of society's rules and guidelines and adhere to others, confirming the seventh wisdom of sociology that some rules are made to be broken, but some are not. And sometimes it is not even clear whether a particular act is deviant. *Deviance* refers to violation of a social norm and *conformity* to adherence to social norms. *Deviance* and *conformity* are not absolute terms. Rather, they are terms that we apply to people and behaviors based on a wide variety of circumstances, determining which rules are made to be broken and when we may break them, and which ones aren't and why.

RANGE OF TOLERANCE

Some norms are *prescriptive*—they tell us what we should do. For example, informal norms that encourage Americans to say "excuse me" after bumping into another person, as well as formal laws that require us to pay a portion of our income each year in taxes, both fall into this category. Not doing these things would be considered deviant.

Other norms are *proscriptive*—they tell us what we should not do. They also range from informal rules such as "Don't put your feet up on the dinner table," to potent religious commandments such as "Thou shalt not kill," to even more powerful *taboos*, which are prohibitions against behaviors that most members of a society consider so repugnant they are unthinkable. Doing any of these things is generally considered deviant.

An emphasis on norms in defining deviance and conformity (sometimes called the *normative approach*) illustrates how members of society evaluate behavior in reference to some preestablished standard of behavior. It also implies that there is some set of absolute norms, the violation of which automatically constitutes deviance. Many people believe that deviance and conformity are objective conditions that need only to be identified. Others insist that defining deviance and conformity is a subjective process that relies on interpretation. Many view deviance and conformity as labels placed on some actions and people by others with the power to do so.

Although we tend to think in simple dichotomies, social life is rarely divided into neat, discrete categories of good and bad, right and wrong, or deviance and conformity. From a sociological viewpoint, deviance and conformity are socially defined; rather than viewing them as two opposing categories, it is more insightful to think of them as representing the two ends of a continuum. As sociologist Émile Durkheim ([1893] 1964) concluded, even in a nation of "saints," some saints would be considered "less holy" than others.

We expect people to conform to social norms because this allows us to anticipate what others will do in certain situations and provides guidelines for what we are expected to do. In most societies, however, people are not expected to adhere to every single norm in every situation; in some cases, adhering to one norm may even require violation of another. For example, when a friend asks your opinion of a bad haircut, you might find that the norm of politeness conflicts with the norm of honesty, thus complicating your response. Similarly, every spouse has learned to avoid answering the question "Do these pants make my butt look big?" Consequently, members of society establish a *range of tolerance*, or a scope of behaviors considered acceptable and defined as conformity, although they may involve violation of a norm. For example, despite posted maximum speed limit signs, police departments and even individual officers establish acceptable ranges beyond the maximum speed that they are willing to tolerate. Although you may have violated a norm, an officer who gives you a ticket for driving one mile per hour over the speed limit is just as likely to be considered deviant by fellow officers as by you.

Sociologist Ruth Cavan (1961) created a behavioral continuum model that illustrates how societal members create an acceptable range of tolerance around a social norm. Society's range of tolerance varies from one culture to another. Whereas the previous example is familiar and clear in illustrating the flexibility of speed limits to most American drivers, it would be confusing and serve as an example of the rigidity of American traffic laws to most European drivers, especially those from Germany, where speed limits are rarely posted and almost never enforced. Sociologists also point out that deviant and criminal activities such as recreational marijuana use and ticket scalping often are tolerated by both the public and law enforcement (Hathaway and Atkinson 2001).

Most deviance is relatively minor in significance and is treated as such. Sociologists call behaviors that fall so far beyond the range of tolerance *extreme deviance*, because they involve beliefs, behaviors, or physical traits that are so unacceptable that they elicit extremely strong negative reactions. Examples of extreme deviance include extreme body modification, believing that one has been kidnapped by extraterrestrials, being hugely obese, believing in white supremacy, endorsing adult–child sexual contact, committing acts of terrorism, cannibalism, and engaging in sadomasochistic sexual practices, to name a few (Goode and Vail 2008; Thompson and Gibbs 2017). This concept illustrates that people can be defined as deviant for what they *think* and *are* as well as for what they *do*.

Cavan's model shows how *overconformity* as well as *underconformity* can be viewed as deviance. For example, a student who never missed a single class period, completed all assignments before they were due, knew the answer to every question, and scored 100 percent on every examination and paper would appear to be the model conformist. Most of the other students would probably think the student was a bit weird, and they might gossip about or ridicule the student. Just as maximum speeds are enforced if exceeded beyond reasonable limits, so too are minimum speeds, and a driver is more likely to be pulled over and issued a citation for driving 30 miles per hour on an interstate highway than for driving 75.

RELATIVITY OF DEVIANCE

What is considered conformity at one point in time may be viewed as deviance at another. This illustrates the importance of *time* in defining deviance and conformity. Folkways governing fashion and grooming are excellent examples of how norms change over time.

The *place* where behavior occurs is also an important determinant of whether an act is viewed as appropriate or deviant. Whistling, shouting, cheering, and booing are acceptable at a football stadium but would evoke strong disapproval in the Mormon Tabernacle, at the Wailing Wall in Jerusalem, or at the end of a college lecture. *Situation* often takes precedence over place in determining the appropriateness of actions. For example, although whistling, shouting, and booing may be deemed appropriate at a football stadium during a baseball game, they would not be okay when it is the site of a religious crusade. Likewise, texting is acceptable at home, but not in class, in church, or while watching a child's soccer match, although it is becoming more and more acceptable.

Perhaps no other variable is more influential in defining deviance and conformity than the cultural context in which behavior occurs. The importance of culture becomes very apparent when people socialized in different cultures come into direct contact. It should be clear that norms vary greatly from one culture to another, and definitions of deviance and conformity vary among different groups and subcultures within a culture. In all cultures, however, at least three elements are important in defining deviance and conformity: the actors, their audience, and the media.

An individual's age, sex, race, ethnicity, social class, physical appearance, demeanor, and other variables all may enter into the deviance–conformity equation. In everyday life, we can see that certain behaviors considered deviant in children (e.g., smoking, drinking, and gambling) may be tolerated in adults. Likewise, a double standard may tolerate premarital sexual activity with many partners for boys, but not for girls. Members of racial and ethnic minorities often find that their behaviors are scrutinized more closely than those of the dominant group, and they are more likely to be labeled deviant for participating in activities tolerated in others. A person's social class also may affect deviant labels and may provide the resources that in court could mean the difference between acquittal and life imprisonment or execution.

DEVIANCE AND STIGMA

Stigma is any characteristic that sets people apart and discredits or disqualifies them from full social acceptance and participation. Sociologist Erving Goffman (1963) identified three principal types of stigma experienced by those considered beyond society's range of acceptability.

The first category is known as *Abominations of the Body*. This category includes any physical limitation, deformity, or other visible and identifiable physical characteristic deemed beyond "normal." For example, people may be stigmatized because they are too fat or too thin; too short or too tall; or because they have a noticeable scar or birthmark or use a wheelchair. Goffman notes that even though others may be sympathetic toward those in this category, they still may regard them as deviant and sanction them.

The second category is *Blemishes of Individual Character*. This category includes those who are stigmatized on moral grounds, such as those who are thought to be dishonest, liars, cheaters, or thieves, as well as people who suffer from mental disorders, alcoholism, drug addiction, or even a terminal illness such as AIDS. The latter is particularly stigmatized if it is believed to be linked to some other type of deviant behavior associated with the disease (e.g., smoking and lung cancer, or illegal drug abuse or homosexual promiscuity and AIDS) (Nack 2000).

The third category is referred to as *Tribal Stigma*. This category includes all those who are discredited because they are members of a socially disapproved category or group. For example, many people are stigmatized because of their race, ethnicity, religion, sexual orientation, or affiliation with a group or organization deemed outside the mainstream. Sometimes family members of deviants are stigmatized simply because of their relationship to the norm violator (May 2000). Furthermore, an entire category of people can be stigmatized by the actions of a very few.

In today's global society, many people confuse diversity with deviance and seek to punish those who pose no real threat to society simply because they are "different." Critical thinking and sociological understanding can expand the range of tolerance, but they must compete with a variety of popular theories that often take narrower and more punitive approaches to deviance.

Sometimes, entire categories of people are viewed as deviant by those who are intolerant of social and cultural diversity. Although most of us are aware of the prejudice, discrimination, and inequality faced by the poor, racial and ethnic minorities, women, and the elderly, we may be less cognizant of the fact that the same is true for millions of people who may be labeled deviant because of their sexual orientation, physical or mental infirmities, religious beliefs, or other characteristics considered outside the mainstream. This devaluation results in *stigma*—a powerful social label that negatively affects every aspect of a person's life. It also sometimes leads to *hate crimes*—criminal acts against people and their property that are motivated by racial and ethnic prejudices and other social biases.

THE POWER OF MEDIA

Media play a powerful role in defining social reality. In today's global society, virtually all parts of the world are linked by mass media and social media. Consequently, the audience involved in defining an act as deviance or conformity is potentially comprised of millions of people from hundreds of cultures. Controversial cases involving police shootings have often been recorded on cell phones, with snippets put online or on television, where millions of people may define the situation without benefit of the context, the entirety of the interaction, or any knowledge of facts in the case.

Today, media images are fundamental to public perceptions of deviance and conformity. Folk wisdom tells us that a dog biting a person is not news, but a person biting a dog is. Because we are inundated with stories about the most bizarre forms of deviance, we tend to forget that the vast majority of norm-violating behavior is fairly mundane and often of little consequence. Media sensationalism—especially in the tabloids, on the internet, and on popular TV shows—contributes to the popular belief that people can be divided into two neat and distinct categories: deviants and conformists. Numerous sociological studies indicate that public perceptions of morality and immorality, and conformity and deviance, as well as what constitutes crime and who is likely to be a criminal, are shaped by media portrayals and social constructions of reality presented by the media (Cavender 2017; Dotter 2002; Lowney 2017). The media also tend to equate deviance and crime and to reinforce stereotypes about deviants and criminals—that they are almost exclusively from lower socioeconomic classes and most are minorities; that they are all violent; and that controlling them costs taxpayers huge amounts of money. These stereotypes do not hold up under scrutiny. In fact, each year, white-collar and occupational crimes account for more lost revenue than all the burglaries, larceny-thefts, auto thefts, and arsons combined (FBI 2018).

Popular wisdom often equates deviance and crime—two related but distinct concepts in sociology. *Deviance* refers to *all* norm violations. *Crime*, on the other hand, refers only to violations of one type of norm: laws. Even the majority of violations of laws involve civil laws covering contracts, real estate, and other noncriminal activities. Consequently, *crime*, which is any act that violates a criminal law, is divided into violent offenses (against persons) and nonviolent offenses (against property). Therefore, we can see that whereas all crime is deviance, not all deviance is crime.

CYBERPORN, CYBERSEX, AND INTERNET ADDICTION

However pornography and sexual deviance might be defined, the internet has them—in abundance. Every day, millions of people access websites that feature live online sex acts, triple-X-rated videos, and a multitude of interactive sites that provide access to adult porn, teen porn, pseudo-child pornography, child pornography, cartoon sex, bestiality, and almost any other form of sexually explicit material imaginable (Bernay 2008). Globally, porn is a $97 billion a year industry, with between $10 and $12 billion of that coming from the United States (NBC News 2015). Law enforcement experts estimate that approximately 50,000 sexual predators per day prowl the internet and lurk in chatrooms looking for victims (LaRue 2008). In virtual worlds, people can create avatars that can date, mate, marry, have children, and get divorced—or kill one another if that is the desired mode of separation. Although some contend that online pornography and cybersex are harmless or, even if harmful, are protected by the First Amendment, others insist that they are insidious forms of deviance that harm women and children, participants and nonparticipants, and erode the moral fiber of society (Bernay 2008; Nelson 2012).

There is a long history of moral crusades against pornography. Many people believe that the use of *pornography*—sexually explicit materials intended solely for sexual arousal—not only is morally deviant but also leads to crimes of violence against women and children. They cite studies contending that pornography dehumanizes sexuality, degrades those who make and use it, and desensitizes consumers to sexual violence (e.g., Attorney General's Commission on Pornography 1986; Hughes and McMickle 1997; Jensen 2004; LaRue 2008; Nichols 1997; Taverner 2009). Yet numerous other studies dispute these claims, indicating that sex offenders are no more likely to be users of pornography than anybody else, and claiming that pornography may have beneficial effects in helping some people explore and understand their sexuality (Diamond 2010; Featherstone 2008; Jensen 2004; McElroy 1997; Strossen 1995).

If we look at the issue of pornography cross-culturally, defining it and assessing its social impact become even more difficult. For example, in Islamic countries such as Iran, censorship is very stringent, and the government bans any material that shows partial nudity or is sexually suggestive. In countries such as Japan, Amsterdam, and Denmark, where censorship is almost unheard of, explicit sexual magazines, videos, and other materials are unregulated and extremely popular. Interestingly, rates of abuse and violence against women are much higher in the Islamic countries where pornography is suppressed or banned than in Japan, Amsterdam, and Denmark, where almost "anything goes" (Diamond 2010; Wekesser 1997).

Another problem in attempting to relate pornography to violence or other forms of deviance is the vast "underground" network involved in its manufacture, sale, and distribution. Although many types of so-called "soft-porn" can be purchased in most bookstores, delivered to a subscriber's home by mail, or accessed online, this is not true of much of the estimated $8 billion per year industry in the United States alone that includes everything from 900 phone sex numbers and explicit materials available over the internet, to triple-X videos that contain everything from bestiality and pedophilia to rape and murder (Spencer 2012). Today, thousands of computer bulletin boards, chat rooms, and other sexually explicit and "deviant" materials are also available in cyberspace (Bernay 2008; Durkin and Bryant 1995; Taverner 2009; Wekesser 1997). Quinn and Forsyth (2005) suggest that because of the internet and other technologies, we may have to rethink and redefine what constitutes conforming and deviant sexual behaviors. Although it is not scientific research, data from the United States indicate that while consumption of online pornography has increased dramatically over the past two decades, violent sex crimes have steadily decreased over that same time period (FBI 2018).

Some researchers suggest that internet use can be addictive, and borrow language from research on drug addiction to differentiate among internet *use, abuse, dependency*, and *addiction* (Fortson, Scotti, Chen, Malone, and Del Ben 2007). Although internet addiction is a relatively new area of research, mounting evidence suggests that "the Internet can easily be the medium of excessive, addictive, obsessive, and/or compulsive behaviors" and that because of "perceived anonymity and disinhibition," internet sex may be particularly addictive (Griffiths 2001:340).

"Hey, wait a second! Aren't we friends on Facebook?! You're Ralph's cousin, right? Yeah, we just friended each other last month."

POPULAR EXPLANATIONS OF DEVIANCE

For much of history, deviance and conformity were explained in theological terms. Deviant behavior was attributed to demonic possession, and it was believed that the devil or evil spirits took possession of people's bodies and souls. There is evidence that Stone Age humans drilled holes in the skulls of wrongdoers so that evil spirits could escape, and that the ancient Hebrews, Egyptians, Greeks, and Romans all practiced rites of exorcism.

Today, many people still equate deviance with sin and the devil. A Galveston preacher, for example, told authorities he put his baby daughter in a microwave oven and cooked her for 20 seconds because "Satan attacked him and saw him as a threat" (AP Galveston 2007). Others allude to demonology in a more figurative way, linking deviance and crime with declining moral values, and many blame the mass media—especially television, which has emerged as a contemporary demon.

The *medical model* views deviance as analogous to illness and uses terminology associated with disease. From this view, if society is to understand and control deviance and deviants, *symptoms* associated with the problem must be identified, *diagnoses* must be made, and appropriate *treatments* must be *prescribed*. In keeping with the medical model, each treatment elicits a *prognosis*, and eventually, the deviant (*patient*) is either *cured, made better*, or declared *incurable*.

Today, it is common to hear the terms *sick* and *deviant* used interchangeably, especially in bizarre and heinous crimes—mass murders, serial killings, acts of cannibalism, and others. This medical model approach to deviance is part of a sweeping *medicalization* of society, whereby problems once thought of as social or behavioral in nature are now attributed to disease.

The widespread use of the term *mental illness* and the view that deviants are "sick" demonstrate the power and pervasiveness of the medical model. Part of its popularity is due to the fact that members of the public hold biology, chemistry, and other sciences linked to medical research in high esteem, and often confuse psychology (a social science) with psychiatry (a medical specialty). Moreover, powerful organizations and money are involved, and the medical establishment has claimed "ownership" of most contemporary forms of deviance. The media have assisted this process by embracing and disseminating research findings and promoting medical explanations, no matter how tenuous, controversial, and questionable they may be.

Mainstream media are prominent sources for moral entrepreneurship, the promotion of moral crusades, and the creation of moral panics. Howard Becker (1963) pointed out that norms are the products of people's efforts to define deviance and deviants. He calls these rule creators *moral entrepreneurs*: social reformers who are not satisfied with existing rules because they believe that some type of behavior is taking place that should be controlled or eliminated. Moral entrepreneurs often have an absolute view of right and wrong, and believe that what they view as wrong is not only deviant but also truly evil. Such strong feelings often evoke a *moral crusade*, an effort to identify wrongdoing, inform others of its existence and potentially dire consequences, and establish rules or laws to eliminate the behavior and punish the wrongdoer. Effective moral crusades rely on the creation of *moral panic,* the belief that the very survival of society is threatened by a particular type of deviant or deviance. Ironically, moral crusaders against the media often rely on various forms of media to promote their cause.

In addition to the media's role in defining deviance, sociologists are interested in the popular view that the media and technology help create, promote, and perhaps even cause deviance. The mass media—television, movies, magazines, radio, comic books, advertising, video games, and various types of popular music—have been linked to such problems as robbery, burglary, poor grades at school, antisocial fantasies, drug abuse, rebellion, declining test scores, lack of moral standards, poor diet, passivity, hyperactivity, wasting time, desensitization to violence, amorality, war, rape, and murder. Technology, especially the internet, has been linked to pornography addiction, predatory crimes, internet fraud, identity theft, cyberbullying, suicide, and even internet addiction.

SOCIOLOGICAL THEORIES OF DEVIANCE AND CONFORMITY

Sociologists who use the structural functionalist perspective view both deviance and conformity as integral components of the basic structure of society. Because norms provide guidelines for human behavior, their violation almost always has important consequences for the deviant and the rest of society. From a structural functionalist perspective, some of these social consequences are dysfunctional (having a potentially disruptive impact) and others are functional (contributing to the overall functioning of society). Functionalists contend that when norms are violated, people may be harmed or injured; norms may be threatened; enormous financial, social, and emotional costs may be incurred; and social order often is disrupted (Liska and Warner 1991; Thompson and Bynum 2017).

Because of their negative consequences, most of us are well aware of these dysfunctional aspects of deviance, but we may be unaware that social deviance can also be functional and have positive consequences for society and individuals. Émile Durkheim ([1895] 1982) viewed deviance as an integral part of social structure and believed that even severe forms of deviance, such as crime, could be functional because they enhanced social cohesion and solidarity. Moreover, functionalists note that in some cases deviance may reaffirm and reinforce norms because the deviants are punished; may promote social solidarity as people unite either against or on behalf of the deviants; may provide a contrast effect because conformity assumes meaning only when it is contrasted with deviance; may act as a "safety valve," relieving pressure and preventing more serious deviance; and may lead to innovation and social change (Dentler and Erikson 1959; Thompson and Bynum 2017).

An early version of the structural functionalist approach to deviance is found in Herbert Spencer's assertion that deviance is a form of *social pathology*. Like most functionalists, Spencer viewed society as having a basic structure that included a variety of interconnected and interdependent parts. To Spencer, a problem in one part of the organism affected the entire organism. Building on Spencer's *organic analogy*, many early sociologists viewed deviant behavior as a form of social pathology, a problem that potentially threatens the survival of society. Crime, mental illness, drug abuse, suicide, and other forms of deviance were viewed as social pathologies in need of study and remedy. Spencer's approach to deviance provided a theoretical basis for the structural functionalist approach to deviance that later became known as *structural* or *strain theories*, the view that deviance is a result of the tensions or strain experienced by people because of their position in the social structure.

To Robert Merton (1938), the primary causes of deviance were social situations in which people, because of their place in the social structure, were unable to pursue socially accepted goals through culturally approved means. According to Merton, Americans are socialized from birth to strive for material possessions (e.g., nice homes, new cars, fashionable clothes, expensive jewelry) and high social status (usually based on the prestige of one's occupation). Although Americans are encouraged to internalize these measures of success, some find it impossible to attain them by culturally approved means (staying in school, hard work, thriftiness, and deferred gratification). When individuals experience the strain associated with the discrepancy between socially approved goals and the approved means of pursuing them, anomie results.

Albert Cohen (1955) and Richard Cloward and Lloyd Ohlin (1960) expanded on Merton's anomie theory of deviance. Focusing on juvenile delinquency, they theorized that the reason lower-class boys may become involved in property offenses and even violent crimes is because they find few legitimate opportunities to achieve some of the middle-class goals (especially material possessions) to which they aspire. These blocked opportunities lead to the formation of deviant subcultures that provide increased social status through illegitimate means and support deviance such as dropping out of school, joining gangs, stealing, dealing drugs, or otherwise pursuing status and material possessions through illegitimate means.

Deviant subcultures are not unique to juveniles. Practitioners of many forms of deviance (e.g., religious cults, drug users, nudists) may feel "cut off" from larger society and consequently find it functional to band together for social purposes, mutual support, and protection (Clinard and Meier 2016).

Although structural functionalist theories provide important sociological insight into deviance and conformity, a common weakness of this perspective is that it infers that there is widespread consensus about what constitutes deviance and conformity and assumes that everyone is socialized to have common values, aspirations, and goals. These assumptions downplay the impact of social inequality and ignore the diversity of a complex global society—two things addressed by the conflict theories of deviance.

Karl Marx ([1867] 1967) argued that society is comprised of two distinctive social classes and that a person's social class largely determines every aspect of life. From this view, norms do not arise out of general consensus, but represent the values and interests of the ruling class and are designed to exploit and control members of the working class. According to Marx, the ruling class treat as deviant any actions that threaten their privileged position. Consequently, any norms at odds with those of the ruling class are viewed as deviant (and usually illegal) and will be punished. Conflict theories of deviance view deviance as arising when groups with power attempt to impose their norms and values on less powerful groups. Contemporary conflict theories focus on power, thus concentrating more on the origin of norms and their enforcement than on the behavior of individuals; hence, they are theories of *deviance* more than theories of *deviant behavior* (Clinard and Meier 2015).

In most cultures, power is differentially distributed on the basis of age, race, sex, religion, and politics as well as social class. In work environments, supervisors and bosses enjoy more power than employees, and in academic environments, at least in terms of academic decisions, administrators have more power than the faculty, and teachers have more power than students. Contemporary conflict theorists focus much of their attention on the role that power plays in creating and enforcing the rules of society and consequently defining deviance and conformity.

Power theories explain deviance in two very important ways. First, those in power have more opportunity to make and enforce the norms that govern their and others' behavior. Hence, they often have the power to say what and who are and are not deviant. Second, because of their loftier social positions, only certain people have the power to commit certain types of deviance.

Turning to the first point, conflict theorists insist that criminal justice systems reinforce inequality and define as deviant any behavior that threatens those in power. Criminologist Jeffrey Reiman (2017) asserts that the American criminal justice system creates an image of crime that portrays the poor as dangerous to individual safety and a threat to the security and stability of society. According to Reiman, this ideological

Sociological Theories of Deviance and Conformity | 171

approach to crime diverts attention from those in power, allowing them to continue their participation in white-collar crimes and other forms of elite deviance. Asserting that "nothing succeeds like failure," Reiman (2017:5) developed the *Pyrrhic defeat theory*, which contends that those in power have designed the criminal justice system to fail because "the failure of the criminal justice system yields such benefits to those in positions of power that it amounts to success." In other words, as long as crime rates are high; prisoners are not rehabilitated; and fear for personal property and safety remains high, very little attention is focused on who makes the laws, how they are enforced, and why crimes committed by the poor and powerless are punished severely while those committed by the wealthy and powerful are largely ignored.

Only certain people in society can commit *elite deviance*, which includes all aspects of white-collar crime as well as other deviant acts perpetrated by those in power. These include environmental pollution, deceptive advertising, fraud, insider trading, manufacturing harmful products, political corruption, and a host of other deviant activities. Elite deviance is not new, and the general public has long been aware of political scandals, corporate crimes, and other forms of crime and deviance committed by those in power. What does the conflict perspective contribute to the understanding of elite deviance? The answer lies in what has always been sociology's major strength: rather than focusing on the individuals who commit elite deviance and explaining their actions as being a result of individual immorality, greed, or pathology, the conflict perspective focuses on the basic social structure and identifies social inequality as the major explanation for this type of deviance (e.g., Quinney 1975, 1980; Reiman 2017; Simon 2018; Turk 1969; Vold 2009).

Drawing on the work of C. Wright Mills (1956, 1959), conflict theorists attribute elite deviance to a social structure in which those who control the dominant social institutions—governments, militaries, major national and multinational corporations—have amassed inordinate amounts of wealth, power, and prestige that allow them to protect their vested interests, control the mass media, and promote their values over those of less powerful social institutions, such as the family, education, and religion. The conflict perspective also contends that the power elite who control those dominant institutions use their wealth, power, and prestige to control and manipulate the mass media to reinforce their definitions of deviance and conformity (Dotter 2002; Simon 2018).

The interactionist perspective views deviance and conformity as flexible and symbolic terms that must be defined and redefined through the process of interaction. From the interactionist perspective, three of the most important explanations of deviance and conformity involve labeling, social learning, and social control.

As their name implies, *labeling theories* view deviance and conformity as labels assigned to certain people and certain acts. From this perspective, attention is shifted from the actor and the act to the audience. Labeling theories are less concerned with explaining what causes deviant behavior than with understanding how labels are applied and why some norm-violating people and behaviors are labeled as deviant while others are not.

Edwin Lemert (1951) emerged as one of the leading proponents of the labeling approach with his analysis of how being labeled deviant may shape subsequent behavior. According to Lemert, *primary deviance* occurs when an individual violates a norm and is viewed as deviant but rejects the deviant label and maintains a conformist conception of self. If the person's self-concept is unaltered by the deviant label, they are no more likely to engage in future deviance than before the label was attached. Lemert acknowledged that others' perceptions are important, and it is difficult to maintain a conformist self-image after being labeled deviant. As a result, many people become involved in *secondary deviance*, which is the internalization of a deviant label and the assumption of a deviant role. Lemert argued that social control, which invariably involves the application of the deviant label, may be more likely to lead to future deviance than to prevent it.

Howard Becker (1963) developed a *career model of deviance* that demonstrates how the application and subsequent internalization of the deviant label leads to continued and increased deviance. Becker's emphasis on the developmental process underscored the idea that deviance often becomes a *master status*, a status that overpowers and in many cases supersedes any other statuses an individual holds that might run counter to it.

Edwin Schur (1971) pointed out that individuals often internalize the deviant identity to the extent that they, too, view themselves as generally deviant rather than deviant in relation to a specific act or attribute. Describing this process as *role engulfment*, Schur explained that people often become so absorbed in their deviant identity that this shapes their subsequent behavior, and they fulfill expectations associated with the deviant role. Likewise, Becker concluded that treating a person as generally rather than specifically deviant produces a self-fulfilling prophecy.

Social learning theories contend that all behavior (including deviance) is learned through social interaction. They assume that some people learn to become deviant through the complex process of socialization (Holt 2011). One of the most prominent social learning theories is *differential association theory* (Sutherland and Cressey 1978).

Many sociologists consider Edwin Sutherland to be the first criminologist to provide a sociological explanation of individual-level and macro-level differences in crime and delinquency, with his *differential association theory* (Laub and Sampson 1991). Sutherland argued that deviant behavior is learned through interaction with other deviants in a social context where deviance is viewed as acceptable. Differential association theory elaborates on the old adage "Birds of a feather flock together" by showing that our behavior is influenced by the people with whom we associate. The theory stresses that primary relationships, such as those with our parents, siblings, and close friends, have the greatest impact on our behavior.

Ronald Akers (2011) pointed out that depending on with whom an individual associates, norm-violating behavior may be *differentially reinforced*, either positively rewarded or negatively sanctioned. For example, suppose a teenage girl shoplifts a tube of lipstick. If she is not caught, she may experience a sense of gratification by getting something she wanted for nothing. If her friends praise her deviant behavior, she is likely to shoplift again. On the other hand, if her friends are outraged by her behavior and threaten to withdraw their friendship, she is much less likely to repeat the deviant behavior. To Akers, then, *differential reinforcement* is the key to deviant or conformist behavior and acts as a method of social control.

In his *social bond theory*, Travis Hirschi (1969) concluded that the main reason why some people do not commit deviance is that they have developed a strong *social bond*, consisting of an attachment to parents, school, church, and other institutions aligned with conformity; a commitment to conventional norms; an involvement in conventional activities; and a belief in the validity of social norms. Hirschi asserted that the stronger a person's social bond, the less likely they are to become involved in deviant activities. Conversely, the weaker the social bond to conformist groups and institutions, the easier it is for the individual to violate society's norms.

Walter Reckless (1961) contended that during the socialization process, individuals develop the first barrier against deviance, which he called *inner containment*. Inner containment is the extent to which an individual internalizes the norms, attitudes, values, and beliefs of their culture. Most people can control their impulses to deviate. For some, however, inner containment is not strong enough, so society provides a second layer of control in the form of *outer containment*, which consists of parents, teachers, police officers, and others who serve as agents of social control. Reckless's *containment theory* also recognizes the importance of the social environment. In some social situations, people with weak inner containment are subject to a vast array of external agents of social control. In many others, outer containment is minimal, and if an individual's inner containment is not sufficiently strong, deviance is likely to occur.

Gresham Sykes and David Matza (1957) theorized that much deviant behavior can be explained by people's ability to rationalize it and hence neutralize their inhibitions. From this perspective, individuals sometimes ignore conventional norms because they view them as flexible guidelines for behavior rather than as rigid rules. Depending on the situation, the greater the ability of an individual to rationalize (and therefore neutralize) norm violation, the more likely they are to engage in deviant behavior. Sykes and Matza identified five *techniques of neutralization*:

1. *Denial of Responsibility.* People may rationalize deviant acts by claiming they were caused by forces beyond their control. For example, have you ever explained to your professor that you were late for class or missed an exam because of a flat tire, a faulty alarm clock, or heavy traffic?
2. *Denial of Injury.* If a person cannot deny responsibility for a deviant act, they may argue that no harm was done. Usually, the less serious the infraction, the greater the chance it will be neutralized, but this technique is also used to rationalize crimes such as vandalism and shoplifting.
3. *Denial of the Victim.* When somebody is hurt and harm cannot be denied, the deviant may rationalize that the victim deserved to be hurt. Rapists, for example, often contend that their victims were "asking for it," and social attitudes and legal processes may reinforce that idea (Davis and Stasz 1990). Victims of sexual harassment, sexual abuse, and sexual assault often find themselves being blamed for the deviance committed against them.
4. *Condemnation of the Condemners.* A common assertion by many deviants is that those who condemn them are even more worthy of condemnation. This argument often is used by prison inmates, who assert that police and judges are corrupt and that white-collar and corporate criminals commit more serious offenses but almost never serve hard time.

5. *Appeal to Higher Loyalties.* Many forms of deviance can be rationalized as altruistic acts for the good of a particular group or for some higher cause. Terrorists, for example, rationalize their deviance as serving some higher cause and greater good.

A shortcoming of all of these sociological theories is that they were developed by men, who primarily conducted their research on males. Feminist theories provide an important gender dimension to the understanding of deviance and conformity.

Traditionally, females have been linked to nonviolent deviant behaviors such as running away from home, shoplifting, drug use and abuse, prostitution, and other more stereotypical behaviors associated with feminine roles. The *liberation hypothesis* contends that females traditionally have not committed as much crime, delinquency, and other forms of deviance because of the rigid gender roles and fewer opportunities afforded them. As gender roles change and become more equitable, girls and women are afforded more deviant opportunities. Official crime and delinquency data tend to support this hypothesis, showing that although male rates have remained constant or declined, female rates have increased in most categories (FBI 2018).

SOCIAL CONTROL

Every society creates ways to encourage conformity and deter deviance. *Social control* refers to the mechanisms people use to enforce prevailing social norms. This process involves the imposition of *positive sanctions* to reward conformity (e.g., encouragement, awards, medals, certificates, diplomas) and *negative sanctions* to punish deviance (e.g., discouragement, ridicule, fines, imprisonment). In most societies, far more effort goes into negatively sanctioning deviance than into positively rewarding conformity.

Some sociologists contend that deterrence is the most important element of social control and that social control is the most important aspect of sociological inquiry. *Deterrence theory* states that deviance will be deterred if negative social sanctions (especially punishment) are perceived to be certain, swift, and severe (Gibbs 1975). Deterrence theorists differentiate between *specific deterrence*, punishments that discourage the individual from committing similar acts in the future, and *general deterrence*, which discourages others from committing similar acts. Ideally, social control mechanisms should accomplish both specific and general deterrence.

One of the most effective methods of regulating human behavior is for people to internalize society's values and norms and voluntarily restrain themselves. Most people voluntarily conform most of the time. What psychologists refer to as "conscience" represents the sense of guilt we feel when we violate or even consider breaking social norms. Sociologists take this reasoning a step further, explaining that we not only take into account the norms, values, and beliefs of others but that we also anticipate social reactions to our acts before we commit them.

When voluntary social control is insufficient and folkways or mores are violated, informal social control measures may be implemented. *Gossip*, for instance, is a very effective means of penalizing behavior. In small towns or groups where everybody knows everybody else, gossip may be a powerful deterrent to straying from the straight and narrow.

Ridicule, or *shame*, is another common and effective method of informal social control. Few people enjoy being the butt of others' jokes. Research indicates that shame, especially in the form of informal but pervasive social control by others, is linked to conformity (Scheff 1988).

Perhaps one of the most effective methods of informal social control is *ostracism*—excluding someone from social acceptance or group membership. In small, interdependent communities such as those created by the Old Order Amish, primary interaction is essential to daily living, and shunning amounts to "social death" (Hostetler 1980; Thompson 1986).

Informal social control can be very powerful and is often all that is necessary to dissuade deviance and encourage conformity. With today's emphasis on media and technology, social media have become powerful agents of social control, where people can be publicly shamed and ridiculed almost instantaneously for appearance, thoughts, ideas, or behaviors. When formal norms are violated, however, informal social control may be supplemented and reinforced by formal controls.

Sociological wisdom teaches us that *some rules are made to be broken, but some aren't*. From a sociological view, specific norms and behaviors—either conforming or deviant—are much less important than the social processes involved in creating norms and defining them as one or the other. Perhaps the only certainty for the future is that, in all societies, people will continue to be set apart for different treatment because of their perceived levels of deviance and conformity.

Sociological Wisdom 8

#TheOnlyDifferenceThatMattersIsTheDifferenceThatMatters

EMPHASIZING DIFFERENCES

ALL SOCIETIES, PAST AND PRESENT, are characterized by *social differentiation*, a process in which people are set apart for differential treatment and opportunities by virtue of their statuses, roles, and other social characteristics, including age, race, sex, and social class, to name but a few. Sociological wisdom tells us that *the only difference that matters is the difference that matters*. In nature these differences emerge instinctively. For example, the ostrich cannot fly but is gifted with unusual speed afoot and is incredibly strong, which helps it elude its enemies. In human societies, however, people often emphasize differences that really do not or should not matter. For example, for over a century it was considered appropriate for men to be pilots, but women were assumed to be incapable of flying an airplane. The major factors that differentiate men from women are a Y chromosome and their genitalia, neither of which matter in the ability to fly a plane. Thus a difference that should not matter did matter, but only because people decided that it mattered. Today, in countries like the United States, women fly airplanes routinely because Americans realize that the difference between the sexes does not matter when it comes to flying. In other countries, however, women still are not only prohibited from flying airplanes but are not allowed to drive automobiles. Social differentiation sets the stage for *social inequality*, a condition in which people have unequal access to wealth, power, and prestige. As Daniel Rossides (2009:12) noted, even in the simplest societies "the old are usually given authority over the young, parents over children, and males over females." Although this may not be fair, and these differences do not truly matter, it is inevitably the way societies work. Even in the United States, where we emphasize values such as "liberty and justice for all," and "all *men* are created equal," we soon realize that the word "all" does not mean everyone, as people are treated differently and unequally based on many social variables. Perhaps one of the most notable is social class.

IMPORTANCE OF SOCIAL CLASS

Social stratification is a form of inequality in which categories of people are systematically ranked in a hierarchy on the basis of their access to scarce but valued resources. All societies distinguish between categories of people who are entitled to a greater share of wealth, power, and prestige, and categories of people who are less deserving. In the principal types of stratification systems, however, one of three factors of inequality (wealth, power, or prestige) tends to receive special emphasis. Stratification systems also differ in the relative permeability of boundaries between social strata. In *closed systems*, boundaries are relatively impermeable—statuses are ascribed, and custom, law, and public attitudes tend to place severe limitations on social mobility. In *open systems*, boundaries are less firm, social statuses are largely determined by achievement, and legal and ideological supports give people opportunities to change their social ranking.

The shift from an agrarian to an industrial economy led to the development and spread of a new form of worldwide stratification called the *class system*, in which the economic factor and achieved statuses are the principal means of ranking. Class systems are open to social mobility, and boundaries between social strata are somewhat unclear. They may take several forms, depending on political and economic conditions, history, and culture. Most contain a small upper class, which owns the bulk of a nation's assets and has a great deal of influence and power. Beneath this level, there may be major differences in the size, wealth, and power of the middle class as well as the conditions of those at the bottom of class hierarchies.

In the United States, many believe that people can be sorted into three major social class categories—a tiny segment of the population that is super-rich, an equally small number of very poor people, and the vast majority of the population that is financially "comfortable"—especially when compared with people in most other nations.

Sociologist Max Weber (1946) was among the first to argue that economic status, or wealth, is not the only factor that

CLASS CLOWNS

Upper   Middle   Working

determines a person's rank. Power and prestige are also basic ingredients in the ranking process, and each dimension can operate independently of the others in determining social rank.

Weber believed that differences in wealth lead to the formation of classes that have similar lifestyles, or ways in which their members consume goods and express their social worth. Differential wealth also gives social classes different *life chances*, or opportunities for securing such things as health, education, and long lives. We often use the word *wealth* to mean "money," but Weber defined it more broadly. To Weber, *wealth* includes a person's or family's total economic assets. In advanced industrial societies, wealth in the form of stocks, real estate, trusts, yachts, and other goods and services is vitally important to class standing. For most people, however, income, which includes money earned in the form of wages and salaries, is the primary economic asset.

Power is the second dimension of class ranking. *Power* is the ability to realize one's will, even against resistance and the opposition of others. Sociologists differentiate between *personal power*, the ability to make decisions that affect one's life, and *social power*, the ability to make decisions that affect the lives of others. Sociologists agree that, like wealth, power is unequally shared. Those who take a *pluralist perspective* maintain that classes and interest groups vote in their own interests and sometimes vote against others to keep them from dominating the political process. Conflict theorists disagree, maintaining that power is concentrated at the top. Some sociologists go even further, maintaining that there is a "governing class" in the United States whose members are drawn from the upper class. But political power only hints at the extent of the upper class's influence and power. Their members also dominate America's giant industries, banks, foundations, and virtually all other important policy-making institutions. These and other "duties" help boost the prestige of the upper class as well.

Prestige, which is the respect and admiration people attach to various social positions, is the third dimension of stratification. In every society, some categories of people are regarded as deserving more respect and honor than others, because of ascribed statuses (e.g., race, sex, ethnicity), achieved statuses (e.g., occupation, marital status), possessions, or personal qualities (e.g., holiness, intelligence). In the United States, such things as material possessions, education, family background, and occupation have a major impact on everyone's class ranking.

SOCIOECONOMIC STATUS

There are often inconsistencies in the three dimensions of stratification. A person may rank high in one dimension but low in another. For example, in terms of occupational prestige, police officers and social workers have maintained mid-level rankings, and firefighters have moved toward the top of occupational prestige. These are low-paying jobs but deemed socially important, and people in these positions often have power over people in more prestigious occupations.

Over the years, sociologists have used three major methods to identify social classes. One of the earliest used was the *reputational method*, which asked selected members of a group to socially rank people in their community. The *subjective method* asks people to locate themselves in the class system. The *objective method* assigns individuals to social classes on the basis of more objective measures. One objective approach is *socioeconomic status*, a ranking that combines income, occupational prestige, level of education, and neighborhood to assess people's positions in the stratification system.

By measuring socioeconomic status, we can make distinctions among people—for example, people in different occupations—and can also demonstrate how people in the same line of work may rank differently.

For instance, if only occupational prestige is used, two professors may be judged as occupying the same social rank. If socioeconomic status is used, however, their rankings may be very different, for one may live in a rental apartment while the other, who ranks higher, may have inherited a fortune and live in a prestigious neighborhood. This method produces a hierarchy that can be used to distinguish the major social classes in the United States.

Although it is difficult and risky to assign specific figures to them, American social classes are distinguished in large part by wealth and income. This distinction is particularly important in differentiating those at the top of the class hierarchy from those at lower levels. Whereas the majority of Americans depend on wages and salaries, the wealthiest Americans derive most of their revenues from income-producing assets.

Common sense tells us that wealth and income go hand in hand: the higher one's income, the more wealth one will accumulate. But remember sociology's admonition that *things are not necessarily what they seem*. Star athletes, famous entertainers, and some college football coaches make millions of dollars per year, but although they may enjoy a high standard of living, they may accumulate little or no wealth. And it is important to remember that athletes sometimes suffer career-ending injuries and, even under the best circumstances, have short-lived careers. Popular entertainers often fade fast, and college coaches can be cult heroes one year and the next year may get fired.

Sociologists often identify five major class groupings in the United States, each with very different life chances and lifestyles. Mobility from one class to another is possible, and many Americans believe upward social mobility is common, but actually most people remain within one of these social classes throughout their entire lifetime.

The upper class constitutes around 5 percent of the population but accounts for more than 22 percent of total income. More importantly, members of the upper-upper class have a net worth in the hundreds of millions and billions of dollars. Household wealth, however, is not their only resource. Upper-class families also dominate corporate America and have a disproportionate influence over the nation's political, educational, religious, and other institutions. Of all social classes, members of the upper class also have a strong sense of solidarity that stretches across the nation and even the globe. In the life course, many enroll in the same private prep schools and attend a handful of prestigious Ivy League colleges. They also are active in the same social clubs and vacation at the "right" retreats and resorts around the world. There are several subgroups within the upper class. At the top are Old Money families whose wealth goes back a century or more. Some members of this exclusive group still manage giant corporations. Many elite families, however, take a less active role in business, using trusts, real estate income, and other inherited investments to fund lavish lifestyles; philanthropic activities; and, in some cases, public service.

Just below them are families of great wealth who have made their fortunes in the past generation or so. They are often called New Money, and some of their more prominent members would include the Walton family (Wal-Mart), Microsoft billionaire Bill Gates, and Facebook founder Mark Zuckerberg. Much of their wealth is in stock and stock options in their own corporations.

Prominent government officials, CEOs of major American corporations, media and sports celebrities, and others who make many millions form the next tier of the upper class. They may or may not have elite backgrounds. The bottom rung of the upper class includes millionaires, who exist in virtually every community: bank and factory owners, large-scale farmers, even lottery winners who have amassed instant fortunes. This group also includes professionals whose incomes exceed a quarter of a million dollars per year.

The upper middle class constitutes about 15 percent of the population and includes corporate executives, physicians, attorneys, white-collar management, and professional employees. In many American communities, this group represents the elite, for small-town America may have relatively little contact with the upper class. Members of the upper middle class often belong to country clubs, live in expensive homes in elegant neighborhoods, and are active in politics and community affairs.

A large and diverse lower middle class (approximately one-third of the population) occupies the next rung on the social ladder. Its members emulate the upper middle class and share many of its values, but they lack the resources to copy their more affluent lifestyles. Many in the lower middle class worked their way through college and have degrees from community and state colleges and universities. Teachers, bank employees, mid-level supervisors, and salespeople make up a large part of this class. Although most are white-collar, nonmanual workers, they have considerably less autonomy and on-the-job decision-making power than upper-middle-class professionals. In terms of America's core values, members of the lower middle class play it by the book. People in this class tend to live in modest but well-groomed homes and neighborhoods and they try to keep up with the Joneses.

The working class (30% of the population) includes both blue-collar and clerical workers who work for low wages in unpleasant and sometimes dangerous environments, usually under close supervision. Truck drivers, machine operators, laborers, and service and factory workers are all members of the working class. For most, job security is tenuous, and many of the benefits routinely enjoyed by the middle classes are rare or nonexistent. Although few have more than a high school education and their jobs are often demeaned by others, many blue-collar workers take pride in doing "real work." Their self-respect hinges on hard work, but members of the working class are most vulnerable to layoffs and long periods of unemployment. With the globalization of the economy, many have also lost a large share of the benefits that were once associated with manufacturing and union jobs, such as health care and pensions. For many, there is the ever-present threat of impoverishment and a free fall to the very bottom of the class system.

The lower class includes the "poor," who constitute about 14 percent of the population. If all people who lose their jobs and enter the ranks of the poor in any given year are counted, however, the figure is probably closer to 20 percent. The working poor, according to the government, are those who work 27 weeks per year but have family incomes below the poverty line (see U.S. Bureau of the Census website). Most work at jobs—sometimes two or three—that are erratic, pay minimum wage, and have no benefits, and nearly half of the nation's poor family heads did not work at all during the early twenty-first century because of family responsibilities, illness, or disability (Mangum, Mangum, and Sum 2003). At the very bottom of the class system are the chronically unemployed, the homeless, and people on "welfare," who are so much in the news today. This group is estimated to number slightly less than 3 million people, or about 1 percent of the U.S. population (U.S. Bureau of the Census 2018). Some contend that there is even a category below the lower class, the *underclass*, who are chronically unemployed, sometimes homeless, and live in poverty.

RACE, ETHNICITY, AND MINORITY GROUPS

In nature, diversity enhances survival of species. For human relationships, however, the record has been mixed. Some groups welcome those defined as racially or ethnically different; many others greet them with rejection, exploitation, and oppression. For some minorities, unequal treatment has meant violent death and mass slaughter; for others, it has brought a more or less permanent assignment to the bottom of the social ladder—not because of a lack of ability or effort, but because of ascribed racial or ethnic statuses.

Over the years, research finds that most Americans believe race to be a "biological concept" based primarily on skin color, although they must admit that they rarely have encountered a person with skin that was truly white, black, yellow, or red in color, with most people's skin being various shades of brown.

According to biologists, a *biological race* is a population that differs from others in the frequency of certain hereditary traits. Because races are open, and gene flow has taken place among them for millennia, no race has exclusive possession of any gene or genes, and there are no "pure races." Likewise, although there may be genetic variation in populations, there is no scientific evidence that the possession of a few distinctive genes by any segment of the population has any significant effect on human behavior. In other words, this is a difference that should not matter. Of course, we cannot see genetic variation within populations; the current system uses observable physical differences.

In the United States, many African Americans have European ancestors, and many of those who define themselves as "white" have African, Asian, and Native American ancestors. In fact, the most popular genographic research projects that trace DNA indicate that everyone on the globe can be genetically traced to a group of people in Africa some 60,000 years ago (Wells 2009). These tests provide information about ancestry and may tell us something about ethnicity, but contrary to popular belief, they indicate very little about race. In terms of people's biological makeup and physical appearance, this means that individuals in one race are not easily distinguishable from others. To establish racial divisions, therefore, people must make choices. First, they must decide which physical traits are significant. Then—despite the fact that no clear boundaries exist—they must promote the understanding and gain general social agreement that they do exist and that they matter. This process is what interests sociologists, for when people assign meanings to physical differences—whether they are real or imaginary—whether they matter or not—they become socially significant.

To sociologists, race is a social construction, and *races* are categories of people set apart from others because of socially defined physical characteristics. This is true in the United States and globally, where groups use physical traits such as skin color, hair texture, and other incidental biological traits and transform them into significant symbols of purported racial differences. Social races may seem to be about biology, but they are in fact pseudobiological classification systems.

The U.S. Census Bureau considers "Race" and "Hispanic Origin" to be separate and distinct categories. Consequently, in the 2000 census, the question on Hispanic origin asked respondents to list separately their "race." The 2000 census marked a fundamental change in how people record and perhaps perceive "race" in the United States. For the first time in over two centuries, the Census Bureau did not demand that people choose a single racial group, but permitted each person to mark one or more races. For the first time, the Census Bureau also split the Asian/Pacific Islanders into two separate categories, and it combined the Indian, Eskimo, and Aleut categories into "American Indian or Alaska Native." These same categories were used again in the 2010 census.

The new government racial classification system is anything but simple. A former director of the U.S. Census who became a professor of public affairs at Columbia University criticized the racial classifications used by the bureau, indicating that they remain based on archaic arbitrary categories that confuse race with ethnicity and nationality, as well as ignoring the reality of hybrid America (Prewitt 2013). Nevertheless, the U.S. government announced it would keep the same racial classifications in the 2020 census (Wang 2018).

Whereas race refers to a category of people who share socially recognized physical characteristics, *ethnicity* refers to statuses based on cultural heritage and shared "feelings of peoplehood" (Gordon 1964:24). An *ethnic group* is a category of people set apart from others because of distinctive cultural customs and lifestyles. Most important for all ethnic groups is that their members have a consciousness of kind and a belief in a common origin and shared fate.

As a rule, it follows that when an ethnic group approximates the culture of the dominant society, acceptance will loosen the bonds of ethnic identity. Conversely, ethnic groups that the dominant group perceives as being vastly different experience rejection and persecution, which in turn often strengthens ethnic consciousness and enhances ethnic solidarity.

In everyday life, people may emphasize ethnicity or downplay and ignore it. In many parts of the nation, ethnic traditions are nurtured within large urban neighborhoods, such as Irish American neighborhoods in Boston and Polish American neighborhoods in Chicago. But in many other parts of the nation, increasing proportions of persons refuse to claim an ethnic identity or, when filling out census forms, mark the category "Other" (Prewitt 2013; Tomasson 2000).

At other times, dominant groups may define a group as being both racially and ethnically distinct—which often serves as a double handicap. Ethnic groups also may be redefined as "races" for political or economic purposes. For example, when the Nazis found it impossible to distinguish Jews from their German neighbors on physical grounds, they mandated that all Jews wear yellow stars. The fact that they could not identify them did not dissuade the Nazis from arguing that Jews were "biologically inferior," nor did it hinder their wartime attempts to exterminate all members of the "Jewish race."

Because ethnicity is based on cultural distinctions, members of ethnic groups often are able to join the majority by adopting the dress, manners, and customs of the dominant group. By contrast, because racial identities are based on socially defined physical characteristics, racial minorities often find it more difficult to blend with the dominant group and gain full social acceptance (Powell 2005; Schaefer 2015).

The word *minority* has many meanings. Some people treat minorities as groups or categories of people that comprise less than half of some population. Defined in this way, *numerical minorities* are everywhere: redheads, CPAs, teenagers, rock musicians, and even sociologists are all numerical minorities. Sociologists are interested in these statuses, but when they use the term *minority group*, they mean a category of people who are set apart for unequal treatment because of physical or cultural characteristics.

Although there are many kinds of minorities, including religious groups, people with disabilities, the elderly, and others, race and ethnicity are particularly important minority statuses. Sociologists have identified five basic qualities of racial and ethnic minority groups: (1) identifiability, (2) membership based on ascription, (3) group awareness, (4) differential power, and (5) differential and unequal treatment.

Prejudice refers to preconceived judgments about a category of people. All forms of prejudice employ stereotypes that ignore the great variation in individual behaviors and focus on a handful of traits that all group members supposedly possess. People usually have positive prejudices about their own group and the dominant group—whether or not they are members. By contrast, they tend to have negative prejudices toward minority groups because they are "different" and are usually viewed as inferior.

Racism, which includes *beliefs and attitudes that one racial category is inherently superior or inferior to another*, is the most potent form of prejudice. Typically, racist beliefs include the notion that minorities are "inferior" because of physical and social traits that are intrinsic to those minority groups. Racism is more than attitudes, however; it involves differential power as well. Some scholars contend that "white" power and privilege are maintained by a majority belief that whites as a people do not have a race and that racial identity (and associated penalties) is something others have (Fears 2003:AO1).

Early scientists once believed that prejudice was a basic part of our biological makeup. After almost a century of research, however, most social scientists agree that prejudice is socially learned and that numerous factors, including personality factors, culture, and group competition and conflict, contribute to prejudice and discrimination.

To social psychologists, unsatisfied expectations and desires are fertile ground for prejudice and discrimination. According to the *frustration–aggression hypothesis*, people are goal directed, and when their desires are blocked, they become angry and frustrated and seek to find an outlet for their hostilities. If people cannot pinpoint the source of their problems, or if they discover the source is too powerful to challenge, they may direct their anger at a *scapegoat*, a weak, convenient, and socially approved target. Historically, scapegoats (usually minorities) have shouldered the blame and have paid terrible penalties for "causing" society's ills.

A noteworthy characteristic of all autonomous racial and ethnic groups is *ethnocentrism*—the tendency to evaluate the customs of other groups according to one's own cultural standards. Groups that share values, norms, and beliefs with the dominant group are highly regarded, whereas those judged to violate important norms are scorned and rejected.

People are not born with prejudices. They acquire them during the socialization process. The remarkable persistence of prejudicial attitudes toward minorities owes much to the fact that prejudice and interaction patterns are mutually reinforcing. When *stereotypes*, which are static and oversimplified ideas about a group or a social category, define a group as being "very different" from one's own group, then their members tend to be avoided. If we rarely encounter members of an out-group, we will have few opportunities to modify our prejudices, and negative stereotypes will persist. By contrast, there is some evidence that when different racial and ethnic groups interact on relatively equal terms, there is a tendency for members of both sides to become less prejudiced. But even in such cases, fears of the gradual homogenization of diverse cultures and threats to traditional ethnic identities may lead to the deterioration of intergroup relations, which is so evident in many parts of the world today (Amir 1969; Clore et al. 1978; Cordell and Wolf 2010).

Whereas prejudices are *attitudes*, discrimination refers to *acts*. *Discrimination* is unequal treatment of people because of their group membership. In everyday life, people sometimes discriminate in favor of a group, sometimes against a group.

SEX AND GENDER

Another source of social inequality is based on sex and gender. Many people use these terms interchangeably, but although the two are related, anthropologists and sociologists make important distinctions in their meaning. *Sex* is based on biological and physical differences between females and males; *gender* refers to a cultural understanding of what constitutes *masculinity* and *femininity* in a society.

Humans have 23 pairs of chromosomes. Two of these are the sex chromosomes, X and Y. The normal chromosomal pattern in females is XX; in males it is XY. During prenatal development, different hormones trigger physical changes in the male and female genitalia and reproductive systems. In rare cases, a hormone imbalance during this period may produce a child born with either ambiguous or some combination of male and female genitalia. Most scientists agree that gender identity is partly innate (linked to chromosomal influence) and partly cultural—a result of socialization (Wade and Ferree 2015; Kimmel and Messner 2018). Individuals whose gender identity matches their sex at birth are referred to as *cisgender*. A growing number of people, however, feel that their biological sex does not match their gender identity (National Center for Transgender Equality N.d.; Wade and Ferree 2015). These individuals are referred to as *transgender* individuals whose gender identity differs from the sex of their birth. If they undergo surgery to change their biological sex, they become *transsexual*.

Later in life, people develop sex-linked disparities in height, weight, body and facial hair, physical strength, and endurance. Idealized body types become associated not only with maleness and femaleness, but also with masculinity and femininity (Lorber and Martin 2013). And although research suggests that the brains of females and males may be both structurally and operationally different, most researchers acknowledge that women and men are far more alike than they are different (Fine 2011; Lindsey 2016). Because we cannot see people's chromosomes, hormones, or brains, all sex-linked differences matter less than the cultural and social expectations linked to them.

Males and females are biologically and physiologically distinct at birth; these differences become more pronounced as humans develop to maturity, but they do not explain the important social and cultural distinctions that are made on the basis of sex. The most important differences between the sexes are acquired through socialization as we all learn to fulfill our *gender roles*, the social and cultural expectations associated with a person's sex. Gender is a fundamental part of the social structure, and masculinity and femininity are products of human definition, social and cultural interpretation, and social interaction (Thorne 2007). Consequently, when new parents-to-be have their so-called "gender-reveal" parties, they are not really revealing gender at all. They are revealing the baby's sex. Gender will develop after the baby is born as it develops and assumes a gender role. These gender roles affect every aspect of our lives, from our eating behavior and the type of neighbor we are likely to be, to our political and religious leanings, to how long we live and our cause of death—in short, the way we think about and live life itself.

Masculinity refers to attributes considered appropriate for males. In American society, these traditionally include being aggressive, athletic, physically active, logical, and dominant in social relationships with females. Conversely, *femininity* refers to attributes traditionally associated with appropriate behavior for females, which in America include passivity, docility, fragility, emotionality, and subordination to males. Research conducted by Carol Gilligan (2016) and her students indicates that children are acutely aware of and feel pressure to conform to these powerful gender stereotypes by the age of four. Barrie Thorne (2007:317) confirms that by preschool age, boys and girls have defined themselves in regard to both sex and gender and prefer the company of "their own kind." And Peggy Giordano's research indicates gender roles are firmly in place by adolescence (Giordano, Longmore, and Manning 2006). Some people insist that gender traits such as male aggressiveness are innate characteristics linked to sex and do not depend on cultural definitions (Maccoby 1980). However, the preponderance of research indicates that females and males can be equally aggressive under different social and cultural conditions, and that levels of aggression vary as widely within the sexes as between them (e.g., Butler 1999; Wilton 2005). Rachel Simmons (2003) in her book *Odd Girl Out* contends that girls are just as naturally aggressive as boys but have been taught to hold their aggression in.

In an effort to reduce social differentiation and inequality based on sex and gender, some people advocate *androgyny*, a blending of masculine and feminine attributes. Androgyny is not role reversal but embraces the full range of human emotions and behaviors rather than only those traditionally considered appropriate to a specific sex. This involves redefining gender roles and attaching new meanings to the concepts of masculinity and femininity. It also means no longer categorizing everybody all the time by sex and gender (Ridgeway and Correll 2000).

Despite more androgynous views of gender and the weakening of some gender stereotypes, powerful cultural distinctions between masculinity and femininity persist. Today, women must "prove" that they are capable of performing traditional "men's work" in the military and in the fields of law, medicine, science, sports, and politics. Similarly, social and cultural attitudes often discourage or ridicule men who pursue "feminine roles" such as homemaker, secretary, nurse, flight attendant, and housekeeper.

Sexism refers to the ideology that one sex is inherently superior or inferior to the other. It fosters both individual and institutionalized prejudice (attitudes) and discrimination (actions). Sexism, much like racism and ageism, is an ideology that supports the differential and unequal treatment of individuals based on ascribed characteristics—in this case, their sex.

Sexism does not apply exclusively to females; in some cases, males are victimized by sexism as well, as they find their pursuits socially limited by attitudes, norms, rules, regulations, and policies based on traditional gender expectations (Benatar 2012; Franklin 1988; Goldberg 1976; Pollack and Shuster 2000). Carol Gilligan (2016:53) noted, "Both sexes suffer when one is not understood—this is not a zero-sum game." But sexism, like any other "ism," is about power, and in the United States the sexism experienced by women is far more prominent than the sexism men may experience. In American society, sexism permeates all major social institutions, including the family, religion, education, the workplace, sports, politics, government, the military, and the mass media. As males and females grow older, they often find that, regardless of their sex or gender, they may face several forms of inequality.

AGE AND AGEISM

"Act your age" is a common admonition in American society. The phrase reminds us that normative expectations vary according to age. Although we tolerate certain behavior from some individuals because they are "too young to know better" or "old and senile," we do not permit others, because of their age, to do the same things. Diana Harris (2007) suggested that we use *social clocks* based on age to mark appropriate times for certain life activities.

For the elderly, age-related folkways govern everything from appropriate dress to sexual behavior and overall lifestyle. Most people would be shocked to see an 80-year-old woman attired in a leather miniskirt, five-inch heels, and a tube top. Similarly, American folkways encourage older people to slow down, take care of themselves, be cautious, be uninterested in sex, and be concerned about their grandchildren or gardens. Folkways also govern other people's attitudes and behavior toward the elderly. We expect younger people to be helpful and deferential in their interactions with older individuals.

The elderly also find that age-specific mores are applied to them. Older couples who divorce after 50 years of marriage may find their actions far more upsetting to others than the divorce of a young couple who have been married for only a few years. Likewise, despite the fact that people can and do remain sexually active throughout the life course, social expectations encourage the elderly to abstain from and lose interest in sex (Lindau et al. 2007). Sex norms for the elderly also are gender related; a flirtatious 70-year-old woman may be viewed as "cute" or "fun-loving," whereas a flirtatious man of that age is more likely to be considered a "dirty old man." Mores also govern other people's actions toward the elderly. Children are viewed as having a moral obligation to care for their elderly parents—at least financially, if not physically—and failure to do so rarely goes unnoticed and unsanctioned by gossip, ridicule, and other informal means.

Many laws are age specific. For example, Social Security laws specify when an individual is entitled to benefits. In 1967, Congress passed the Age Discrimination in Employment Act (ADEA), which prohibits the denial of job opportunities to people aged 40–65 solely on the basis of age. In 1978, the law was amended to extend to age 70, and today it includes everyone over age 40. Criminal laws rarely distinguish between the elderly and other adults—but law enforcement does. Except for serious violent crimes, police officers are reluctant to arrest the elderly, district attorneys hesitate to prosecute them, and judges and juries are disinclined to sentence them to jail. This does not mean that criminal activities by the elderly are ignored. The FBI's official crime data indicate that increasing numbers of people over age 65 are arrested each year, especially for property crimes (FBI 2018). An increasingly aged prison population provides new and interesting challenges for correctional officials in the form of special diets, health care, and other age-related needs—compounded by the fact that in most cases, elderly inmates are housed in the same institutions as 20-year-old violent and predatory inmates.

There is some disagreement over whether the elderly constitute a minority group. Earlier, we indicated that a minority group is a category of people set apart on the basis of ascribed status who are readily identifiable, feel a strong sense of cohesiveness, have less power than the dominant group, and suffer unequal treatment in the form of prejudice and discrimination. According to these criteria, the American elderly definitely qualify. As with other minority groups and subcultures, prejudice and discrimination against the elderly are bolstered by a supporting ideology: *ageism*, the belief that people in a particular age category are inferior to people in other age categories. Ageism plays on stereotypes that portray the elderly as nonproductive, physically decrepit, suffering from a variety of debilitating diseases, sexually impotent, and mentally impaired.

Before the twentieth century in America, few people interacted with anyone older than 65. The elderly were perceived as tired, weak, senile, and decrepit, and people rarely encountered elderly who violated the stereotype. Today, elderly Americans are everywhere, riding bicycles, jogging, hiking, camping, playing sports, attending concerts, giving art shows, and working in fast-food restaurants. It is difficult for younger people to adhere to negative stereotypes of the elderly when they see these myths debunked every day. Yet the elderly remain one of the few minority groups that are still considered fair game for comedians and others to negatively stereotype for fun and profit.

An important social development has been the formation of organizations whose goals center on the destruction of myths about the elderly and the prejudice and discrimination aimed at them. The American Association of Retired Persons (AARP), founded in 1958, began as a fledgling organization of retirees who circulated a newsletter that focused on topics such as how to apply for Social Security benefits and how to choose a retirement village or nursing home. By the mid-1990s, it boasted over 3,600 chapters and a membership of 32 million, and today it numbers over 37 million. Transforming numbers into power, the AARP is politically active, promoting legislation related to Social Security, Medicare, the elimination of mandatory retirement, and other matters affecting the elderly. The AARP also flexed its muscles in the 1980s by endorsing political candidates and contributing money, time, and energy toward electing officials viewed as sympathetic to its cause. Since the 1994 elections, almost all politicians have felt tremendous pressure to assure the elderly that Social Security and Medicare were off-limits as targets for cuts.

In the early 1970s, Maggie Kuhn formed the *Gray Panthers*, an organization with the goal of eliminating ageism in all its forms. Initially met with curiosity and humor, the Gray Panthers became a viable force on the American political scene. At the top of their agenda was the elimination of mandatory retirement, and the Gray Panthers were a significant force behind the passage of the 1978 and 1986 amendments to the ADEA, which all but eliminated mandatory retirement except for law enforcement officers and a few other occupations. The Gray Panthers also attacked substandard conditions in nursing homes, archaic inheritance laws, inadequate health care, and other forms of segregation and discrimination against the elderly. Until her death in 1995, Kuhn continued to advocate the elimination of ageism and the creation of enhanced social status for the elderly in recognition of their wisdom, experience, and meaningful contributions to society. Part of her focus was on media portrayals of the elderly. Kuhn criticized the media for portraying the elderly as senile, useless, and sexless. These portrayals not only have encouraged older people to buy into these stereotypes but also have shaped a generation of young Americans' impressions of the aged and the aging process (cited in Davis and Davis 1985:xi).

Social stratification exists among the elderly, just as it does in all other age categories. In fact, inequality is greatest among elderly people. The poorest 20 percent of the elderly, who are primarily unmarried women, minorities, and the physically impaired, possess only 5.5 percent of all of the elderly's resources, whereas the wealthiest 20 percent own 46 percent of the total (U.S. Bureau of the Census 2017). Retirement or loss of work because of ill health, decreased physical abilities, or other age-related factors can be economically devastating. Although it is a myth that the vast majority of the elderly are poor, those over age 65 have a lower median income than all other adult categories between ages 25 and 64, and elderly members of African American, Hispanic, and other minority groups fare far worse than elderly white Americans (Novak 2018; U.S. Bureau of the Census 2018). In short, the public perception that inequality narrows after age 65 is inaccurate, and for the aged, even more than for other age cohorts, it is true that the rich get richer and the poor get poorer (Moos 2006; U.S. Bureau of the Census 2018). Still, contrary to popular notions, the majority of the elderly do not languish in poverty, and each new generation of elderly seems to fare better financially than the previous ones.

Some pessimism exists about the future of Social Security and whether there will be sufficient funds to support the baby boom cohort when its members reach retirement age. Although these fears seem reasonable, as about one-fifth of the population will be retired by the year 2025, and the younger workers may be unwilling or unable to pay higher taxes to support retirees, evidence suggests that most baby boomers will be less dependent on Social Security benefits and will enjoy better economic conditions during old age than any previous cohort (Hillier and Barrow 2015).

From time to time, we hear shocking reports of abuse of the elderly. In the past, *elder abuse* was associated with isolated cases of mistreatment of residents in nursing homes by unscrupulous and uncaring staff. During the 1980s, however, an alarming phenomenon came to light. Elderly people are more likely to be abused by family members than by strangers (Payne 2011). When the definition of elder abuse is expanded to include verbal abuse and financial exploitation, it may affect over 1 million cases across the nation each year (Hooyman and Kawamoto 2015:133). Reported cases of elder abuse have increased in almost every state (National Center on Elder Abuse 2015).

Elder abuse, which is the mistreatment of older persons, takes several forms. The most obvious and shocking is *physical abuse*, including pushing, shoving, rough handling, beating, physical assault, and rape. *Psychological abuse*, consisting of threats, verbal assaults, intimidation, and isolation, is not as violent and attracts far less attention, but can be equally devastating. The elderly also may suffer *neglect*, in which they are deprived of adequate food, medication, or other goods and services, or *financial exploitation*, in which their money is misused, stolen, mismanaged, or squandered.

The extent of elder abuse is impossible to determine because of imprecise definitions, inadequate systematic research, and the ability of abusers to disguise or cover up the abuse (Wood 2006). Bruises, lacerations, and broken bones can be attributed to falls and accidents, and even if victims complain of maltreatment, their accusations may be attributed to senility, the influence of medications, or other discrediting factors. Whereas school officials, social workers, medical personnel, and others are legally required to report suspected child abuse, there is no such protection for the elderly.

The National Center on Elder Abuse serves as a clearinghouse on elder abuse data and publishes information on the prevention of elder abuse. It produces a newsletter, operates a website, and sponsors an annual World Elder Abuse Awareness Day. In 2003, a nonpartisan coalition of national, regional, state, and local advocacy groups was formed, called the Elder Justice Coalition. This organization is dedicated to promoting public understanding of the problems of elder abuse, and encouraged the passage of the Elder Justice Act of 2003, which was introduced in both houses of Congress. This bill established dual Offices of Elder Justice in the U.S. Department of Health and Human Services and the U.S. Department of Justice, and an Office of Adult Protective Services within the U.S. Department of Health and Human Services. These offices are charged with coordinating elder abuse prevention on a national basis and enhancing law enforcement response to elder abuse cases when reported (NCEA 2015). Signed into law by President Obama in 2010 as part of the Patient Protection and Affordable Care Act, among other things the law provided federal resources to prevent; detect; treat; understand; and, where appropriate, intervene in and prosecute elder abuse.

From the conflict perspective, the elderly, like any other minority group, face social isolation, prejudice, and discrimination. In a capitalist society, productivity becomes an important measure of an individual's value to society. If older people are viewed as less productive, they fall lower in the social hierarchy than their younger counterparts, who are considered more productive. Declines in income and wealth in old age are usually accompanied by lower status and less power.

INTERSECTIONALITY

Sociologists often focus on *intersectionality*, the overlap among various forms of inequality and oppression. For example, established practices of sexism are often interconnected with other forms of prejudices and discriminations, including racism, ethnocentrism, ageism, sexual orientation biases, and inequalities associated with social class (Bates 2016). This can result in what sociologists call *double jeopardy*, or being disadvantaged or stigmatized because of more than one social characteristic. Consequently, a homeless woman may suffer more stigma than a homeless man. If a third variable is added, such as race or ethnicity, it may be argued that a homeless woman of color will experience even more prejudices and discrimination than one who is white. Indeed, racial and ethnic minorities make up a disproportionate number of homeless people in the United States.

It should be no surprise that women and men experience the aging process differently. So do members of different races, ethnic groups, and social classes. Although the physiological and biological aspects of aging are quite similar for women and men, blacks and whites, rich and poor—thinning and graying hair, wrinkled skin, age spots, loss of muscle tone, and others—how individuals and society respond to these changes is quite different. There is a clear cultural double standard when it comes to aging and sex: men grow more distinguished looking, whereas women simply grow old. Sociologists Lisa Wade and Myra Marx Ferree (2015) summarized the two standards of beauty for men as compared with only one for women: boys can seamlessly make the transition from boyhood to manhood, exchanging the smooth skin and hairless body of a boy for the rugged lines and coarse good looks of a man; conversely, women are expected to maintain the single standard of beauty and flawlessness established in girlhood—every line, every wrinkle, and every gray hair diminishing their desirability.

The media have long reflected this double standard, as 40-something newswomen are often marginalized while 50-year-old newsmen are only beginning to hit their peak. Similarly, female celebrities who dominate prime-time television are rarely over 40 and, if so, are most likely to be cast in roles as mothers or grandmothers, rarely the central female figure. Add being a member of a racial or ethnic minority, and the inequality seems to multiply exponentially, not only in the media but in real life.

Some might rightfully argue that social inequality is inevitable in every society; others insist that it is patently unfair. And though the gap between the richest and poorest is growing larger, the United States and many other nations are seeing increased emphasis on differences regarding race, ethnicity, sex, sexual orientation, gender, and age. Now more than ever, it is important to emphasize the eighth wisdom of sociology: *the only difference that matters is the difference that matters.*

Sociological Wisdom 9

#NothingEnduresButChange

CREATING SOCIAL CHANGE

THE YEAR IS 2019. Blockbuster music artists Elton John and Neil Diamond announce to the world that although they will continue to write and record songs, they will no longer go on tour. Elton John is retiring from live performances because he wants to spend more time with his family, and Neil Diamond because he has been diagnosed with Parkinson's disease. That same year, however, disappointed concertgoers still have plenty of opportunities to see and hear their favorite artists in concert as legendary Billie Holiday is on tour selling out venues across the United States as concertgoers clap, cheer, and sing along to her top-selling hits, "Them There Eyes," "Billie's Blues—I Love My Man," "Solitude," and "Strange Fruit." Additionally, fans can watch Michael Jackson moonwalk across the stage; Elvis Presley sing a duet with Celine Dion; Christina Aguilar team up with one of her idols, Whitney Houston; and country music fans can sing along with their beloved Tammy Wynette. Live concert performances are alive and well—or so it seems. However, sociological wisdom teaches us *nothing endures but change*. These are not live performances. Michael Jackson died in 2009, Elvis in 1977, and Whitney Houston in 2012; Tammy Wynette passed in 1998, and the aforementioned Billie Holiday died six decades earlier in 1959. How can live audiences watch dead celebrities perform in person? Is this some technological dream of the future? Yes and no. The future is now, as celebrity holograms have become all the rage, linking the past to the future. Although this technology is primarily aimed at entertainment, it could just as easily be adapted to inspire social change and shape collective behavior as future civil rights movements might once again be visually and verbally inspired by Dr. Martin Luther King Jr., and women's movements' crowds could rally around the likes of Susan B. Anthony and Betty Friedan.

The ancient Greek philosopher Heraclitus mused about our ninth sociological wisdom, "*Nothing endures but change.*" Many Americans are certain that technology holds the key to the future—either for better or for worse. The latest pronouncements from Silicon Valley or Microsoft about the technological wonders of the future are often treated by the press and the public not as possibilities, but as statements of fact. For example, sociologist Arthur Shostak (2000:3) cites one futurist who predicted at the turn of the century that technology would change an astounding "90 percent of our culture and society" in the next 10 years. Indeed it did. Few sociologists would disagree that new technologies are bringing sweeping changes to societies everywhere on earth. However, despite the idea that technology is the major and perhaps even the only significant agent of social change, many other factors are involved.

We can use a variety of sociological perspectives to examine the complex factors that contribute to social change. They include the powerful economic and political organizations that produce and control many of the technological wonders of the Information Age. There are several other key agents of change, such as the globalization, demography, wars, and natural disasters. Sociology emphasizes collective behavior and social movements, or "politics from below." In both forms of collective action, large numbers of ordinary people join forces to challenge the mainstream and to promote or resist change.

SOCIAL CHANGE

Social change is a process through which patterns of social behavior, social relationships, social institutions, and systems of stratification are altered over time. Everything changes, and, like nature, all societies are in a constant state of flux. The rate of change, however, varies from one society to another. For much of human history, change was slow, and though hunting-gathering societies adopted new ways and relinquished customs and traditions, they did so very gradually over the course of centuries or even millennia.

With the origin of agriculture and the emergence of cities, the pace of change quickened, and with industrialization, social changes that once had taken generations or more occurred in the space of decades, or even a few years. C. Wright Mills's (1959:4) comment that no society on earth had experienced such "earthquakes of change" at such a rapid pace as contemporary American society is even more poignant today than when he wrote it some six decades ago.

Macro-changes are gradual, large scale, and, because they take place over long periods of time, imperceptible to people as they go about their daily lives. *Modernization*, a process through which societies become more internally differentiated and complex as they move from simple to complex social institutions, is a good example of this kind of macro-change. Other kinds of macro-change may take less time, spanning only a few generations, such as the shift from industrial societies based on manufacturing to postindustrial societies based on information and service economies.

Micro-changes involve small, rapid changes produced by the countless decisions people make as they interact with others in the course of their daily lives. Micro-change occurs in the everyday lives of millions of ordinary people, as people make business, family, and countless other decisions. With the exception of movers and shakers whose decisions may have an immediate effect on our lives, the small acts of ordinary people may slowly and imperceptibly alter social institutions and, eventually, entire societies.

Like other aspects of culture, people's understandings of the future are paradoxical. While the future is the repository of people's collective hopes and dreams, it also represents people's collective fears. Consequently, although some individuals and groups view change as positive and beneficial, others perceive it as harmful and a potential threat to their interests,

Damn change and newfangled ideas...if mindless back breaking work was good enough for my ancestors it's good enough for ME!

needs, and "futures." Even when there is widespread agreement, and change is carefully planned, it often has social consequences that were never intended or imagined.

Change may be desired and pursued or reviled and resisted—but it can never be halted. The speed and direction of change, however, are never random. As Clark Kerr observed, every society "moves towards its future in terms of its past, its own institutions, and traditions" (cited in McCord 1991:58). Put another way, when societies confront a new situation, they do so in a context of existing sociocultural constraints that influence their members' perceptions and choices (Barrett 1991).

SOURCES OF SOCIAL CHANGE

In addition to wars, some of the most important sources of change are the physical environment, technology, population, cultural innovation, and social conflict. The *physical environment* includes cataclysmic events such as floods, droughts, volcanic eruptions, and earthquakes. Human activities, especially urban and industrial activities in the last two centuries, which have produced acid rain, global climate change, massive deforestation, desertification, and holes in the ozone layer, also produce social change and have the potential to cause profound changes during this century.

Technology, which is the application of knowledge for practical ends, has been a powerful force for social change since the invention of the first tool. Lasers, fiber optics, biotechnology, genetic engineering, computer-assisted technologies, and other technological advances have the potential to vastly improve the quality of people's lives. Although technology can enhance our lives, it also has the potential to give government and other giant organizations powers of surveillance and social control that were impossible and even unimaginable just a few years ago.

Population and *changes in the size and composition of populations, migration*, and other *demographic forces* are also important sources of change. *Cultural innovation*, including discovery, invention, and diffusion—*or cultural borrowing*—is an important source of social change as well. Tourism, international commerce, and the global telecommunications industry have introduced the world to a steady stream of Western products, goods, ideas, and values—especially consumerism, individualism, and popular culture. Diffusion is rarely a one-way process, and goods and ideas from all of the world's cultures affect the foods we eat, the clothes we wear, the music we listen to, and most other aspects of American culture and society.

Social conflict in a global society includes racial, ethnic, religious, and gender conflicts, as well as nationalist struggles. Because they have strong vested interests in the status quo, elites often resist change and suppress subordinates who desire it. When elites become divided or lose legitimacy, however, significant social change becomes possible. War and terrorist activities also can bring sudden change, and so can ordinary people—when they join forces to alter the conditions of their lives.

Novel ideas and radically new visions of the world sometimes emerge during periods of intense conflict and social turmoil. The Industrial Revolution in the nineteenth century, for example, provided fertile ground for a "new science" that could explain the remarkable social changes that were taking place in Europe and America. The growth and respectability of science also generated a great deal of optimism that sociology—like the natural sciences—would discover "laws" that would not only explain social change but also lead to the creation of "better societies" (Turner and Killian 1987).

With the widespread distribution of clocks and watches during the Industrial Revolution, linear views, which hold that time proceeds in a straightforward, nonrepetitive fashion, became popular. Businesspeople, of course, favored linear models because they facilitated industrial production and the pursuit of profit. In linear models, time can be divided into discrete units and "made better use of," or it can be "lost," "wasted," or "squandered." Linear views also make planning important, and the "future"—not the past—is the dominant orientation.

Borrowing models from the biological sciences, many sociologists subscribed to the popular theory called *unilineal evolution*, which held that all forms of life—and, by analogy, all societies—"progressed" from simple to complex forms, with each form an *advance* over its predecessors. Just as biologists classified life forms according to complexity, social scientists developed ranking systems of their own, each showing humankind's "steady ascent up a ladder of predictable stages" (Caplow 1991:11).

One popular nineteenth-century scheme emphasized that all societies passed through three main stages: *savagery, barbarism,* and *civilization*. Auguste Comte, often referred to as the founder of sociology, argued that all societies passed through *theological, metaphysical,* and *positivistic* stages, and that European societies were in the last stage—which was the highest and final stage of human development.

Herbert Spencer, a contemporary of Comte, also was influenced by biological theories of evolution. Coining the term "survival of the fittest" before it became associated with Charles Darwin and biological evolution, Spencer saw the survival of organisms and societies as linked to their ability to *adapt* to a changing environment. To Spencer, Western societies had advanced to the highest social level because they were "better suited" to nineteenth-century conditions than non-Western ones. These ideas gained widespread popularity during European colonization and industrial expansion, and they added ideological support when European colonial powers redefined their activities from conquest and exploitation to the moral duty of a "superior race" to assist natives in making the difficult journey from "savagery" to "civilization."

Not everyone was convinced that industrialization and the new emphasis on competition, profit, and self-interest would lead to social advancement. German sociologist Ferdinand Toennies ([1887] 1961) maintained that modernization led to a progressive loss of community, or *Gemeinschaft*, whereby social life was characterized by primary ties and a strong sense of solidarity. These bonds were replaced by fleeting and impersonal ties based on self-interest, or the modern *Gesellschaft* social type (Toennies [1887] 1961). Toennies argued that modern societies might give people greater opportunities and material benefits, but the costs would include a growing sense of isolation, uncertainty, and powerlessness, which had the potential to produce unmanageable social problems, social decay, and collapse.

Another classical theorist, Émile Durkheim, did not agree that economic competition would lead to chaos. He argued that new varieties of *social solidarity*, or feelings of collective conscience, would emerge to maintain social order. According to Durkheim's ([1893] 1964) two-part model, in simple societies every member performed the same tasks, was interchangeable, and shared similar beliefs and values. Homogeneity, or *mechanical solidarity*, served to integrate society. During the nineteenth century, it was clear that industrialization, increased population growth, and competition were destroying traditional forms of social solidarity. Durkheim argued that those who survived the bitter economic competition were progressively assuming specialized roles and exchange relations with one another, and thus were in the process of developing *organic solidarity.* This same theme was echoed in the works of Robert Redfield (1941, 1953), who viewed society as evolving from "folk" to "urban," and Carl Becker (1933), who linked social change to the transition from "sacred" to "secular." Likewise, industrialization and modernization also have transformed small-scale, *traditional societies* into modern *mass societies* everywhere on earth.

During the twentieth century, unilineal models that described social change as continuous and inevitable were replaced by more sophisticated and less ethnocentric ones. Current *neo-evolutionary theories* acknowledge that societies differ according to levels of social complexity and that, over time, there has been a general trend toward *social differentiation*, in which various social institutions (economic, religious, political, and others) have become separate and distinct from one another.

Unlike nineteenth-century evolutionary theorists, however, neo-evolutionists neither describe one form of society as superior to another nor maintain that societies inevitably progress to some higher state. Likewise, few associate modernization with an inevitable shift in the opposite direction: from a nostalgic past of warm personal relations to the cold indifference of the city. Instead, they stress that there are many paths to development and change. Perhaps the major proponents of contemporary evolutionary thinking are Gerhard and Jean Lenski, who contend that at various stages of history, technological and economic changes have set in motion a series of other changes, including population growth, increased population density, more complex organizations, and new ideologies (Nolan and Lenski 2014).

Like most nineteenth-century social theorists, Karl Marx was influenced by evolutionary theory. He agreed with Hegel's idea that social change came about as a result of the dialectic involving *thesis* (idea or proposal), *antithesis* (counter thesis), and *synthesis* (a new thesis that reconciles the conflict and starts the process all over again). Marx argued that societies had to adapt to survive, and stressed that the economy served as the foundation for the social order. He also believed that societies inevitably advanced toward a higher and final state—in his model, from class to a classless society.

In Marx's model of revolutionary change, as capitalists bought off competitors, they would grow stronger and more ruthless in their search for profits, and workers would suffer progressively lower wages, higher rates of unemployment, and poverty and destitution. This, in turn, would produce rising levels of alienation, discontent, and severe economic crises—each more serious than the last—until in the end, workers everywhere would recognize their common enemy and join in a revolutionary movement to overthrow capitalists and the system of private property, ultimately taking charge of the economy and running it for the good of all.

Marx overemphasized economic factors in his model of revolutionary change. In her study of revolutions in France, Russia, and China, Theda Skocpol (1979:19) found that where revolutionary change occurred, not only were there serious economic crises and class conflicts, but in all cases, national political and economic elites were unable to meet the challenges of transnational or international relations, which "helped shape revolutionary struggles and outcomes."

The collapse of the Soviet Union supports Skocpol's thesis. Not only did national economic crises and internal conflicts fuel revolutionary change in the Soviet Union and Eastern Europe, but so did military competition with the United States. This led to massive spending by both nations, which helped bankrupt the former Soviet Union and put severe economic pressures on Western economies. Despite short-term gains, however, most conflict theorists agree that although capitalism seems to be prospering at present, "crises can only be put off, not evaded entirely" (Collins and Makowsky 2010:44). While modern conflict theorists continue to explore the social consequences of class conflict, they have expanded their analysis to include all forms of social conflict—racial, ethnic, religious, gender, age, and others.

For most of human history, cyclical understandings of social change dominated people's thinking. Before the invention of clocks and the Industrial Revolution, the basic rhythms of people's lives were attuned to the repetitive cycles of nature. The sun rose and set; the seasons changed; and these and other natural cycles guided people's everyday lives and influenced their understandings of social change. Even today, many Native Americans make no clear distinctions between the past and future. To them, they are one and the same, because—like nature—history is forever repeated in endless cycles.

Sociologist Pitirim Sorokin (1941) used the cyclical theory of change, arguing that civilizations oscillated among three types of "mentalities," or worldviews: *ideational*, which emphasizes faith and spirituality; *sensate*, which stresses practical and utilitarian approaches to reality; and *idealistic*, which balances the practical and the transcendental. According to Sorokin, in all cultural systems, change occurs when a particular mode of thinking reaches its logical limits: for example, when a sensate society becomes too hedonistic, and sensual people "turn to ideational systems as a refuge" (Ritzer 2013:202).

Cyclical understandings of change have experienced something of a revival among New Age groups, as well as in popular expressions such as "Everything that goes around comes around." Most modern sociologists, however, believe that in addition to describing change, we must take the next step and explore the complex processes that have taken us from the Stone Age to beyond the Space Age.

Few sociologists subscribe to a single "grand theory" of social change. Some borrow elements of neo-evolutionary theory, and stress adaptation and economic factors in the process of change. Most also emphasize class-based and other forms of conflict both within and among nations. Likewise, instead of attempting to explain change in terms of a single factor, most agree that the complex interaction among many factors—both internal and external to a nation—produce change, although in varied specific historical and social contexts, specific factors may sometimes exert more influence than others.

Interactionists tend to view change as being a result of ideas and the process of redefining meaning and reality through social interaction. For example, Toennies' ideas reflect a change in the feeling of a society rather than its structure. Similarly, Max Weber pointed out how social change is often linked to a change in worldview, as what may have been considered as traditional "truth" becomes redefined and replaced by another version of truth. These ideas are reflected in Weber's work on bureaucracy and the increasing rationalization of society, as well as his works on capitalism, religion, and society. Interactionists also focus on how social change can be initiated at a micro level and then have major impact on a macro level. Acts such as the refusal by Rosa Parks to go to the back of the bus, linked with the charismatic personality and peaceful protests initiated by Dr. Martin Luther King Jr., provided the catalyst for social change in the area of civil rights not only for African Americans but also for other racial and ethnic minorities as well as women. Ritzer (2015) pointed out how the simple act of Ray Kroc combining with the McDonald brothers eventually led to creating one of the largest food chains in the world and to the *McDonaldization* of society, which had a lasting impact on the fast-food industry, other retail businesses, and almost every aspect of modern life.

Not surprisingly, feminists view social change from a gendered perspective. The central question posed by most feminist sociologists is why, despite such monumental social change both in the United States and worldwide, patriarchy persists in so many social arenas (Gottfried 1996). The United Nations included a resolution to promote equality between women and men, but it was not until 1975 that it held the first World Conference on Women. Three subsequent conferences over the next 30 years found that worldwide sex and gender discrimination had changed very little.

When ordinary people join forces to protest and challenge the status quo, they too can become powerful agents of social change. *Collective behavior* consists of relatively spontaneous and noninstitutionalized responses by a large number of people to uncertain and problematic situations. *Social movements* involve organized, goal-directed efforts by a large number of people to promote or resist change outside of established institutions.

COLLECTIVE BEHAVIOR

Most of our lives are spent in small social groups or large formal organizations where we interact with others in patterned and predictable ways. During the course of our everyday lives, we also become part of *collectivities*—large numbers of people who interact briefly and superficially in the absence of clearly defined norms—such as shoppers at a supermarket or mall (Miller 2013).

Most early scientific approaches to collective behavior focused on "crowd psychology." For example, Gustav LeBon's ([1895] 1960) *contagion theory* stressed powerful and "contagious" emotions, which, when combined with the anonymity of the crowd, enabled people to act irresponsibly or even brutally. According to contagion theory, this transformation occurs through the power of suggestion, which makes people susceptible to crowd emotions.

Although most social theorists agree that emotions are important in such crowds, few believe there is *total uniformity* in people's moods and behaviors in crowds, or even that there is a common emotional response in crowds (McPhail 1994; Miller 2013). Ralph Turner and Lewis Killian (1987:27), however, agree with contagion theory in one regard: the more uncertain the situation, the more individuals become susceptible to "the suggestions of others."

Convergence theory maintains that mobs are comprised not of ordinary citizens caught in the grip of powerful emotions, but of segments of the population who already share certain attitudes and interests that predispose them to converge and act in violent and destructive ways. Sociologists, however, have found little difference between the attitudes and beliefs of participants and nonparticipants in most forms of collective behavior.

According to *emergent norm theory*, in situations where collectivities become crowds, people are neither overwhelmed by emotions, nor are they simply imitating one another. Instead, they look to one another during interaction for clues as to how they should behave, and establish new or emergent "group norms of judgement" (Turner and Killian 1987:27).

Neil J. Smelser's (1962) *value-added theory* requires both an understanding of crowd dynamics and an examination of the larger social context in which collective behavior occurs. According to Smelser's model, several conditions increase the likelihood of collective behavior. One condition known as *structural conduciveness* is where institutions are organized in such a way that they encourage collective behavior. For example, democratic states that permit legal rallies and assemblies are structurally more conducive to rioting and mob behavior than authoritarian regimes that outlaw and brutally repress all public gatherings. In much the same way, the mass media can dramatize events, heighten emotions, and encourage crowd behavior, rumors, fads, and fashions. *Social control factors* such as government inactivity, confusion, and vacillation or active encouragement by elites may boost collective behavior and is a second condition. The third condition, *structural strains*, includes any social condition that strains social relations, such as poverty, injustice, discrimination, and economic uncertainty. *Generalized beliefs* about their situation define the nature of the problem, identify who is responsible for it, and offer some plan of action. Finally, *mobilization for action*, which usually occurs when leaders emerge and mobilize curious or sympathetic observers into active participants. Often a *precipitating event* triggers collective behavior—such as Dr. Martin Luther King Jr.'s assassination in 1968, which touched off urban riots in 125 cities across the United States.

Following John Lofland's (1985) model, sociologists have combined two major characteristics in classifying various forms of collective behavior: (1) the *dominant emotion* expressed (joy, anger, fear, and other emotions) and (2) the *type of collectivity* involved. In a *crowd*, people are in close proximity; in a *mass*, large numbers of people are widely dispersed (Turner and Killian 1987).

Some kinds of crowds produce collective behavior, whereas others do not. *Casual crowds*, such as a gathering of people who witness an accident, may share a common focus, but too briefly to qualify as collective behavior. *Conventional crowds*, in which people are gathered to watch a sports event, concert, or theater performance, also do not qualify, but for the opposite reason: these events occur so often that they are routine and governed by established norms. But even conventional and casual crowds can quickly change to emotionally charged, nonconforming crowds—either expressive or acting (Blumer 1969a).

An *expressive crowd* gathers for the purpose of expressing emotions. As Turner and Killian (1987:98) noted, "The crowd creates a permissive setting in which the individual can express feelings more freely and with less regard for conventional formality." Rock concerts and sports events, for example, are common settings where members of expressive crowds chant, hug perfect strangers, and even take off their clothes in response to the joyous mood.

Unlike expressive crowds, in which emotional release is the only goal, *acting crowds* are emotionally aroused gatherings that direct their attention and activity toward some event or goal. For example, if expressive members of a crowd at a rock concert notice that police officers are attempting to remove an overly exuberant fan, anger may replace joy, and in minutes they may become an acting crowd.

In *mob behavior*, an acting crowd threatens violence or engages in violent and destructive acts; it is referred to as a *mob*. If the violence becomes widespread, sustained, and includes large numbers of people, it is called a *riot*. McPhail (1994b:25) contends that during riots "violent actors are neither hapless victims of structural strains nor [victims] of psychological deindividuation. [Instead] purposive actors adjust their behaviors to make their perceptions match their objectives." Social media play an important role in motivating collective behavior and can contribute to the motivation of mobs and revolutions (Trottier and Fuchs 2015).

Revolutions are "attempts by subordinate groups to transform the social foundations of political power" (Kimmel 1990:6). Successful revolutions include the American and French Revolutions and the street protests and uprisings in Iran that toppled the Shah's regime and ushered in the Islamic Republic.

In a *panic*, which is a "collective flight based on a hysterical belief," fear, rather than anger, is the predominant emotion (Smelser 1962:131). Panics occur whenever crowds believe they must immediately escape a perceived danger or avoid being excluded from a highly desired event. The panics most of us are familiar with involve fires in theaters, nightclubs, or businesses, where exits are limited and people develop the belief that the only course of action is immediate escape by any available means. Increasingly in contemporary society, crowd members panic when they fear they are being excluded from some desirable event or perhaps denied a consumer product.

The least common and most dramatic form of crowd behavior is *mass suicide*. Historically, such events have been associated with members of apocalyptic religious communities who are convinced the end of the world is imminent and an armed assault by a hostile government force is about to take place. This was the context of the 1978 mass suicide of more than 900 members of the People's Temple sect in Jonestown, Guyana, who committed suicide by drinking cyanide-laced Kool-Aid (Robbins 1986). Although the exact cause of the conflagration that took the lives of David Koresh and almost 90 members of the Branch Davidians is uncertain, the Waco tragedy involved an armed millenarian group that found itself threatened and under siege by government forces (Haught 1995).

Unlike crowds, in which people affect one another directly, in *mass behavior* people are not in the same locality, yet through a common source of information or communication medium, they can indirectly influence one another. Personal networks remain important, but television, mobile phones, and other forms of communication have become key agents in many forms of mass collective behavior. Although the media may promote collective action, they can discourage it as well. For example, Gary Fine and Ryan White (2002) examined how the mainstream media use "human-interest stories" to create collective attention, provoke public discussion, and foster communal identification. Media favorites for over a century include stories about people and animals that have become trapped, a child lost in the woods, a missing climber, or a baby who needs unusual medical attention. But human-interest stories—just like media stories that detail the trials and tribulations of celebrities—rarely produce collective action. In fact, because these stories are highly personal and seem to have little social importance, "the call for collective action and political action is muffled and muted." Today, important forms of collective action include fads, fashions, rumors, urban legends, and mass hysteria.

Fads are short-term, frivolous, and unconventional collective behaviors that usually provide pleasure and involve only a small segment of the population. Many challenge tradition and authority—such as young people dressing like popular rock stars. College students "streaking" and youths dyeing their hair green or purple are other examples of fads. Some fads are more respectable and more profitable to businesses and other interests.

Fashions are relatively enduring styles and behaviors that enjoy widespread popularity, often in cycles, such as dress and hairstyles, and automobile and home designs. Fashions are acutely sensitive to shifting economic and demographic trends. In the United States, shifts in the values, tastes, and concerns of baby boomers are of special importance. In the 1960s, for example, many youthful and rebellious baby boomers found miniskirts and bikinis fashionable. Early in the twenty-first century, more affluent baby boomers switched to Jacuzzis, BMWs, Harley-Davidsons, and designer sunglasses. Today, fashions reflect concerns such as the powerful emphases on saving, dieting, fitness, travel, and other leisure activities.

Rumors tend to be the opposite of fashion in many ways. Whereas fashions are often associated with the "high-brow" domain, popular rumors are "low-brow" and commonplace—the stuff of ordinary people, popular culture, tabloids, and "reality TV." *Rumors* are unconfirmed items or media reports that spread by word of mouth and cannot be verified. They can arise on a large scale in periods of change or when people lack reliable or trustworthy information. Rumors reflect people's deep-seated concerns, prejudices, hopes, and fears. They also can be spread by activists and others to alert the public to social problems or to promote or resist change. "Organ-stealing" rumors have been one collective response to these threats. This urban legend has been perpetuated by story lines on popular television shows and spread like wildfire on the internet.

Many rumors are introduced on television, but the internet and social media are the favored sources. Websites and social media spread both facts and rumors about corporations, the government, celebrities, and a host of other public concerns each day. Because of their growing influence in contemporary life, website rumors about corporate activities are especially popular. For example, at the turn of the century, a rumor in the form of mass emails claimed that if a person mailed a pair of worn-out Nikes to the Nike headquarters, they would receive a brand new pair. Millions of old shoes were mailed before people learned the rumor was a hoax.

Urban legends are complex popular tales that often contain implicit warnings and messages. For example, tales of alligators in sewers, fried rats in buckets of chicken, severed human fingers in soft drink bottles, and other urban legends have been around for quite some time. Today, warnings of dangerous computer viruses that will destroy hard drives, empty bank accounts, or create some other high-tech tragedy circulate almost daily. A few may be true; many are fake. Such stories express collective anxieties and concerns about mass society and things beyond people's control—such as the hidden dangers of modern technology and the subtle costs of the hurried pace of modern life. These legends are enhanced on the rare occasion when one of them actually occurs.

Many rumors also are fabricated or sustained by businesses, the government, and other organizations and movements. Rumors are most easily and rapidly spread through email, over the internet, through social media or other electronic means. A rumor can be spread in nanoseconds, making it almost impossible to rectify the bogus information before it has been spread to millions of people around the globe.

At first glance, *mass hysteria*, which involves widespread anxiety and the frantic reactions of large numbers of people to some perceived threat, seems to be completely irrational and to have no logic. Typically, the dangers involved—witches, UFOs, and Satanists—are either greatly exaggerated or nonexistent. James Richardson and colleagues (1991) argue that to understand these forms of hysteria fully, it is useful to take into account some of the more organized and goal-oriented forms of collective action that sociologists call *social movements*.

For example, the *anticult movement*—a religious movement aimed at containing the spread of New Age and other novel approaches to religion—promoted the idea that Satanists had infiltrated almost every American community. About the same time, the *childsaver movement* focused public attention on missing and abducted children, introducing the public to a whole range of issues, perhaps including some—such as UFO abductions and UFO medical experiments—that never happened. The fact that some parents, school officials, police officers, and segments of the public became convinced that Satanists and sinister aliens from outer space had become a threat to society attests to the power and influence of these and other social movements.

SOCIAL MOVEMENTS

Social movements are organized, goal-directed efforts by a large number of people to promote or resist change outside of established institutions. Unlike fads, riots, panics, and other forms of spontaneous social action, social movements are relatively enduring and have an organizational base, leadership, and an ideological blueprint for collective action. Because they are well-organized and enduring social movements have been major agents of social change (Della Porta and Diani 2006; Eitzen and Stewart 2007; Schaeffer 2014).

Social movements are "noninstitutional challenges to the mainstream." Unlike the activities of lobbyists, political parties, and interest groups, which are integral parts of the political order, social movement organizations are not part of the formal political process. Instead, they are political outsiders, and their ideas and alternative visions of the future are either at the margins of mainstream society or excluded and deemed socially unacceptable (Lofland 1996; Meyer 2006).

Establishment officials typically ignore emerging social movements—at least initially. If their ideas become widespread and somewhat socially acceptable, officials may ridicule movement leaders and their ideas. They often do so with the help of the media—which may frame movement leaders and their ideas as silly, outrageous, unpatriotic, or even treasonous. Those that strike a chord with the public, however, may receive much closer scrutiny from authorities: perhaps close monitoring of movement leaders and their activities, and sometimes even official and unofficial violence. Successful movements must find ways to overcome these and other obstacles, as well as challenges from competing social movements (Eitzen and Stewart 2007; Lofland 1996; Meyer 2006; Schaeffer 2014).

According to *relative deprivation theory*, social movements appear when people feel deprived relative to others or the way life was in the past. In fact, social movements are more common in relatively affluent societies than in those experiencing severe poverty. Often, they occur when conditions are improving, but expected benefits are not materializing as rapidly or to the degree that people wish.

Sociologists who adopt the *resource mobilization* perspective disagree that grievances and alienation are at the heart of social movements. For example, McCarthy and Zald (1977) contended that whereas discontent is widespread in all societies, collective action is relatively uncommon. They maintained that when deprived groups mobilize, it is not because of rising levels of discontent but because they have found effective ways to mobilize people and resources—leadership, money, organizing skills, and media coverage—to their causes. The resource mobilization perspective places special emphasis on the strategies and tactics used by leaders to mobilize resources from within and outside their ranks, rally supporters, neutralize external challenges, and gain the support of elite groups.

David Snow and Robert Benford (1988) pointed out that a movement's success is also dependent on ideology and what they termed *frame alignment*. This is a process in which the values, beliefs, and goals of potential recruits are made congruent and complementary to a movement's value orientation and put into the service of the movement (Snow et al. 1980, 1986). According to Snow and Benford (1988), commitment to a social movement is an ongoing, interactive process, in which leaders must provide potential recruits with reasons why they should join or remain members. To be successful, a movement must develop "core framing," which negotiates the nature of a problem, who is responsible for it, and an alternative set of arrangements and plans for action (Benford and Snow 2000:615). In effect, movements are engaged in the production of meaning for participants, and their relative success depends on how well their messages compete with those of other movements and, most importantly, with those of the established political forces they attack (Eitzen and Stewart 2007; Schaeffer 2014).

Social movements should be considered part of the political process because they, like political parties and interest groups, seek to affect public policy. But unlike parties and interest groups, which are part of the formal political process, social movements include "irregular players" who have fewer resources than their competitors and minimal access to traditional avenues of influence and power. As Robert Goldberg (1991:3) observed, "Aware of power realities, movement leaders mobilize recruits to pursue goals in unorthodox and innovative ways."

Depending on their tactics and relationships with authorities, whether they look to the future or the past, and how much change they advocate, social movements can be classified into four ideal types. *Reform movements* are the most common and socially acceptable type. They aim at limited reforms to existing institutions, such as the Children's Rights Movement, which has worked for several centuries to improve the health and welfare of American children (Hawes 1991). Reform movements attempt to work within established political channels, although they often have militant branches. *Utopian movements* seek to create "perfect societies," often by establishing communities apart from the larger society that promise to fulfill *all* of their members' needs and desires, as well as serving as models for future social behavior.

Revolutionary movements have both utopian visions and specific plans for governing a society once they have assumed power. Revolutionary movements have as their goal the elimination of old institutions and their replacement with new ones that conform to a radically different vision of society. Few revolutionary movements succeeded in achieving their visions, but those that have (e.g., the American and French Revolutions) brought extraordinary changes that have reshaped societies virtually everywhere on the globe.

RESISTANCE TO CHANGE

Resistance movements, or *countermovements*, seek to reverse or resist change and restore "traditional values" that presumably prevailed at some time in the past. Resistance movements often emerge to resist reform movements. For example, Phyllis Schlafly's conservative Eagle Forum opposes the goals of the National Organization for Women (NOW), and there are other well-organized movements both for and against abortion rights, gun control, capital punishment, civil rights, and gay rights. These movements and others have websites where they dispense information, sign up recruits, and link to other social movements' sites. When grievances are widely shared, and there are abundant resources to attract many followers, social movements and countermovements proliferate (McAdam et al. 1988). Moreover, successful movements typically produce many separate social movement organizations (SMOs) with the same general goals but diverse tactics.

There are two major kinds of SMOs: volunteer and professional. The former are supported and run by ordinary women and men who volunteer their time, money, and services and who are committed to a cause that directly affects their lives. For example, homeowners can join forces to stop a company from dumping toxic chemicals in their neighborhood. By contrast, professional SMOs are formal organizations, such as the National Association for the Advancement of Colored People (NAACP) or the National Audubon Society, that include full-time professional activists who derive much of their income from foundations, grants, and agencies, in addition to contributions from the people they represent.

McCarthy and Zald (1973) believe that the success of many professional SMOs hinges not so much on how deeply their members feel about issues as on gaining the support of elite groups. In fact, many contemporary professional SMOs have relatively few active members.

They rely on expertise donated by think tanks, on media support, and on funds supplied by foundations and middle- and upper-class "conscience constituents," who contribute to but do not directly benefit from a movement's success (McCarthy and Zald 1977; McCrea and Markle 1989). Of course, being indebted to such groups presents new dilemmas for the movement that leaders must resolve if the movement is to persevere and achieve its goals.

In his study of the Civil Rights movement, Aldon Morris (1984) found that many were also attracted to Dr. Martin Luther King Jr. because he possessed *charisma* as well as the talent to articulate his visions of a new society devoid of racism. At the same time, King was able to mobilize the support of churches, labor unions, the media, and others essential for the movement's development and growth. Many voters seemed attracted to Barack Obama, and his campaign slogans related to change in the same way, causing his first presidential campaign to resemble a social movement in many ways (*Life* 2009).

Early on, leaders must overcome what is known as the *free-rider problem*: many people who stand to benefit from a movement let others do the hard work while they sit on the sidelines. Leaders try to gain the support of free riders by winning "quick victories" and concessions from authorities (Chong 1991). Leaders can also gain new recruits and resources by aligning their causes with churches, colleges, and other powerful organizations (Schaeffer 2014).

In his book *Soul of a Citizen*, Paul Loeb (1999:34–35) contends that the media and popular culture portray famous civil rights activists such as Rosa Parks as larger-than-life figures who come out of nowhere to take dramatic stands. Such portrayals imply that unique individuals, acting alone, have the greatest social impact. Yet Rosa Parks—whose refusal to give up her bus seat to a white man helped set in motion the Montgomery, Alabama, bus boycott—had a long history of social activism. As Loeb (1999) and many social researchers have found, prior to this historically important incident, Parks had spent many years helping lead the local chapter of the NAACP, and she had close links to union, church, and many other groups and social movements. Loeb (1999:37) argues that we should honor heroes such as Rosa Parks, but we should recognize that "social change is the product of deliberate, incremental action whereby we join together to try to shape a better world."

Social networks that facilitate participation in social movements are fundamental to recruitment as well (Cable 1992; Knoke and Wisely 1990). There are three kinds of networks: networks of individuals, networks of organizations, and networks of collectivities and events, according to Diani and McAdams (2003:4). Though people may recognize the benefits of joining social movements, most tend to participate out of a sense of obligation to family members, friends, and associates who already belong. Member commitment, in turn, is bolstered by a variety of group processes, such as group decision making, group discussions, and confrontations with authorities, which often enhance protesters' "commitment to the cause and their belief in the noninstitutional tactics that further the cause" (Hirsh 1990:243).

To augment their resources and gain new sources of funding and recruits, successful movement leaders—especially in professional SMOs—commonly employ a strategy called *bloc mobilization*, whereby resources are shared with other organizations with similar beliefs and goals. By sharing computer mailing lists, underdogs now have instant access to thousands or even millions of potential supporters and contributors, as well as access to political friends in high places, celebrities, and experts.

In 1975, William Gamson completed an in-depth study of 53 social movements active between 1800 and 1945. He found that several factors were related to a movement's success. First, large, bureaucratically organized movements were somewhat more successful than small, loosely organized ones. Historical conditions, such as wars and depressions, boosted social movements as well. Movements that effectively used "strategic violence" tended to fare somewhat better than their more peaceful counterparts. Of course, violence is a double-edged sword that may backfire and generate public outrage rather than support. Finally, single-issue challengers advocating minor reforms generally do much better than movements that demand significant social change (Della Porta and Diani 2006; Goldberg 1991; Schaeffer 2014).

Robert Goldberg's (1991:230) study of the Ku Klux Klan, NOW, the Berkeley free-speech movement, and five other twentieth-century movements generally supported Gamson's findings. However, Goldberg found that three interrelated variables were critical to a movement's fate: the support of powerful sponsoring groups and organizations; linking a movement's ideology to a society's core values and traditions; and a multitude of resources to overcome government attempts to silence or co-opt the movement's leadership and either make them part of the political establishment or get them to return to "normal life." Eitzen and Stewart (2007) contend that for social movements to succeed, they must also involve committed activists organized from the bottom up.

Although the forces opposed to grassroots protest and challenge are formidable, it should be obvious that some social movements, such as the Civil Rights and feminist movements, have brought significant changes to American society. Even obscure grassroots movements may generate important changes in people's lives. For example, Sherry Cable (1992:39), who studied a women's environmental protest movement in rural Kentucky, found that by assuming leadership roles, rural activists not only forced a local tannery to stop polluting local streams but also "experienced changes in their perceptions and grievances, of themselves, and of their own SMO roles." Many of the women also experienced a sense of empowerment that led to additional changes in their domestic lives.

Moreover, even movements that appear to have been crushed, such as Poland's Solidarity movement during the early 1980s, may set in motion a series of events that pave the way for significant political change. According to Piotr Sztompka (1991:156), even at its low point, when its leaders were in prison, Solidarity had already "succeeded in infusing the system with the 'logic of reform,' enlarged the scope of participation in political life, and transformed the balance of forces in political elites."

Perhaps, as Goldberg (1991) noted, the United States and other major industrial nations have become more tolerant of protest movements because they see themselves as beneficiaries of social movements and collective activities in Eastern Europe and elsewhere. Whether these movements will persist, die out, or spread to other parts of the world is uncertain, though there is plenty of evidence that democratic ideals that legitimate protest are spreading across the globe. Moreover, waves of protests, strikes, and "food riots" are becoming more common throughout the developing world as international economic competition intensifies.

Boswell and Dixon (1990) contended that in the absence of intense state repression, protests and rebellions will increase as nations modernize; income inequality and class polarization become more pronounced; and greater resources become available to the lower classes for organizing protests. Verta Taylor (2000:227) contends that the United States is becoming a "social movement society," in which grassroots protests are "routine" and serve as vital sources of community, meaning, and multicultural citizenship. There is also some evidence that protests are spreading worldwide because intervention by national elites is becoming less cost effective and more politically hazardous because of the unprecedented rise of mass anti-interventionist and human rights movements (Kowalewski 1991).

Perhaps the safest prediction for the future is to embrace the ninth wisdom of sociology. In the future, as in the past, it is wise to assume that *nothing endures but change*.

Sociological Wisdom 10

#NothingLastsForever

SUSTAINING THE PLANET

IN 2018, THE UNITED NATIONS issued a startling report on the devastating and irreversible consequences of climate change, warning that by as soon as 2040, the world will experience worsening food shortages, massive wildfires, dramatically more destructive weather changes, and a mass die-off of coral reefs (Davenport 2018). The report, compiled by an international team of distinguished scientists, was designed to warn world leaders about the catastrophic results of climate change in order to stimulate them to take positive immediate action to help sustain the planet. One would assume that all world leaders would immediately unite to take affirmative steps to address this looming crisis, but a few nations, including the United States, which dramatically altered its previous position, refused to acknowledge the reality of climate change and its resulting devastation of nature, insisting that the world could continue to rely on nonrenewable and unsustainable resources. This, however, belies the sociological wisdom that *nothing lasts forever*.

FORCES OF NATURE

Although many world leaders indeed promised to take positive action, the ink was barely dry on the report before Donald Trump, President of the United States, openly criticized its conclusions and concluded that even if the climate were changing, which he seriously doubted, there was not evidence that those changes were linked to human activities (Davenport 2018). Yet, well before the United Nations' report was issued, there was much evidence to the contrary.

In August 2005, Hurricane Katrina barreled across the coastlines of Louisiana, Mississippi, and Alabama, leaving in its wake over 1,800 people dead and over $75 billion in property damage. Entire cities disappeared; schools, hospitals, municipal buildings, supermarkets, and locally owned businesses and industries ceased operation—some never to be reopened. Thousands who were fortunate enough not to lose their lives lost their livelihoods. Hurricane Katrina and its aftermath, like most natural disasters, seemed inexplicable and unavoidable, and it was believed that certainly after such a disaster, the United States would never be caught off guard again.

In 2017, Hurricane Harvey struck the Gulf Coast, and over a four-day period deposited over 40 inches of rainfall in the Houston metropolitan area alone, tying it with Hurricane Katrina for the costliest hurricanes on record at approximately $125 billion (National Hurricane Center 2018). Although Harvey caused fewer deaths than Katrina, almost as many people were placed in rescue situations and ultimately displaced. Then came Hurricane Maria later the same year. Although the continental United States was spared, American territories, including the Virgin Islands and Puerto Rico, were severely damaged, and the death toll was significant.

Hurricanes Katrina, Harvey, and Maria exposed America's social stratification system and class differences, but these are not the only sociological lessons to be learned from such a disaster. The breached levees, flooding, looting, price gouging, and even the ferocity of the hurricanes were as much social disasters as natural ones. Moreover, the fierceness of hurricanes, frequency of tornadoes and flooding, uncontrollable wildfires, and a host of other seemingly "natural" disasters signal potentially catastrophic global consequences if governments, corporations, groups, and individuals refuse to recognize human contributions to creating the problem and their role in creating the social change necessary if the planet is to survive.

People band together in tribes, villages, towns, and cities to increase their personal safety, to have access to goods and services, and to enhance the quality of their lives. Ironically, the same forces that bring people together—population growth, urbanization, and technology—also alter the environment and may threaten the quality of life as well as life itself.

DEMOGRAPHY

Sociologists are keenly interested in *demography*, the scientific study of the size, composition, distribution, and changes in human population. These factors have far-reaching consequences, including but not limited to food and gasoline prices, likelihood of marriage and divorce, having children, type of housing, career choices, life expectancy, and quality of life (Weeks 2016:4). Demographers are interested in a number of population factors, but they concentrate on fertility, mortality, migration, and population composition and density.

Fertility is the extent of reproduction in a society. It is usually expressed as *crude birthrate*, the number of live births per year for every 1,000 people in a specific population. With this standardized formula, we can compare countries or compare birthrates in a single country over time. Demographers are also interested in *mortality*, or death. They calculate *crude death rate* as the number of deaths per year for every 1,000 people in a specific population.

Birthrates and death rates ignore the numbers of people who move from one place to another. To obtain these figures, demographers must look at *migration*, or population movement across political boundaries. Demographers calculate a *migration rate* as the number of emigrants (people leaving a country) subtracted from the number of immigrants (those entering it) per 1,000 people in the population. From a sociological viewpoint, migration rates depend on two interacting factors. *Push factors* are undesirable events or situations, such as droughts; famines; plagues; and political, economic, and social upheaval. These encourage people to leave a country for a better life elsewhere. Conversely, *pull factors* attract people. These may include enhanced economic prospects, political and religious freedom, and aesthetic and creature comfort factors such as climate, landscape, and amenities.

Demographers do not simply count people; they are also concerned about how population factors affect people's lives. The *composition of a population* refers to the numbers and types of people, classified by characteristics such as age, sex, race, and ethnicity. *Population density* describes how a population is dispersed geographically (e.g., the number of people per square mile).

One of the simplest measures of population composition is the *sex ratio*, the number of males per 100 females. In most countries, the sex ratio is below 100 because women have longer life expectancies than men. In the United States, the sex ratio is approximately 95, indicating that there are about 95 males for every 100 females.

The age composition of the population is undergoing dramatic changes. The fact that the worldwide population is becoming increasingly aged is more than an interesting demographic fact. In the United States, for example, more people are entering the over-65 age bracket, and the elderly will soon become the single largest population category. This demographic shift has created increased demands and problems related to health care, Social Security, housing, and other social issues regarding the elderly.

POPULATION GROWTH

The world's population stands at over 7.7 billion people, and it is increasing by approximately 75 million a year, with over 130 million babies born each year (Population Reference Bureau 2019). Population growth is of major concern to sociologists, because many believe that as the number of people on the planet increases, the quality of life goes down.

Population *growth rate* is the difference between the numbers of people added to and subtracted from a particular population, expressed in annual percentages. In most industrialized nations today, the population growth rate is less than 1 percent; in many developing nations it is over 3 percent. Worldwide, birthrates are declining, but the population is growing at an annual rate of approximately 1.1 percent (World Health Organization 2018).

Growth rate figures do not tell the whole story; another important measure of population growth is its *doubling time*, the number of years it takes for a population to double in size. The United States will double its current population in roughly 90 years, reaching 600 million around the end of the twenty-first century. A country with a 1 percent growth rate will double its population in approximately 70 years, and a country with a 2 percent growth rate in about 35 years. If current trends continue, over 80 countries will double their populations in 30 years or less. The world's population has doubled over the past 40 years and, at current rates, could double again in the next half-century (World Health Organization 2018).

In 1968, Paul Ehrlich, a professor of biology at Stanford University, wrote *The Population Bomb*. The book's cover depicted an infant inside a glass "bomb" with a lit fuse, and proclaimed, "While you are reading these words five people, mostly children, have died of starvation—and forty more babies have been born." Ehrlich calculated that if trends continued, in over 900 years, the earth's population would grow to 60 million billion people. This would be "about 100 persons for each square yard of the earth's surface, land and sea" (Ehrlich 2017:4). Ehrlich pointed out that world population growth has far outpaced increases in food production, and he predicted that by the 1990s, there would be thousands of deaths due to starvation and malnutrition. Ehrlich insisted that the problem is more than a matter of food production and population growth; he noted that the quality of the environment, especially the availability of clean air and water, is also an important variable.

Ehrlich offered his version of preventive checks to control population growth. His primary recommendation was the implementation of government policies to limit population growth, and he encouraged people to join *Zero Population Growth (ZPG)*, an organization dedicated to reaching the population replacement level of approximately two children per family.

Paul Ehrlich teamed with his wife, sociologist Anne Ehrlich, to write *The Population Explosion* (1990), which declared that the population bomb had been detonated. The Ehrlichs pointed out that although birthrates have declined in many industrialized nations, worldwide population growth is still out of control. Moreover, while each year brings over 100 million more mouths to be fed, there are "hundreds of billions fewer tons of topsoil and hundreds of trillions fewer gallons of groundwater" than existed in 1968, when Ehrlich sounded his initial alarm (Ehrlich and Ehrlich 1990:9).

In a later work, the Ehrlichs contended that the world's population figure of 6 billion at that time was about three times the "optimal" number and has taken, and will continue to take, a severe toll on the world's nonrenewable natural resources, the environment, and even the climate (Ehrlich and Ehrlich 2006).

The theory of demographic transition is not so bleak. *Demographic transition theory* contends that population growth develops through three distinct stages: (1) high birth and death rates, (2) high birthrates and low death rates, and (3) low birth and death rates. Demographic transition theory implies that eventually all countries will progress through all three stages. While it is far more optimistic about population growth than Ehrlich's theory, population trends portend dire consequences. In the meantime, because so many countries are caught in the demographic trap of stage 2, millions of people die of starvation and disease as population outstrips the available land, pure water, and food supplies. Nevertheless, research indicates that as these less-developed countries experience modernization, there is a general decline in birth and death rates, thus lending support to demographic transition theory (Crenshaw, Christenson, and Oakey 2000).

Benjamin Franklin estimated in 1751 that America's population was doubling approximately every 25 years. He remarked that if population expansion continued at such a high rate, "The greatest number of Englishmen will be on this side [of] the water" (Divine, Breen, Williams, Gross, and Brand 2013:96).

Accurate population data for the American colonies are difficult to ascertain; it was not until 1790 that the first systematic census was taken. Thereafter, it has been taken every 10 years. Since the first official census, which counted 3.9 million Americans, the U.S. population has expanded continuously. It grew quite rapidly at first, almost doubling by

1810 and almost tripling, to approximately 9.6 million, by 1820 (Nam and Gustavus 1976). By 1900, the U.S. population had reached 76.2 million; then growth rates dropped, reaching an all-time low during the Great Depression of the 1930s.

The years following World War II witnessed a demographic anomaly in the United States: the *baby boom*. Birthrates jumped dramatically during the late 1940s and 1950s. In 1950, the U.S. population numbered over 150 million for the first time. The *baby boomers*, the age cohort in the United States comprising those born roughly between 1945 and 1964, continue to leave an indelible mark on society as they progress through the life stages. During the late 1960s and early 1970s, demographers recorded another noticeable increase in birthrates (although smaller than the original baby boom) as the baby boomers began having children. The media dubbed this demographic event the *baby boom echo*, but by the late 1970s, birthrates had once again declined. Then came the *Millennials*, those born roughly between 1981 and 1996. Millennials surpassed Baby Boomers, becoming the largest single age cohort in the United States, consisting of approximately 83 million people.

URBANIZATION AND SUBURBANIZATION

Cities have been in existence for approximately 9,000–10,000 years, and human cultural development is directly linked to them. In fact, the word *civilization* comes from the Latin *civis*, which means "a person living in a city."

Even though much of the world's population remains rural, when human accomplishments are chronicled, it is the cities that capture the most attention. The first cities developed in the fertile valley of the Tigris and Euphrates Rivers, and cities formed along the Indus River and parts of ancient China as long as 4,000 years ago. These cities resembled overgrown villages of 5,000–10,000 people more than modern-day cities. Nevertheless, these early population centers served many of the same functions that contemporary cities do, including providing a centralized government, property rights, an expanded division of labor, and a relatively stable market for the exchange of goods and services. Important empires throughout the world were marked by the growth of cities. In ancient times, while Greek citizens lived throughout the countryside, the cities of Athens and Sparta epitomized Greek life, and they are still remembered for their contributions to Western culture. As populations have grown throughout the world, cities have increased in importance. In 1950, fewer than 30 percent of the world's population lived in cities; in the twenty-first century, that percentage has already risen to just under one-half; and the United Nations and Population Institute predict that by the year 2025, for the first time in human history, well over half (approximately 60%) of the world's population will live in cities (Knight Ridder 2006).

The rise of cities is linked to (1) agricultural improvements that reduce the number of workers needed in food production; (2) stabilization of political and economic institutions, which enhances safety and the distribution of goods and services; (3) improvements in transportation and communication, which enhance trade and social interaction among large numbers of people; and (4) the rise of industrial and postindustrial economies, which demand concentrated populations to provide labor and services. As cities grow and increase in importance, society undergoes the powerful social force of *urbanization*.

Many Americans have romantic notions of moving to the country to escape the hustle and bustle of city life, but the United States is becoming increasingly urbanized. In 1790, only about 5 percent of Americans lived in cities, and fewer than 25 cities had a population of more than 25,000. Two hundred years later, those figures had substantially changed. Over three-fourths of the U.S. population live in towns or cities, and another 20 percent live within the sphere of influence of a city. The United States clearly has experienced *urbanization*, the movement of masses of people from rural to urban areas and an increase in urban influence over all spheres of culture and society.

The U.S. Bureau of the Census continues to classify any demographic entity with a population over 2,500 as urban and any under 2,500 as rural, but these figures are almost meaningless in understanding urbanization in the United States today. Sociologists recognize that the number of people residing within the political boundaries of cities is less important than the complex communication, transportation, economic, and social networks that link people in cities and towns to those in suburbs and surrounding rural areas. Acknowledging this fact, the U.S. Bureau of the Census collects and analyzes data from *metropolitan statistical areas (MSAs)*, a city, or a city and its surrounding suburbs, with a population of 50,000 or more. The Census Bureau refers to the largest MSAs (those containing over a million people) as *consolidated metropolitan statistical areas (CMSAs)*.

From the beginning of the twentieth century through the mid-1960s, urbanization patterns reflected a steady migration from rural to urban areas. Since the mid-1960s, however, while cities have continued to grow, most migration has been into the fringe areas around major cities. The traditional concept of the city grew inadequate to describe American urbanization, and the newer term *metropolis* was coined to describe the bulging urban areas that were once cities.

A metropolis is a major urban area that includes a large central city surrounded by several smaller incorporated cities and suburbs that join to form one large recognizable municipality. The greater metropolitan area of New York City, for example, has a population of over 16 million and includes people who live in the city's five boroughs—Manhattan, the Bronx, Brooklyn, Queens, and Staten Island—as well as surrounding suburbs in Long Island and Westchester Counties and in the states of Connecticut and New Jersey. Similarly, Los Angeles has absorbed the communities of Anaheim, Beverly Hills, and several other satellite cities; today, metropolitan Los Angeles includes over nine separate cities and 60 self-governing communities. Even the Dallas/Fort Worth metroplex, which cherishes its Western tradition and rural roots, boasts a population of over 6.8 million and includes the cities of Garland,

Mesquite, Irving, Arlington, Plano, Frisco, and Las Colinas, to mention only a few, as part of its greater metropolitan area.

As major metropolitan areas have continued to absorb smaller surrounding cities, an even larger urban unit has developed. The *megalopolis* consists of two or more major metropolitan areas linked politically, economically, socially, and geographically. Along the Eastern Seaboard, a chain of hundreds of cities and suburbs now stretches from Boston through Washington, DC, to Richmond, Virginia, in an almost continuous urban sprawl. Similarly, much of Florida is almost one continuous city, from Jacksonville through Tampa to Miami. Dallas and Fort Worth, once two distinct cities 30 miles apart, are now linked by an international airport and a nearly unbroken band of businesses, industries, and suburban communities. Urban sprawl joins Chicago to Pittsburgh. Along the West Coast, a huge megalopolis stretches from San Diego through Los Angeles and up to San Francisco and Oakland, with only a few breaks. Migration patterns reflect a move from older cities in the Northeast (sometimes dubbed the rust belt because of its decaying factories) to cities in the sun belt of the South and the Southwest. In fact, over half the U.S. population growth during the 1980s and 1990s occurred in three states: California, Texas, and Florida. It is predicted that if these trends continue, even more megalopolises, or "supercities," will emerge in the Sun Belt states.

Prior to World War II, fewer than one-fifth of the U.S. population lived in *suburbs*, residential areas surrounding cities, which expand urban lifestyles into previously rural areas. By 2000, however, almost half of all Americans were classified as suburbanites. The rush to the suburbs by urban dwellers and rural residents alike can be explained by several factors. After World War II, Americans wanted to raise the families they had deferred during the Great Depression and the war—and they produced a huge baby boom and a demand for housing. The expansion of interstate highway systems, including loops around major cities, made it easier for disenchanted city dwellers to leave the congestion of the city and move into surrounding neighborhoods, from which they could easily commute to their jobs. The shortage of desirable housing in many cities, combined with rapid economic expansion and the availability of cheap land, government-subsidized loans, and moderately priced housing in outlying areas, made suburban living attractive and economically practical for working-class and middle-class families.

Another important variable was the idyllic stereotype of suburban living promoted by the media. According to television, motion pictures, and popular magazines, the suburbs provided all the amenities of urban life yet were far enough from the central city that people could avoid the hassles and problems of the city.

Perhaps the greatest problem facing major cities is generating enough revenue to provide adequate services and protection for their residents. Suburban growth exacerbated the financial woes of many cities, because urban dwellers who leave the city limits reduce the city's property tax base but still demand services. Most cities raise taxes to compensate for shrinking revenues, but tax increases encourage more residents and businesses to flee the city and locate in the surrounding suburbs.

Urban decay hits the central city as major businesses move from the downtown area to more profitable suburban locations. Old buildings often remain vacant and deteriorate or become multiple-unit slum housing, low-rent hotels, "adult" bookstores and theaters, centers for drug distribution and other criminal activities, and repositories for the urban homeless.

Poverty is accompanied by other urban problems, especially chronic unemployment, homelessness, violent crimes, alcohol and drug abuse, suicide, terrorism, and other forms of deviance. The number of homeless is almost impossible to determine. Although estimates vary from 500,000 to over 3.5 million, today, most agree that this may be a conservative estimate, with some studies estimating that approximately 5 million people, almost one-third of them children, are likely to experience homelessness in a given year (National Law Center on Homelessness and Poverty 2015).

There have been numerous attempts to revitalize central cities. During the 1950s and 1960s, federal funding assisted many cities in urban renewal projects intended to clean up inner cities. Most of these projects involved razing dilapidated buildings and replacing them with modern high-rise office buildings and apartment complexes. Though these efforts seemed successful, they rarely solved the problems of inner-city decay. The street people, drug dealers, and prostitutes who had inhabited those areas did not disappear—either they were displaced to other parts of the cities, or they vanished during the daytime and reappeared after dark.

In their effort to eliminate urban blight, city planners often ignored the fact that many inner-city areas provided an important ecological niche for minorities, who had created their own cities in the form of ethnic enclaves. The razing of old tenement buildings and shops meant the destruction of meaningful social networks and communities that were "home" to thousands of urban residents.

Urban distress is one of the most perplexing and challenging problems that city officials and residents face. A number of cities that attempted revitalization in the 1980s were heralded as "success stories" in the 1990s, but based on objective indicators of the economic and social well-being of their residents, with the possible exception of Atlanta, Baltimore, and Boston, there is no evidence that these cities have performed any better than other cities with similar problems that did not undergo revitalization. In fact, in some cases, the so-called revitalized cities have performed even worse (Wolman, Ford III, and Hill 1994).

Urban sociologists, as well as architectural historians and other experts on cities, contend that revitalization of a city requires far more than simply the beautification and regentrification of its streets and buildings. Rather, for cities to be socially viable, they must not only have a solid infrastructure that meets all of the economic and political needs of their inhabitants, but they must also be able to take on an important sense of *place* in the hearts and souls of those who live there (Hutchison, Gottdiener, and Ryan 2015; Jacobs 1992; Rykwert 2000).

The suburbs—once viewed as the great escape from the cities—are not immune to problems associated with urban living. As increasing numbers of people flee the cities, suburban areas are running out of affordable housing, and many building sites originally designated for single-family dwellings now contain apartment complexes and condominiums. Multiple-unit housing brings the traffic and noise associated with urban living. Moreover, as more members of racial and ethnic minorities move to the suburbs, once-homogeneous neighborhoods are encountering racial strife and religious controversies.

Real estate speculation, accompanied by the recession of the 1980s and the economic crisis of 2008–2009, resulted in the bankruptcy and closing of some large suburban shopping malls. Some suburban commercial districts mirror the urban decay of the central city. Mortgage foreclosures also hit suburban areas fairly hard. Suburban crime rates have increased, especially the rates of property crimes, such as burglary and vandalism. Many suburban neighborhoods grew up around small municipalities outside the main city, and their police forces and volunteer fire departments are ill equipped to handle the burgeoning growth of the suburbs. Likewise, many suburban schools are woefully overcrowded; their small tax base cannot support rapid enrollment growth.

ECOLOGY AND THE ENVIRONMENT

Sociologists' interest in cities began with the inception of the discipline, but in 1929, Pitirim Sorokin and Carle Zimmerman (1929) identified the need for a specialty within general sociology to study cities. They created *urban sociology*, a subdivision of sociology that identifies, studies, and explains the specific traits of urban social phenomena. Even before the creation of urban sociology, however, sociologists compared and contrasted rural and urban societies.

Ferdinand Toennies developed a theoretical continuum to analyze the differences between rural and urban living. At one pole is *Gemeinschaft*, a community characterized by a relatively small population, a simple division of labor, face-to-face interaction, and informal social control. At the other end is *Gesellschaft*, a society made up of a large population characterized by loose associations, a complex division of labor, secondary relationships, and formal social control. According to Toennies ([1887] 1961), *Gemeinschaft* communities share a strong sense of community, common values, and a commitment to strive for the common good. Cities, on the other hand, tend to be *Gesellschaft* communities and more heterogeneous in values, with much less emphasis on common goals. Toennies's ideas influenced Durkheim and other

European sociologists who sought to understand the social experiences of people undergoing the rapid industrialization that accompanied the Industrial Revolution.

Émile Durkheim ([1893] 1964) made a similar distinction between rural and urban societies, but he focused on social solidarity, or the extent to which members of a society are bound together. He believed that a society's social solidarity was based on its level of division of labor. In predominantly rural societies, where there is very little division of labor, people are bound together through *mechanical solidarity*, characterized by tradition, unity, consensus of norms and values, and strong informal pressure to conform. Durkheim contrasted this with highly diverse urban areas, where people are bound by *organic solidarity*, characterized by a highly sophisticated division of labor that makes individuals interdependent with one another. Both Toennies' and Durkheim's ideas provided a theoretical foundation for urban and rural sociology in the United States.

Urban studies in the United States gained momentum during the 1920s and 1930s and became closely identified with *human ecology*, a subfield of sociology that focuses on recurring spatial, social, and cultural patterns within a particular social environment—in this case, cities. Human ecologists view a city as an *ecosystem*, a community of organisms sharing the same physical environment. Spatial relations are the analytical basis for human ecology, which focuses on the physical shape of cities, the economic and social relations between cities, and social relations and interactions. The study of human ecology became synonymous with the Chicago School of sociology. Its founders and early proponents developed theories and applied them to urban studies, especially within their local sociological laboratory: the city of Chicago.

The founder of the Chicago School of human ecology was Robert Ezra Park (1916), who joined the Department of Sociology and Anthropology at the University of Chicago in 1914 and established a research agenda that dominated urban studies for decades. An influential work associated with the Chicago School was an essay by Louis Wirth entitled "Urbanism as a Way of Life." Wirth (1938) asserted that rather than being a simple reflection of a shift from rural to urban residency patterns, *urbanism* entailed a way of life in which the city affects how people feel, think, and interact. Urbanization refers to an increase in the proportion of people living in cities; *urbanism* reflects changes in attitudes, values, and lifestyles resulting from urbanization. According to Wirth, urbanism affects people negatively because the city's large size, high population density, and great heterogeneity lead to impersonality, anonymity, and such individual problems as loneliness, alcoholism, and suicide.

Ernest Burgess, a sociologist at the University of Chicago, was interested in how the ecological arrangement of cities affects the economic resources of groups and individuals and the degree to which people can profitably use urban space. He noticed that land use influences residential patterns and segregation based on race, social class, and other characteristics of people and places of business. According to Burgess's (1925) *concentric zone model*, cities develop in a series of zones represented by concentric circles radiating out from the central business district. Zone 1 is the central business district—the heart of the city and the center of distribution of goods and services; it is the location of important businesses, financial institutions, and retail outlets. Zone 2 is the zone of transition because it is subject to rapid social change. In many major cities, this area has been where immigrants first settled and established urban enclaves, such as a Chinatown or Little Italy. Zone 2 often reflects the cultures of numerous foreign countries, and as a result of the marginality experienced by many of its inhabitants, it is characterized by high rates of delinquency, crime, alcoholism, drug abuse, suicide, and other forms of deviant behavior. Factories also often locate in and around zone 2, adding increased rail and truck traffic, more transients, and pollution. The zone of transition is marked by urban decay, in part because speculators and absentee landlords who own the land and buildings there do not invest in their maintenance.

Factory workers and other blue-collar laborers live in zone 3, which contains residential hotels, apartments, trailer parks, and other working-class housing. As immigrants become assimilated, find jobs, and can afford permanent housing, they often move into zone 3.

Zone 4 is a middle-class and upper-class residential area. Since World War II, people living in zone 4 have found it inconvenient and undesirable to drive downtown to shop, bank, and receive necessary services, so branch banks, shopping malls, medical clinics, hospitals, and other services have sprung up in and around zone 4.

Zone 5 is a commuter zone, where people live in suburban areas or smaller incorporated towns far enough away to avoid the undesirable elements of the city (e.g., crime and drugs), yet close enough to enjoy its amenities (e.g., theater, professional sports, and necessary goods and services) as well as to commute to their places of work.

Burgess's ecological model provided sociological insight into urban development. Since then, other urban sociologists have offered models they believe more accurately illustrate the process. According to Homer Hoyt (1939), the center of the city develops in much the way Burgess described. But Hoyt proposed that cities grow outward in several wedge-shaped sectors, each reflecting different land uses and the congregation of fairly homogeneous populations based on race, ethnicity, and social class. Hoyt contended that suburban middle-class housing is not likely to develop next to inner-city ghettos, but instead develops outward from lower-middle-class housing areas. Likewise, after these middle-class neighborhoods have developed, wealthier suburban housing often develops adjacent to them. Factories and other forms of industry are not allowed to locate in these housing areas and therefore develop in another sector, usually along major arteries of transportation such as major highways and railroad lines.

C. D. Harris and Edward Ullman (1945) offered yet another explanation of urban development with their multiple-nuclei model. According to their model, cities evolve from several nuclei that shape the character and structure of the areas surrounding them. For example, the central business district serves as one important nucleus while a college or university across town serves as another. If the community has a prison, it may serve as another distinct nucleus for development, and a major manufacturing plant would provide the nucleus for yet another area. The models proposed by Burgess, Hoyt, and Harris and Ullman are just that: models representing ideal types. They may or may not accurately describe the specific developmental patterns of actual cities. Nevertheless, they provide important sociological insight into how spatial relationships and different land uses affect population patterns and social life.

Human ecologists also apply the *ecological perspective* to how urban development affects the environment. The *ecological perspective* provides a theoretical model for analyzing the interdependence between human beings and the physical environment. In the case of human society, two of the most important ecological factors are growth in population and our ability to alter the environment through technology.

As human populations grow, we alter our physical environment in order to obtain sufficient food and shelter. In the United States alone, billions of acres of land once covered with trees, grasses, flowers, marshes, and streams have been covered with asphalt, concrete, steel, wood, and glass to build cities and residential areas and to create millions of miles of highways. Moreover, worldwide, there is mounting evidence that population growth is the most significant cause of environmental damage, ranging from topsoil loss and diminishing water supply to *global climate change* (Nierenberg 2003; Robbins, Hintz, and Moore 2014).

In many developing nations trapped in stage 2 of demographic transition, overpopulation threatens to bring about widespread starvation and millions of deaths. As population increases and urban areas expand, farmers are forced onto marginal lands. They may burn forests to grow crops or raise cattle, or may cut down the trees for fuel. Either way, deforestation often leads to overcultivation and soil erosion. Moreover, larger populations demand not only more food and wood but also more petroleum and other fossil fuels, electricity, water, and other scarce commodities. Although some argue that human ingenuity has enabled the earth to sustain more people at higher living standards than ever before, others insist that we have missed numerous opportunities to confront the problems of overpopulation, food scarcity, renewable energy, and related issues that will continue to plague us during the twenty-first century (Brown 2009; Brown, Larsen, Roney, and Adams 2015).

One of the consequences of overpopulation is the depletion of natural resources. Worldwide, population growth and urbanization have led to problems of deforestation, desertification, and the extinction of many species of plants and wildlife.

Forestland around the globe is being destroyed at a rate of 1 acre per second, and tropical forests are shrinking by 14 million hectares per year (Brown 2009; Gore 1992, 2007). In North America, deforestation results from massive logging operations to provide lumber for housing and pulp for paper; in tropical rainforest areas, it often follows the burning of trees to clear land for crops and animals. Overgrazing, deforestation, and agricultural mismanagement account for almost three-fourths of the damage to the world's soil. And the burning of tropical rainforests may contribute as much as 10 percent of the global greenhouse buildup (Spillsbury 2009; Worldwatch Institute 2014, 2017).

One side effect of the depletion of tree cover and other plants is accelerated soil erosion, resulting in an estimated loss of 26 billion tons of topsoil per year (Schlissel 2009). The U.S. Department of Agriculture discovered in the early 1980s that American farmers were losing 3.1 billion tons of topsoil annually to wind and water erosion, and that for every ton of grain produced, 6 tons of topsoil were lost (Brown, Renner, and Flavin 2009b). Soil mismanagement has also contributed to desertification in many parts of the globe—most noticeably in Sub-Saharan Africa.

Desertification, the creation of a desert in what was once arable land can be partially attributed to the loss of fresh groundwater and the destruction of natural lakes. As overpopulation and expanded use of agricultural irrigation increase the demand for fresh water, water tables are falling at a rate of 20 meters per year. Some natural aquifers are being drained at a rate faster than the water can be replaced (Brown 2006; Worldwatch Institute 2017).

As human population expands, more than half the world's population of other primates is declining (McGavin 2007; Tuxill 1997). Humans' greatest impact on other species, especially other primates, is the alteration of their natural environments for our use. As a consequence, species are becoming extinct at a rate 1,000 times greater than the pace that has prevailed since prehistory; it is predicted that over the next three decades, *every day,* humans will drive 100 species into extinction.

Many distinguished ecologists, such as E. O. Wilson and Norman Myers, are concerned that entire ecosystems are being destroyed (Brown, Flavin, and French 2009; Brown, Renner, and Flavin 2009; Diamond 1990; Linden 1989). Whereas prior periods of extinction were caused by natural disasters such as meteors, earthquakes, or massive floods, the current trend of extinction is almost exclusively caused by humans (McGavin 2007).

Pollution now affects almost every aspect of life. Its most serious manifestations affect the three major givers of life: water, air, and land. The three major sources of water pollution are domestic wastewater, industrial discharges, and agricultural runoff. Urbanization creates a heavy concentration of human waste, which is discharged into sewage systems that empty into nearby bodies of water. Unfortunately, other municipalities downstream rely on those same bodies of water for their major supply of drinking water. Even small amounts of pollutants from paper, chemical, petrochemical, refining, textile, and metalworking industries can be toxic when they are discharged into freshwater supplies. Despite strict regulations and heavy fines, illegal disposal of toxic waste is second in profits only to trafficking in illegal drugs in the United States.

Each year, millions of gallons of petroleum, industrial chemicals, and other toxic substances are either intentionally dumped or accidentally spilled into the world's oceans. One of the most alarming and highly publicized disasters occurred in 1989, when the *Exxon Valdez* oil tanker ran aground, split its hull, and dumped millions of gallons of oil into the pristine waters of Prince William Sound in Alaska. Several years and billions of dollars later, cleanup efforts were still under way, and both plants and wildlife in the area were still suffering repercussions of the spill. The *Exxon Valdez* and other tanker accidents pale in comparison with the intentional dumping of billions of gallons of oil each year during tank cleaning, ballasting, and other routine tanker operations (World Resources Institute 2018). Another major disaster involved the Deepwater Horizon explosion in 2010, which pumped millions of gallons of oil into the Gulf of Mexico and became the subject of a major motion picture that brought worldwide attention to the risks associated with offshore drilling. Meanwhile, an oil leak in the gulf that began six years earlier, the Taylor Oil Spill, continues to this day to spew oil into the ocean at an alarming rate, threatening to surpass the cumulative amount of the Exxon Valdiz and Deepwater Horizon disasters combined

(Willingham 2018). Clean, fresh water is becoming scarcer around the world—a problem that could cause global food prices to soar in the future (Johnson 2000). The United Nations projects that up to 7 billion people in 60 countries will face water scarcity in the next half century (Sawin 2003).

Los Angeles smog has provided material for comedians for decades, but the worldwide problem of urban air pollution is generating very few laughs. Mexico City, one of the largest and most beautiful cities in the world, is almost permanently enveloped in a haze of smog. And at the 2008 Olympics in Beijing, as well as the 2012 Olympics in London, contestants in outdoor events had to battle air pollution in addition to other competitors (AP Beijing 2008; Vaughn 2012). The 2016 Olympics held in exotic Rio de Janeiro experienced so much air and water pollution that some event venues had to be moved, and others were boycotted by some countries fearing for their athletes' health and safety (Brooks and Barchfield 2015).

Emissions of lead, sulfur dioxide, and nitrogen oxides produce air pollution that is aesthetically displeasing as well as threatening to human health. These pollutants are most heavily concentrated in urban areas and have been directly linked to lung damage and respiratory diseases. Moreover, they pose a significant environmental threat because they contain acids that help form acid rain, which is altering the chemistry of streams, rivers, and lakes and has caused irreparable damage to crops and forests (World Resources Institute 2018).

By the end of the 1980s, the United States was producing over 178 million metric tons of municipal waste per year and facing a major problem of waste disposal. The Environmental Protection Agency estimates that one-third to one-half of America's landfills are already full. Another problem is the type of waste materials produced, many of which are not biodegradable. Paper, cardboard, and wood products can be burned, or if buried, they eventually break down into natural elements. Petroleum products, plastics, Styrofoam, and other synthetic materials pose new environmental dilemmas. If burned, they emit toxic gases; if buried, they lie intact beneath the earth's surface for hundreds of years because they are not biodegradable.

In an effort to meet energy needs and decrease dependence on fossil fuels, several nuclear reactors have been brought online since the early 1970s, creating a new environmental and human problem. Fear associated with nuclear energy was underscored in the United States in 1979 when a problem at the Three Mile Island reactor in Pennsylvania forced its closure and the evacuation of nearby areas. Although officials reassured the public that the problem was minor and the plant had never approached a "meltdown," the incident highlighted the potential threat of a nuclear catastrophe. In 1986, the threat of a massive nuclear disaster was realized when the Chernobyl nuclear plant in Ukraine experienced a core meltdown. The North American continent had another scare in December 1994, when Canada's oldest nuclear reactor, the Pickering Nuclear Power Plant near Toronto, experienced an "incident" causing it to be shut down. In 1995, Japan's Monju plant experienced a major accident during start-up testing; in 2007, an earthquake damaged and forced the closure of a nuclear power plant in Kashiwazaki, Japan (Talmadge 2007).

As of January 2015, 30 countries worldwide were operating 437 nuclear reactors for electricity generation (100 of them in the United States), and 71 new nuclear plants were under construction in 15 countries (Nuclear Energy Institute 2015). Nuclear reactors pose a hazardous waste problem even when plants operate safely and efficiently. Radioactive waste was once sealed in lead containers and dumped miles out into the ocean, but nature reminded us that the earth is a giant ecosystem: some of the sealed canisters drifted ashore.

Remote desert areas in Nevada—near nuclear bomb test sites—have become a popular dumpsite for nuclear waste, but Nevada residents and government officials are beginning to fight such practices. Some people have proposed that radioactive waste be launched into outer space or dumped in the oceans, but scientists reminded public officials that the earth is part of a large ecosystem, and when it comes to nuclear waste, "out of sight" should not mean "out of mind." Much of the material we launch into space finds its way back to earth as debris.

Damage to the earth's ozone layer has received increasing attention since the mid-1970s. This layer is a band of ozone molecules in the stratosphere 10–30 miles from the earth's surface; it filters out the sun's most dangerous rays. In 1985, researchers reported the existence of a large hole in the ozone layer over Antarctica, where as much as 50 percent of the ozone had been depleted. Scientists warn that the hole is spreading, and today ozone damage is detectable over populated and agricultural areas. The results could be devastating for human, plant, and animal life. Damage to the ozone layer allows more ultraviolet radiation from the sun to reach the earth's surface. Ultraviolet light has been linked to sunburn, skin cancer, cataracts, and damage to the immune system as well as increased carbon dioxide production, which may contribute to *global climate change*, more often referred to as *global warming*, an increase in the earth's overall average temperature because of a greenhouse effect produced by increased exposure to ultraviolet light (Brown et al. 2009; World Resources Institute 2018; Worldwatch Institute 2017). In 2005, the nonprofit World Resources Institute found, in agreement with a report on global warming authored by 600 scientists, that most scientists believe that the world has gone past a dangerous tipping point in global warming, and pointed out that perhaps the concept should instead be called *global climate change* because the overall warming contributes to other climate changes, including harsher winters (Begley 2007; World Resources Institute 2018; Zabarenko 2006). The United Nations (2018) report stated in no uncertain terms that the most prominent threat to human survival is global climate change.

WHERE DO WE GO FROM HERE?

With today's widespread access to the social media, environmental activists have established a multitude of websites where environmental causes and concerns are defined and discussed, and information is given on how to become involved in environmentalist organizations and contemporary ecological social movements.

Al Gore championed environmental causes during the 2000 presidential campaign, as did Green Party candidate Ralph Nader in 2000, 2004, and 2008. When George W. Bush was elected president and Dick Cheney vice president, both with strong ties to the oil business, environmentalists feared this was a major step backward. Despite assurances from Bush's director of the Environmental Protection Agency that the administration was very concerned about the environment, decisions to rescind some of the restrictions on drilling for oil on protected lands and easing some of the restrictions on various pollutants confirmed many of the environmentalists' fears. In 2006, Al Gore's documentary *An Inconvenient Truth* raised international awareness of the problems of global warning. Barack Obama's election signaled a change in federal approaches to ecological issues, and environmentalists were heartened when he signed the International Treaty on Global Warming (Kyoto Protocol) during the first year of his presidency and vetoed legislation on the Keystone Pipeline during his second term. The election of Donald Trump in 2016, however, dealt a severe blow to environmentalists, as he outspokenly denied climate change; pulled the United States out of the International Treaty on Global Warming; reversed many of the environmental regulations established by the Obama administration; and appointed cabinet members, including the Director of the EPA who favored elimination of the Environmental Protection Agency.

The United Nations Population Division predicts that by 2050, world population will increase to about 9.2 billion people (United Nations 2017). More disturbingly, whereas the United Nations earlier predicted that the world population would stabilize at around 10 billion, it has revised its estimate to closer to 11 billion, or even as high as 14 billion. These projections have prompted concerns that overpopulation and scarcity of food and pure water are the principal threats to the planet's future (Brown 2006; Brown et al. 2009; Block 2015).

Urban sociologists predict that the United States will continue to see an increase in suburban development around large metropolitan areas. Thus, although the population of some major cities may decline, increased suburbanization around those cities may perpetuate their importance. And although some argue that urbanization and even suburbanization are slowing, most sociologists believe they will continue to dominate American life as well as life on other continents (Pieterse 2009; Parnell and Pieterse 2014).

Worldwide urbanization is predicted to grow at unprecedented rates. In mid-2006, the United Nations issued a report announcing that by 2007, for the first time in world history, more people would live in cities than in rural areas, and predicted that by 2030, over 62 percent of the world's population would be urban. The majority of urban growth and new "megacities" (populations of 10 million or more) will be in poverty-stricken developing nations least equipped to deal with them (Knight Ridder 2006; Parnell and Pieterse 2014).

A major concern for the future is the impact that the increased population and concentration of people in cities and suburbs will have on the environment. For the first time in our existence, our lifestyle may threaten the existence of life on the planet (Davenport 2018; United Nations 2018; Worldwatch Institute 2014, 2017).

Although not everyone is this pessimistic, Katsuhide Kitatani, deputy executive director of the United Nations Population Fund, noted that developing countries now produce one-third of the world's carbon dioxide and one-sixth of the world's chlorofluorocarbons (CFCs). By the year 2025, these countries could raise their share to two-thirds of a much higher level of carbon dioxides and more than one-third of a dangerously high level of CFCs. Moreover, some wildlife conservationists believe that more than half of all existing species will be extinct or endangered by the middle of the twenty-first century (Brown 2006; Brown et al. 2009; Diamond 1990; Easton 2018).

These projections emphasize the need for environmental education and resocialization toward an ecological perspective on human life. Environmental problems have renewed interest in the study of demography and ecology, which led one sociologist to contend that ecological demography, a combination of the two subfields, might become the most important paradigm in sociology (Namboodiri 1988)—something that has not come to pass. Scientists around the world are experimenting with methods to reduce the depletion of natural resources, find alternatives to chemical fertilizers and pesticides, halt the process of global warming, recycle waste, protect the ozone layer, and slow the extinction of species. Additionally, the global institutionalization of the principle that nation-states are responsible for environmental protection is bringing about an increase in national activities and policies to protect the natural environment (Frank, Hironaka, and Schofer 2000). Although sociological wisdom tells us *nothing lasts forever*, the very survival of humankind may depend on our ability to sustain the planet.

A Final Note

#SociologicalWisdomOnlyHasValueIfItIsApplied

IN 1906, AMERICAN SOCIOLOGIST Lester Frank Ward distinguished between *pure sociology*, research and understanding for the sake of knowledge, and *applied sociology*, research and understanding in order to improve society and the world in which we live. Although the distinction is often blurred, and the two endeavors are to some extent inherently linked, academic and philosophical arguments over the role of sociology continue to this day. Sociology suffers from many of the same misconceptions as other liberal arts disciplines such as anthropology, philosophy, art history, and several others. Although considered to be intellectually interesting, they are viewed by many as being arcane "navel-gazing" pursuits with little or no practical application. Television sitcoms and stand-up comedians joke that college students with majors in sociology will graduate only to face chronic unemployment. In real life, many parents who sent their children off to universities in hopes of them becoming doctors, lawyers, or accountants are chagrined to learn their hard-earned tuition money is being "wasted" on degrees in the social sciences or humanities. Declining enrollments in some sociology departments may seem to buttress the idea that there is little need for *sociological* wisdom in today's world. But once again, we invoke the first wisdom of sociology that *things are not what they seem*, and then quickly add, *wisdom only has value if it is applied*. One reason that the number of sociology majors is declining is actually due to the *success* and practicality of the discipline, rather than its failure. A number of areas of study that originally were subdisciplines of sociology have proven to be so popular and in demand that they have evolved into full-fledged disciplines, college majors, and careers of their own. Just a partial list of these academic areas and careers include the following:

1. American Studies
2. Criminal Justice
3. Criminology
4. Demography
5. Gerontology
6. Global Studies
7. Juvenile Justice
8. Social Psychology
9. Social Work
10. Urban Studies

Consequently, although the number of sociology majors may be declining in some cases, the number of academic disciplines, majors, and career fields that sociology spawned and that require sociological wisdom are increasing.

University professors are sometimes tongue-tied regarding how to answer when confronted with the question "What can I do with a degree in sociology?" The most simple and accurate answer is "Almost anything and everything." The need for sociological wisdom has never been more obvious or paramount than it is today. Moreover, the knowledge and wisdom generated by sociological research and theories are driving some of the most in-demand careers and professions in the United States and around the world today. That may seem like a pretty bold claim, but take a look at some of the topics covered in this book and how the wisdom gained from studying them sociologically can be applied.

"Students who major in these subjects have a 7% less chance of moving back in with their parents after graduation."

We introduced the discipline of sociology and emphasized its first wisdom as being: *things are not what they seem*. Has there ever been a time in human history when that admonition has been more accurate and more important to understand? In an age when science and technology are at their ultimate heights, many people deny scientific findings and are turning to myths, folklore, conspiracy theories, fear, bigotry, and propaganda as opposed to facts, logic, reason, and truth for resolution of serious personal and social issues. On a daily basis, social media, traditional media, and even government officials, bombard us with so-called "alternative facts," figures, and statistics manufactured to promote a particular ideology or potential public policy. A sociological imagination and the critical thinking demanded by sociology is more important than ever for sorting through the information overload to which we are exposed.

The second wisdom of sociology tells us that we should *analyze with our brain and not with our hearts*. Although people's emotions, feelings, and beliefs are important, and shape the way in which they view the world and their lives, this does not reduce the importance of realizing that we also live in a world where facts matter. Émile Durkheim was one of the first among many sociologists who emphasized that the only way to meaningfully understand the world in which we live was to study *social facts*. Max Weber, with his concept of *verstehen*, emphasized that although we all interpret human behavior and our social world from a subjective viewpoint, we must recognize that truth and seek to distance ourselves from our personal biases in order to study and understand society and human behavior. We described some of the most common quantitative and qualitative research methods by which sociological wisdom is gained today. Knowledge and application of these research skills are in high demand not only in the social sciences, but also in business, industry, and governments. Lucrative careers are available in areas utilizing survey research, content analysis, and evaluation research as private businesses, multinational corporations, political parties, and governments attempt to assess the effectiveness of advertising and marketing campaigns, training programs, human resources policies, and government programs. Careers in the profitable fields of advertising and marketing apply research findings from sociology and social psychology to identify values and social variables that motivate human behavior, particularly in terms of purchasing behavior. On a personal level, being able to distinguish between fact and opinion, truth and expediency, rational reasoning and emotional rationalizing are critical thinking skills that can prevent us from being victims of scams, crimes, and being taken advantage of by unscrupulous individuals, groups, and others.

The third wisdom of sociology teaches us that despite elitist arguments to the contrary, *there is no such thing as an uncultured person*. Everybody has culture, and virtually all human behavior is motivated and influenced by cultural values, norms, beliefs, and traditions. Ethnocentrism sometimes causes people to judge other cultures as not only different but inferior, and in some cases people assume those whose culture is dramatically different from their own, are "uncultured" or have no culture at all. Understanding society and culture as well as the importance of cultural diversity is as important today, if not more so, than at any other time in history. Popular culture is a driving force behind multimillion- and multibillion-dollar industries in entertainment, sports, and social media, to name but a few. At a time when globalization as well as cultural exchange are in full swing, and nation states are more interconnected and interdependent than ever before, many countries, including Western Europe and the United States, are experiencing an unprecedented rise in nationalism, isolationism, separatism, chauvinism, and ethnocentrism. Basic cultural values surrounding freedom, equality, and civility are being questioned and undermined as the norms they represent and produce are being challenged, threatened, destroyed, and redefined on a daily if not hourly basis. Refugees and immigrants, once encouraged and welcomed in democratic societies, are now being refused entry and asylum while also being blamed for preexisting domestic social problems such as poverty, drugs, crimes, and violence. Sociological studies and analysis routinely show that these social issues are deeply ingrained in social structures and policies intended to maintain the status quo and resist cultural and social change.

The fourth sociological wisdom tells us that people are not born with culture, but must learn and internalize it through the process of socialization. More importantly, *when you were born, you were not yet you.* People are not born with personalities making them innately good or evil, civil or uncivil, friendly or unfriendly, confident or timid, but must be taught all of these qualities. Similarly we are taught and must learn how and whom to love, hate, envy, resent, admire, and fear as well as when, where, and why any or all of these emotions may be appropriate or forbidden. Developing social selves is a complex process that begins at birth and continues throughout the entire life course. Our family, schools, churches, peers, and other social institutions and entities all help shape who we are and what we become. In short, they make us who we are. The results of socialization shape and affect our interactions in everyday life in countless mundane and yet important ways.

The fifth sociological wisdom teaches us that individuals must learn that we are not the center of the universe and that *the world revolves around the sun and not us.* In order for an act to be "social," requires that we take others into account before, during, and after interacting with them. We first take into account significant others, but in order to become truly social, we must also be aware of the significance of generalized others. Everybody occupies various social statuses, with accompanying roles that shape and influence who we are and what we do, as well as how and why we do it. Social media and technology have altered and expanded people's social networks exponentially and simultaneously substantially increased the number of people with whom we interact on a daily basis, while somewhat decreasing, or at least changing, the number and nature of intimate relationships experienced.

Sociological wisdom teaches us that despite all our efforts to organize and control it, *the world is a messy place*. Much of our everyday lives and the social structure that impacts them is taken for granted, but the sixth sociological wisdom reveals that we must actively form the groups, organizations, and bureaucracies that we enjoy, appreciate, and take for granted because they organize the world around us and make our lives easier. Conversely, we sometimes curse and resent these same groups, organizations, and bureaucracies because they may complicate our lives and frustrate us with their inefficiency and impersonal response to our personal needs. Understanding this paradox can be invaluable as we interact with these groups, organizations, and bureaucracies on a daily basis. Better understanding of how primary and secondary groups form and work can be beneficial in dealing with family members, classmates, fellow workers, bosses, and those who report to us. Additionally, although technology makes it easier to deal with the DMV, IRS, telephone carriers, and other organizations and bureaucracies, there are still many situations in which we need to interact with real human beings in order to successfully complete a transaction or correct a problem. A fundamental understanding of how these organizations work (and don't work), as well as of the potential power and simultaneous limitations of those with whom we are dealing, can often determine whether our interaction with representatives goes smoothly or terribly awry.

Every society makes rules for living, and the members of every society soon learn that *some rules are made to be broken, but some aren't*. Societal members individually and collectively decide how much leeway they will afford their fellow citizens in regard to their thoughts, actions, and behaviors, determining what is considered deviant and what is not. Sociological wisdom teaches us this range of tolerance varies, by age, race, ethnicity, sex, gender, and social class, and can increase or decrease at a moment's notice. Although sociological wisdom also teaches us that people of all different social categories have far more in common with one another than things that are different, many people seem to fixate on those differences, no matter how minor or inconsequential, until they become significant, resulting in prejudice, discrimination, and inequality.

This understanding leads us to the eighth wisdom of sociology: *the only difference that matters is the difference that matters*. The United States, and many other Western democracies, emphasize values such as freedom, equality, justice, and fairness. Yet those same societies from their inception have limited the freedoms of various categories of people based on their differences and treated some people as being "more equal" than others. Similarly, justice and fairness are not only relative terms but are subjectively defined. Those in power have always been able to determine what is "just" and "fair" while those with limited or virtually no power have been required to submit to those in positions of power and authority. What is the practical application of this sociological wisdom? Rather than whining and complaining about life being unfair, armed with this wisdom, we can acknowledge the inequalities and unfairness and adjust our expectations accordingly and work to make society more just and fair. Despite well-meaning parents, teachers, and self-help gurus, we sometimes must acknowledge the fact that we may not be able to be or do anything we want to be or do, simply because we want it badly enough. Some differences matter. Physical, mental, and social situations place limitations on our opportunities, and sometimes we cannot do or be anything we want, no matter how badly we want it. Those differences sometimes matter. This knowledge, however, also motivates and allows us to address some of life's inequities in order to remove unnecessary and unfair restrictions on some people in order to make life more fair and just, if possible. If people are being discriminated against or treated unfairly because of differences that do not matter, we are morally and socially obligated to help remove those barriers. Whatever progress has been gained regarding racism, sexism, and ageism, was not made by pretending it did not exist or by throwing up hands and declaring that nothing could be done about it. Social reform is a result of a combination of social awareness, social cohesion, and social action. Abolition of slavery, women's suffrage, and the removal of age barriers in employment were all results of increased social awareness and hard-fought battles by individuals who formed groups and mobilized organizations in order to bring about social change. This leads to the importance of another sociological wisdom.

Sociological wisdom also reveals that *nothing endures but change*. The only real constant to the seemingly rigid social structure and social inertia experienced by most societies is that virtually all things inevitably will change. Some change is evolutionary, developing slowly and culminating over a long period of time in gradual increments, and is barely noticeable by many. Other change is revolutionary in nature, seeming to take place overnight, and is overwhelming to some, and initially unacceptable and threatening to many. Nevertheless, sociological wisdom provides us with the tools necessary to adapt, repair, cope, and carry on. In today's world, where many seek to ignore or reverse the effects of globalization, bury their heads in the sand, and retreat to isolationism and nationalism, sociological wisdom can prepare us to adapt to this process, embrace globalization and diversity, and recognize the tremendous potential of different societies and cultures around the world cooperating to create stable governments, economies, and sustainable living conditions. Which brings us to another sociological wisdom.

Nothing lasts forever. Perhaps one of humankind's greatest and gravest follies has been the notion that humans can overcome or control the laws and forces of nature, and that the earth's bounty of natural resources is infinite. All species are genetically programmed to reproduce, but humans seem to be one of the few that think they can do so indiscriminately without potentially dire consequences. For several centuries the increase in human population primarily brought about positive results as critical masses of people were necessary to create tribes, build communities, develop cities, and create safe and sustainable living environments. In portions of the globe, however, uncontrolled population growth accompanied by indiscriminate foraging of finite natural resources has led to dangerous levels of depletion of potable water, deforestation, extinction of species, and potentially disastrous climate change. Those who continue to ignore these developments threaten to severely decrease, and potentially eliminate, life on this planet as we know it. Those applying this sociological wisdom are working diligently at limiting needless devastation of nature, developing sustainable resources, and encouraging values, norms, and lifestyles compatible with future adaptation to both natural and social changes that will inevitably occur.

Back to the premise we presented earlier that sociology suffers from many of the same misconceptions that haunt other liberal arts disciplines such as anthropology, philosophy, art history, and several others. The idea that while they are interesting fields of study, they are merely arcane "navel-gazing" pursuits with little or no practical application needs to be abandoned. Think for a moment of the list of academic disciplines listed earlier, that have been spawned by the so-called impractical pursuit of sociological wisdom. As early as the nineteenth century, Jane Addams practiced applied sociology by establishing the famous Hull House in Chicago to aid the poor and the homeless, and essentially gave rise to the burgeoning field of social work that employs millions of people and helps billions of others around the globe today. Criminology began as a subfield in sociology, and the wisdom generated by its research has given rise to the popular applied field of criminal justice and its related careers and professions, including law enforcement, homeland security, probation and parole, corrections, paralegal work, and a host of others. Moreover, criminological research has shaped governmental laws, policies, and procedures at local, state, national, and international levels.

The knowledge gained from popular college courses and sociological research related to race, ethnicity, sex, gender, and social class has inspired individuals, groups, organizations, clubs, governments, and nations to embrace human differences and see the benefits of diversity instead of its perceived detriments. Try to name any job, career, or profession where knowledge of racial and ethnic differences, sex and gender issues, and the influences of social class on human behavior would not only be beneficial but almost essential for success. Increasingly, leaders in business and industry are acknowledging a long-known social fact that the vast majority of workers are either fired or voluntarily leave their jobs not because of incompetence, but because they cannot get along with their bosses, subordinates, or coworkers. Much of that inability to work with others stems from not acknowledging, understanding, or appreciating other people's values, attitudes, beliefs, and norms, especially if they come from different racial and ethnic or social class backgrounds than our own. And how many jobs, careers, and lives have been destroyed by a basic lack of understanding or appreciation for the differences attributed to sex and gender? Knowledge and application of the sociological wisdom associated with these areas are essential for personal, social, and professional interaction in today's world.

As the population of the United States, and indeed the world, ages, what began as a subarea of sociology that studied aging and the elderly has given rise to gerontology, one of the fastest growing academic fields in colleges and universities worldwide. The reason gerontology is so popular as an academic pursuit is because the job market requiring that type of sociological wisdom is exploding. Geriatric medicine is one of the most prolific medical specialties today, and any business that focuses on an aging population is almost guaranteed financial success. Occupational and physical therapy, much of which is aimed at this group, is in high demand, and students pursuing certification and licensure in those areas most assuredly will have no problem finding jobs and lucrative careers. Real estate developers have discovered that tracts of land once devoted to housing for new families with large yards for playing children and backyard barbecues are now better suited for retirement communities with zero-lot lines and wheel chair–accessible facilities. These well-planned gated communities need to include 24-hour security, paved golf cart lanes, designated areas for shuffleboard and lawn bowling as well as recreational facilities, emergency care facilities, pharmacies, and other businesses or services specifically geared toward an aged constituency. Politicians are learning that they cannot be elected without the support of older voters, and almost no local, state, or national government dares to suggest cuts to Medicaid, Medicare, or Social Security, as they must try to find solutions to shrinking budgets and growing older populations. Simultaneously, sociological wisdom informs them that there is a new breed of politician emerging as millennials are not only taking to the polls to vote but are also running for office and using the tools of social media to campaign, raise money, identify issues, and propose policies.

Sociological wisdom gave birth to the fields of demography, social ecology, urban studies, urban planning, and even human resources, all of which provide important services and meaningful careers. Students who combine double majors or major/minor combinations in business and sociology are finding that job opportunities increase significantly. The stereotype of the shy, socially challenged "bean counter" who is good with numbers and spreadsheets, but not people, is giving way to socially confident accountants, financial planners, and life coaches who combine business acuity with sociological wisdom to help people plan and accomplish their life goals.

Finally, the ancient Greek aphorism "Know thyself" prompted the wise philosopher Socrates to declare "the unexamined life is not worth living" and "wisdom begins with wonder" (Hackett 2016). Certainly, those two admonitions are at the heart of sociological wisdom. We hope that the brief overview of some of the major "sociological wisdoms" contained in this book inspire you to apply them to your life. Again, however, a warning may be advisable. Sociological wisdom can be both a blessing and a curse, as a critical examination of our lives "taken for granted" can be both enlightening and frightening. As we cautioned at the beginning of the book, once armed with sociological wisdom, you may never see the world the same way again. Some may contend that a degree in sociology is worthless, but nothing could be further from the truth. Sociological wisdom can have tremendous value, but *sociological wisdom only has value if it is applied.*

References

Adams, Paul. 2011. *Grouped: How Small Groups of Friends Are the Key to Influence on the Social Web*. Berkeley, CA: New Riders.

Adichie, Chimimanda Ngozi. 2015. *We Should All Be Feminists*. New York: Anchor Books.

Akers, Ronald L. 2011. *Social Learning and Social Structure: A General Theory of Crime and Deviance*. New York: Transaction.

American Sociological Association (ASA). 2015. *Code of Ethics*. Washington, DC: ASA. http://www.asanet.org/about/ethics.cfm.

Amir, Yehuda. 1969. "Contact Hypothesis in Ethnic Relations." *Psychological Bulletin* 71(5):319–342.

Apter, Terri. 2018. *Passing Judgment: Praise and Blame in Everyday Life*. New York: W. W. Norton.

Asch, Solomon E. 1952. *Social Psychology*. Englewood Cliffs, NJ: Prentice Hall.

Associated Press. 2007. "Devil Made Dad Hurt Baby, His Wife Says." *Dallas Morning News*, May 21, p. 3A.

———. 2008. "Air Pollution Gets Worse." *Dallas Morning News*, July 27, p. 17A.

Attorney General's Commission on Pornography. 1986. *Final Report*. Washington, DC: Government Printing Office.

Ballantine, Jeanne H., Floyd M. Hammack, and Jenny Stuber. 2017. *Sociology of Education: A Systematic Analysis*. 8th ed. Boston: Pearson.

Bandura, Albert J. 1977. *Social Learning Theory*. Englewood Cliffs, NJ: Prentice Hall.

———. 2015. *Moral Disengagement: How Good People Can Do Harm and Feel Good about Themselves*. New York: Worth.

Barnier, Amanda J., Louis Klein, and Celia B. Harris. 2018. "Transactive Memory in Small, Intimate Groups: More Than the Sum of Their Parts." *Small Group Research* 49(1):62–97.

Barrett, Richard A. 1991. *Culture and Conduct: An Excursion in Anthropology*. 2nd ed. Belmont, CA: Wadsworth.

Bates, Laura. 2016. *Everyday Sexism*. New York: St. Martin's Press.

Beasley, Chris. 1999. *What Is Feminism? An Introduction to Feminist Theory*. Thousand Oaks, CA: Sage.

Becker, Howard S. 1963. *Outsiders: Studies in the Sociology of Deviance.* New York: Free Press.

Beebe, Steven A., and John T. Masterson. 2016. *Communicating in Small Groups: Principles and Practices.* 11th ed. Boston: Pearson.

Begley, Sharon. 1997. "How to Build a Baby's Brain." *Newsweek* (special issue), February 28, pp. 28–32.

———. 2007. "The Truth about Denial." *Newsweek*, August 13, pp. 20–29.

Bell, Joyce M., and Douglas Hartmann. 2007. "Diversity in Everyday Discourse: The Cultural Ambiguities and Consequences of 'Happy Talk.'" *American Sociological Review* 72(6):895–914.

Benatar, David. 2012. *The Second Sexism: Discrimination against Men and Boys.* Hoboken, NJ: Wiley-Blackwell.

Berger, Peter L. 1963. *Invitation to Sociology: A Humanistic Perspective.* New York: Doubleday.

Bernard, L. L. 1924. *Instinct.* New York: Holt, Rinehart & Winston.

Bernay, Emma, ed. 2008. *Online Pornography: Opposing Viewpoints.* Chicago: Greenhaven Press.

Berns, Roberta M. 2015. *Child, Family, School, and Community: Socialization and Support.* 10th ed. Boston: Cengage.

Blalock, Hubert M., Jr. 1989. "The Real and Unrealized Contributions of Quantitative Sociology." *American Sociological Review* 54(3):447–460.

———. 2013. *Quantitative Sociology: International Perspectives on Mathematical and Statistical Modeling.* New York: Academic Press.

Blau, Peter M. 1963. *The Dynamics of Bureaucracy: A Study of Interpersonal Relations in Two Government Agencies.* 2nd ed. Chicago: University of Chicago Press.

———. 1964. *Exchange and Power in Social Life.* New York: Wiley.

Block, Ben. 2015. "U.N. Raises 'Low' Population Projection for 2050." *Vision for a Sustainable World.* Washington, DC: WorldWatch Institute.

Blumer, Herbert G. 1969a. "Collective Behavior." Pp. 65–21 in *Principles of Sociology*, edited by Alfred McClung Lee. 3rd ed. New York: Barnes & Noble.

———. 1969b. *Symbolic Interactionism: Perspective and Method.* Englewood Cliffs, NJ: Prentice Hall.

Bogart, Leo. 1991. "American Media and Commercial Culture." *Society* 28 (September/October):62–73.

Bolinger, Alexander R., and Julie V. Stanton. 2014. "The Gap between Perceived and Actual Learning from Group Reflection." *Small Group Research* 45(5):539–567.

Bond, Michael. 2014. *The Power of Others: Peer Pressure, Groupthink, and How the People Around Us Shape Everything We Do.* London: Oneworld.

Borgatti, Stephen P., Martin G. Everett, and Jeffrey C. Johnson. 2018. *Analyzing Social Networks.* 2nd ed. Los Angeles: Sage.

Bork, Robert. 1996. *Slouching Toward Gomorrah: Modern Liberalism and American Decline.* New York: ReganBooks.

Bradshaw, Matt, and Christopher G. Ellison. 2009. "Do Genetic Factors Influence Religious Life? Findings from a Behavior Genetic Analysis of Twin Siblings." *Journal for the Scientific Study of Religion* 47(4):529–544.

Brooks, Brad, and Jenny Barchfield. 2015. "Filthy Water a Health Threat to Athletes at 2016 Rio Olympics." *Providence Journal*, July 30. https://www.providencejournal.com/article/20150730/news/150739898.

Brown, Gordon. 2006. "How to Embrace Change." *Newsweek*, June 12, p. 69.

Brown, J. David. 1991. "The Professional Ex-: An Alternative for Exiting the Deviant Career." *Sociological Quarterly* 32(2):219–230.

Brown, Lester R. 2009. *Plan B4.0: Rescuing a Planet under Stress and a Civilization in Trouble.* New York: W. W. Norton.

Brown, Lester R., Christopher Flavin, and Hilary French, eds. 2009. *State of the World 2009.* New York: W. W. Norton.

Brown, Lester R., Michael Renner, and Christopher Flavin. 2009. *Vital Signs 2009: The Environmental Trends That Are Shaping Our Future.* New York: W. W. Norton.

Brown, Lester R., Janet Larsen, J. Matthew Roney, and Emily E. Adams. 2015. *The Great Transition: Shifting from Fossil Fuels to Solar and Wind Energy.* New York: W. W. Norton.

Bryman, Alan. 2004. *The Disneyization of Society.* Thousand Oaks, CA: Pine Forge Press.

Burgess, Ernest W. 1925. "The Growth of the City: An Introduction to a Research Project." Pp. 47–62 in *The City*, edited by Robert Park, R. D. McKenzie, and Ernest Burgess. Chicago: University of Chicago Press.

Butler, Judith. 1999. *Gender Trouble: Feminism and the Subversion of Identity.* New York: Routledge.

Campbell, Anne. 2000. "Cultural Identity as a Social Construct." *Intercultural Education* 11(1):31–39.

Caplow, Theodore. 1991. *American Social Trends.* New York: Harcourt Brace Jovanovich.

Carr, Nicholas. 2011. *The Shallows: What the Internet Is Doing to Our Brains*. New York: W. W. Norton.

Carroll, John B., ed. 1956. *Language, Thought, and Reality: Selected Writings of Benjamin Lee Whorf*. Cambridge MA: MIT Press.

Castells, Manuel. 2002. "The Internet and the Network Society." Pp. xx–xxxi in *The Internet in Everyday Life*, edited by Barry Wellman and Caroline Haythornwaite. Malden, MA: Blackwell.

Cavan, Ruth Shonle. 1961. "The Concepts of Tolerance and Contraculture as Applied to Delinquency." *Sociological Quarterly* 2 (Spring):243–258.

Cavender, Gray. 2017. "Reality Television Constructs Crime." Pp. 29–36 in *Social Problems: Constructionist Readings*, edited by Joel Best and Donileen R. Loseke. London: Routledge.

CBS News. 2007. "Fake Break-up on MySpace Leads to Teen Suicide." *CBS Evening News*, December 5.

Centeno, Miguel A., and Joseph N. Cohen. 2010. *Global Capitalism: A Sociological Perspective*. Malden, MA: Polity.

Chafetz, Janet Saltzman. 1997. "Feminist Theory and Sociology: Underutilized Contributions for Mainstream Theory." Pp. 97–120 in *Annual Review of Sociology 23*, edited by John Hagan and Karen S. Cook. Palo Alto, CA: Annual Reviews.

Chalfant, H. Paul, Robert E. Beckley, and C. Eddie Palmer. 1994. *Religion in Contemporary Society*. 3rd ed. Itasca, IL: Peacock.

Cherry, Andrew L. 1994. *The Socializing Instincts: Individual, Family, and Social Bonds*. Westport, CT: Praeger.

Chestnut, Beatrice. 2017. *The 9 Types of Leadership: Mastering the Art of People in the 21st Century Workplace*. Brentwood, TN: Post Hill Press.

Clinard, Marshall B., and Robert F. Meier. 2016. *Sociology of Deviant Behavior*. 15th ed. Belmont, CA: Cengage.

Clore, George C., Robert M. Bray, Stuart M. Itkin, et al. 1978. "Interracial Attitudes and Behavior at a Summer Camp." *Journal of Personality and Social Psychology* 36:107–116.

Cloward, Richard A., and Lloyd E. Ohlin. 1960. *Delinquency and Opportunity*. New York: Free Press.

Cohen, Albert K. 1955. *Delinquent Boys: The Culture of the Gang*. New York: Free Press.

Connell, R. W. 2000. "Charting Futures for Sociology." *Contemporary Sociology* 29 (March):291–296.

Cooley, Charles H. [1902] 1922. *Human Nature and the Social Order*. New York: Scribner.

Cooley. 1909. *Social Organization*. New York: Scribner.

Corbin, Juliet, and Anselm Strauss. 2015. *Basics of Qualitative Research*. 4th ed. Los Angeles: Sage.

Cordell, Karl, and Stefan Wolf. 2010. *Ethnic Conflict: Causes, Consequences, and Responses*. Malden, MA: Polity Press.

Coser, Lewis A. 1956. *The Functions of Social Conflict*. New York: Free Press.

Cowley, Geoffrey. 2000. "For the Love of Language." *Newsweek* (Fall/Winter special issue), pp. 12–15.

Cowley, Geoffrey, and Mary Hager. 1996. "The Biology of Beauty." *Newsweek*, June 3, pp. 61–66.

Cox News Service. 2008. "'Tweens' Putting Their Lives Online." *Dallas Morning News*, July 24, p. 9A.

Crenshaw, Edward M., Matthew Christenson, and Doyle Ray Oakey. 2000. "Demographic Transition in Ecological Focus." *American Sociological Review* 65(3):371–391.

Crossman, Ashley. 2017. "The Asch Conformity Experiments: What Solomon Asch Demonstrated About Social Pressure." *Thought Co.* https://www.thoughtco.com/asch-conformity-experiment-3026748.

Cylwik, Helen. 2001. "Notes from the Field: Emotions of Place in the Production and Interpretation of Text." *International Journal of Social Research Methodology* 4(3):243–250.

Dahrendorf, Ralf. 1959. *Class and Class Conflict in Industrial Society*. Palo Alto, CA: Stanford University Press.

Darwin, Charles. [1859] 1964. *On the Origin of Species*. New York: Mentor.

Davenport, Coral. 2018. "Major Climate Report Describes a Strong Risk of Crisis as Early as 2040." *New York Times*, October 7.

Davie, Grace. 2013. *Sociology of Religion: A Critical Agenda*. 2nd ed. London: Sage.

Davis, Richard H., and James A. Davis. 1985. *TV's Image of the Elderly: A Practical Guide for Change*. Lexington, MA: Lexington Books.

Davis, Nanette J., and Clarice Stasz. 1990. *Social Control of Deviance: A Critical Perspective*. New York: McGraw-Hill.

DeLamater, John D., Daniel J. Myers, and Jessica L. Collett. 2015. *Social Psychology*. 8th ed. Boulder, CO: Westview.

Delamont, Sara. 2003. *Feminist Sociology*. Thousand Oaks, CA: Pine Forge Press.

DeMallie, Raymond J., ed. 1984. *The Sixth Grandfather: Black Elk's Teachings Given to John G. Neihardt*. Lincoln: University of Nebraska Press.

Dentler, Ronald, and Kai Erikson. 1959. "The Functions of Deviance in Groups." *Social Problems* 7 (Fall):98–107.

Denzin, Norman K. 2009. *The Research Act in Sociology: A Theoretical Introduction to Research Methods*. London: Routledge.

DeVault, Marjorie L. 1996. "Talking Back to Sociology: Distinctive Contributions of Feminist Methodology." Pp. 29–50 in *Annual Review of Sociology*, 22, edited by John Hagan and Karen S. Cook. Palo Alto, CA: Annual Reviews.

Diamond, Jared. 1990. "Playing Dice with Megadeath." *Discover* 11 (April):55–59.

Diamond, Milton. 2010. "Porn: Good for Us?" *The Scientist*, March 1.

Divine, Robert A., T. H. Breen, R. Hal Williams, Arelia J. Gross, and H. W. Brands. 2013. *America: Past and Present* (Combined). 10th ed. Boston: Pearson.

Domosh, Mona, Roderick P. Neuman, Patricia L. Price and Terry G. Jordan-Bychkov. 2011. *The Human Mosaic: A Cultural Approach*. 12th ed. New York: W. H. Freeman.

Donne, John. [1624] 1988. *No Man Is an Island*. London: Souvenir Press.

Dotter, Daniel. 2002. "Creating Deviance: Scenarios of Stigmatization in Postmodern Media Culture." *Deviant Behavior* 23(5):419–448.

Douglas, Jack D. 1976. *Investigative Social Research*. Beverly Hills, CA: Sage.

Dowd, James, and Laura Dowd. 2003. "From Subcultures to Social Worlds." *Teaching Sociology* 31(1):20–37.

Doyle, Sir Arthur Conan. [1892] 1987. *The Adventures of Sherlock Holmes*. Stanford, CT: Longmeadow Press.

Dreben, E. K., S. T. Fiske, and R. Hastie. 1979. "The Independence of Evaluative and Item Information: Impression and Recall Order Effects in Behavior-Based Impression Formation." *Journal of Personality and Social Psychology* 37(10):1758–1768.

Durkheim, Émile. [1897] 1951. *Suicide: A Study in Sociology*, edited by George Simpson. Translated by John A. Spaulding and George Simpson. New York: Free Press.

———. [1893] 1964. *The Division of Labor in Society*. Glencoe, IL: Free Press.

———. [1895] 1982. *The Rules of the Sociological Method*. Translated by W. D. Halls. New York: The Free Press.

———. [1912] 1965. *The Elementary Forms of Religious Life*. New York: Free Press.

Durkin, Keith F., and Clifton D. Bryant. 1995. "'Log on Sex': Some Notes on the Carnal Computer and Erotic Cyberspace as an Emerging Research Frontier." *Deviant Behavior* 16 (July–September):179–200.

Eagleton, Terry. 2000. *The Making of Culture*. Malden, MA: Blackwell.

Easton, Thomas. 2018. *Taking Sides: Clashing Views on Environmental Issues*. 17th ed. New York: McGraw-Hill.

Ehrlich, Paul R. 2017. *The Population Bomb*. Rev. ed. New York: Ballantine.

Ehrlich, Paul R., and Anne H. Ehrlich. 1990. *The Population Explosion*. New York: Simon & Schuster.

———. 2006. *One with Nineveh: Politics, Consumption, and the Human Future*. Washington, DC: Island Press.

Eitzen, D. Stanley, and Maxine Baca-Zinn. 2011. *Globalization: The Transformation of Social Worlds*. 3rd ed. Belmont, CA: Wadsworth Cengage.

Etzioni, Amitai. 1975. *A Comparative Analysis of Complex Organizations*. Glencoe, IL: Free Press.

Evra, Judith Van. 1990. *Television and Child Development*. Hillsdale, NJ: Erlbaum.

Fears, Darryl. 2003. "Hue and Cry on Whiteness Studies' Classes." *WashingtonPost.com*, Friday, June 20, p. A01.

Featherstone, Liza. 2008. "Online Pornography Can Be Harmless." Pp. 29–38 in *Opposing Viewpoints: Online Pornography*, edited by Emma Bernay. Chicago: Greenhaven Press.

Federal Bureau of Investigation. 2018. *Crime in the U.S., Uniform Crime Reports 2017*. Washington, DC: U.S. Government Printing Office.

Feld, Scott L. 1991. "Why Your Friends Have More Friends Than You Do." *American Journal of Sociology* 96 (May):1464–1472.

Felson, Richard B., and M. Reed. 1986. "The Effect of Parents on the Self Appraisal of Children." *Social Psychology Quarterly* 49:302–308.

Fernandez, Roberto M., Emilio J. Castilla, and Paul Moore. 2000. "Social Capital at Work: Networks and Employment at a Phone Center." *American Journal of Sociology* 105(5):1288–1356.

Ferraro, Gary, and Susan Andreatta. 2018. *Cultural Anthropology: An Applied Perspective*. 11th ed. Belmont, CA: Cengage.

Finder, Alan. 2006. "When a Risqué Online Persona Undermines a Chance for a Job." *New York Times*, June 11, p. A1.

Fine, Cordelia. 2011. *Delusions of Gender: How Our Minds, Society, and Neurosexism Create Difference*. London: W. W. Norton.

Fisher, Robert Leslie. 2005. *The Research Productivity of Scientists: How Gender, Organization Culture, and the Problem Choice Process*

Influence the Productivity of Scientists. Lanham, MD: University Press of America.

Fortson, Beverly L., Josephy R. Scotti, Yi-Chuen Chen, Judith Malone, and Kevin S. Del Ben. 2007. "Internet Use, Abuse, and Dependence among Students at a Southeastern Regional University." *Journal of American College Health* 56(2):137–144.

Frank, David John, Ann Hironaka, and Evan Schofer. 2000. "The Nation-State and the Natural Environment over the Twentieth Century." *American Sociological Review* 65(1):96–116.

Franklin, Clyde W., II. 1988. *Men and Society.* Chicago: Nelson-Hall.

Frieden, Jeffrey A. 2017. *Global Capitalism: Its Fall and Rise in the Twentieth Century.* New York: W. W. Norton.

Friedkin, Noah E. 1999. "Choice Shift and Group Polarization." *American Sociological Review* 64(5):856–875.

Garfinkel, Harold. 1956. "Conditions of Successful Degradation Ceremonies." *American Journal of Sociology* 61(5):420–424.

———. [1967] 1991. *Studies in Ethnomethodology.* Englewood Cliffs, NJ: Prentice Hall.

Geertz, Clifford. 1968. "The Impact of the Concept of Culture on the Concept of Man." Pp. 16–29 in *Man in Adaptation: The Cultural Present*, edited by Yehudi A. Cohen. Chicago: Aldine de Gruyter.

Gelles, Richard J. 1997. *Intimate Violence in Families.* 3rd ed. Newbury Park, CA: Sage.

Gerber, Theodore P. 2002. "Structural Change and Post-Socialist Stratification: Labor Market Transitions in Contemporary Russia." *American Sociological Review* 67(5):629–659.

Gibbs, Jack P. 1975. *Crime, Punishment, and Deterrence.* New York: Elsevier.

Gilligan, Carol. 2016. *In a Different Voice: Psychological Theory and Women's Development.* Reprinted ed. Cambridge, MA: Harvard University Press.

Gilligan, Carol, Janice Victoria Ward, and Jill McLean Taylor. 1989. *Mapping the Moral Domain: A Contribution of Women's Thinking to Psychological Theory and Education.* Cambridge, MA: Harvard University Press.

Giordano, Peggy, Monica A. Longmore, and Wendy D. Manning. 2006. "Gender and the Meanings of Adolescent Romantic Relationships: A Focus on Boys." *American Sociological Review* 71(2):260–287.

Gitlin, Todd. 1996. *The Twilight of Common Dreams: Why America Is Wracked by Cultural Wars.* New York: Metropolitan Books.

Goffman, Erving. 1959. *The Presentation of Self in Everyday Life.* New York: Doubleday.

———. 1961a. *Asylums: Essays on the Social Situation of Mental Patients and Other Inmates*. Garden City, NY: Doubleday.

———. 1961b. *Encounters*. Indianapolis, IN: Bobbs-Merrill.

———. 1963. *Stigma: Notes on the Management of Spoiled Identity*. Englewood Cliffs, NJ: Prentice Hall.

Goldberg, Herb. 1976. *The Hazards of Being Male: Surviving the Myth of Masculine Privilege*. New York: Signet.

Goode, Erich and D. Angus Vail. 2008. *Extreme Deviance*. Thousand Oaks, CA: Pine Forge.

Gordon, Milton M. 1964. *Assimilation in American Life*. New York: Oxford University Press.

Gore, Albert. 1992. "The Ecology of Survival." Pp. 492–496 in *Contemporary Issues in Society*, edited by Hugh F. Lena, William B. Helmreich and William McCord. New York: McGraw-Hill.

———. 2007. *An Inconvenient Truth*. New York: Viking.

Gouldner, Alvin W. 1960. "The Norm of Reciprocity: A Preliminary Statement." *American Sociological Review* 25(2):161–178.

Gracey, Harry L. 1977. "Learning the Student Role: Kindergarten as Academic Boot Camp." Pp. 215–226 in *Readings in Introductory Sociology*, edited by Dennis H. Wrong and Harry L. Gracey. 3rd ed. New York: Macmillan.

Greeley, Andrew M. 2002. "The Great Story and Its Discontents." *Society* 40 (November/December):45–48.

Griffiths, Mark. 2001. "Sex on the Internet: Observations and Implications for Internet Sex Addiction." *Journal of Sex Research* 38(4):333–342.

Grossman, Lev. 2005. "Grow Up? Not So Fast." *Time*, January 16, pp. 42–54.

Grusec, Joan E., and Paul D. Hastings, eds. 2008. *Handbook of Socialization: Theory and Research*. New York: Guilford Press.

Hackett, David G. 1990. "Rodney Stark and the Sociology of American Religious History." *Journal for the Scientific Study of Religion* 29(3):372–376.

Hall, Edward T. 1959. *The Silent Language*. New York: Doubleday.

———. 1990. *The Hidden Dimension*. New York: Random House.

Halter, Marilyn. 2000. *Shopping for Identity: The Marketing of Ethnicity*. New York: Schocken.

Hand, Bad. 2010. *Plains Indians Regalia and Customs*. Atglen, PA: Schiffer.

Harris, C. D., and Edward L. Ullman. 1945. "The Nature of Cities." *Annals of the American Academy of Political and Social Science* 242(1):7–17.

Harris, Diana K. 2007. *Sociology of Aging*. 3rd ed. Lanham, MD: Rowman & Littlefield.

Harris, Malcolm. 2017. *Kids These Days: Human Capital and the Making of the Millennials*. New York: Little, Brown and Company.

Hass, Nancy. 2006. "In Your Facebook." *New York Times*, January 8, p. 30.

Hathaway, Andrew D., and Michael F. Atkinson. 2001. "Tolerable Differences Revisited: Crossroads in Theory on the Social Construction of Deviance." *Deviant Behavior* 22 (July–August):353–377.

Haviland, William A., Harold Prins, Dana Walrath, and Bunny McBride. 2016. *Anthropology: The Human Challenge*. 15th ed. Belmont, CA: Cengage.

Hayden, Thomas. 2000. "Sense of Self." *Newsweek* (Fall/Winter special issue), pp. 57–62.

Hickey, Joseph V. and William E. Thompson. 1988. "Personal Space: The Hidden Dimension of Cowboy Demeanor." *Midwest Quarterly* 24 (Winter):264–272.

Hillier, Susan M. and Georgia M. Barrow. 2015. *Aging, the Individual, and Society*. 10th ed. Boston: Cengage.

Hirschi, Travis. 1969. *Causes of Delinquency*. Berkeley: University of California Press.

Holstein, William J. 2003. "BOOK VALUE; How Consumer Culture Sets Up Its Young Ducks." *New York Times*, January 26. https://www.nytimes.com/2003/01/26/business/book-value-how-consumer-culture-sets-up-its-young-ducks.html.

Holt, Thomas. 2011. *Social Learning Theory*. New York: Oxford University Press.

Homans, George C. 1950. *The Human Group*. New York: Harcourt Brace Jovanovich.

———. 1961. *Social Behavior: Its Elementary Forms*. New York: Harcourt Brace Jovanovich.

Hooyman, Nancy R., and Kevin S. Kawamoto. 2015. *Aging Matters: An Introduction to Social Gerontology*. Boston: Pearson.

Hornsby, Anne M. 2008. "Surfing the Net for Community." Pp. 61–100 in *Illuminating Social Life: Classical and Contemporary Theory Revisited*, edited by Peter Kivisto. 4th ed. Los Angeles: Pine Forge.

Hostetler, John. 1980. *Amish Society*. 3rd ed. Baltimore, MD: Johns Hopkins University Press.

Howard, Michael C., and Janet Dunaif-Hattis. 1992. *Anthropology: Understanding Human Adaptation*. New York: HarperCollins.

Hoyt, Homer. 1939. *The Structure and Growth of Residential Neighborhoods in American Cities*. Washington, DC: Federal Housing Authority.

Hughes, Donna Rice, and John D. McMickle. 1997. "Pornography Incites Violent Sexual Crime." Pp. 36–39 in *Pornography: Opposing Viewpoints*, edited by Carol Wekesser. San Diego: Greenhaven Press.

Hughes, Everett C. 1958. *Men and Their Work*. Glencoe, IL: Free Press.

Hulbert, Ann. 2011. *Raising America: Experts, Parents, and a Century of Advice about Children*. New York: Vintage.

———. 2018. *Off the Charts: The Hidden Lives and Lessons of American Child Prodigies*. New York: Knopf.

Humphreys, Laud. 1970. *Tearoom Trade: Impersonal Acts in Public Places*. New York: Aldine de Gruyter.

Hutchison, Ray, Mark Gottdiener, and Michael T. Ryan. 2015. *The New Urban Sociology*. 5th ed. Boulder, CO: Westview.

Irwin, John. 1970. *The Felon*. Englewood Cliffs, NJ: Prentice Hall.

Jackson, Jeffrey M., and Stephen G. Harkins. 1985. "Equity in Effort: An Explanation of the Social Loafing Effect." *Journal of Personality and Social Psychology* 49(5):1199–1206.

Jacobs, Jane. 1992. *Death and Life of Great American Cities*. New York: Vintage.

Jacobs, Jerry, Marie Lukens, and Michael Useem. 1996. "Organizational, Job, and Individual Determinants of Workplace Training: Evidence from the National Organizations Survey." *Social Science Quarterly* 77 (March):159–176.

Janis, Irvin. 1972. *Victims of Groupthink*. Boston: Houghton Mifflin.

Jensen, Robert. 2004. "Pornography and Sexual Violence." *National Electronic Network on Violence against Women, Applied Research Forum*, July:1–8.

Johnson, Dan. 2000. "Clash of Trends: Disappearing Water vs. Super Farms." *The Futurist* 34 (September–October):16–17.

Johnstone, Ronald L. 2015. *Religion in Society: A Sociology of Religion*. 8th ed. London: Routledge.

Jones, Charisse, and Nathan Bomey. 2018. "Sears Files for Chapter 11 Bankruptcy, To Close 142 More Stores." *USA Today*, October 15.

Jones, Stephen R. G. 1990. "Worker Interdependence and Output: The Hawthorne Studies Reevaluated." *American Sociological Review* 55(2):176–190.

Kantrowitz, Barbara. 1997. "Off to a Good Start." *Newsweek* (Spring/Summer special issue), pp. 7–9.

Kaplan, Abraham. 1964. *The Conduct of Inquiry*. Scranton, PA: Chandler.

Katz-Gerro, Tally. 2002. "Highbrow Cultural Consumption and Class Distinctions in Italy, Israel, West Germany, Sweden, and the United States." *Social Forces* 81(1):207–229.

Kiang, Peter Nien-Chu. 1994. "When Know-Nothings Speak English Only: Analyzing Irish and Cambodian Struggles for Community Development and Educational Equity." Pp. 125–145 in *The State of Asian-Americans: Activism and Resistance in the 1990s*, edited by Karin Aguilar San Juan. Boston: South End.

Kimmel, Michael S., and Michael A. Messner. 2018. *Men's Lives*. 10th ed. New York: Oxford University Press.

Kiser, Edgar, and Michael Hechter. 1991. "The Role of General Theory in Comparative-Historical Sociology." *American Journal of Sociology* 97(1):1–30.

Knight Ridder. 2006. "World to Soon Have Urban Majority." *Dallas Morning News*, June 17, p. 2A.

Kolmar, Wendy, and Frances Bartkowski. 2013. *Feminist Theory: A Reader*. 4th ed. New York: McGraw-Hill.

Kottak, Conrad P. 2015. *Anthropology: Appreciating Human Diversity*. 17th ed. New York: McGraw-Hill.

Kozol, Jonathan. 1967. *Death at an Early Age*. New York: Bantam Books.

Kumar, Krishan. 1995. *From Post-Industrial to Post-Modern Society: New Theories of the Contemporary World*. Oxford, UK: Blackwell.

Langmia, Kehbuma, and Tia C. M. Tyree. 2017. *Social Media: Culture and Identity*. Lanham, MD: Lexington Books.

Lamont, Michele, and Marcel Fournier. 1992. *Cultivating Differences: Symbolic Boundaries and the Making of Inequality*. Chicago: University of Chicago Press.

Lanz, Tobias J. 2008. *Beyond Capitalism and Socialism: A New Statement of an Old Ideal*. New York: HIS Press.

LaRue, Jan. 2008. "Online Pornography Can Be Harmful." Pp. 21–28 in *Opposing Viewpoints: Online Pornography*, edited by Emma Bernay. Chicago: Greenhaven Press.

Latané, Bibb, and Steve Nida. 1981. "Ten Years of Research on Group Size and Helping." *Psychological Bulletin* 89(2):308–324.

Laub, John H., and Robert J. Sampson. 1991. "The Sutherland-Glueck Debate: On the Sociology of Criminological Knowledge." *American Journal of Sociology* 96 (May):1402–1440.

Leavitt, Robin Lynn, and Martha Bauman Power. 1989. "Emotional Socialization in the Postmodern Era: Children in Day Care." *Social Psychology Quarterly* 52 (Spring):35–43.

Lemert, Charles. 2012. *Social Things: An Introduction to the Sociological Life.* 5th ed. New York: Rowman & Littlefield.

Lemert, Edwin. 1951. *Social Pathology.* New York: McGraw-Hill.

Lengermann, Patricia Madoo, and Gillian Neibrugge. 2007. *Women Founders: Sociology and Social Theory, 1830–1930.* Long Grove, IL: Waveland.

Lengermann, Patricia Madoo, and Ruth A. Wallace. 1985. *Gender in America: Social Control and Social Change.* Englewood Cliffs, NJ: Prentice Hall.

Lenski, Gerhard. 1988. "Rethinking Macrosociological Theory." *American Sociological Review* 53(2):163–171.

Levine, John M., and Richard L. Moreland. 1998. "Small Groups." Pp. 415–469 in *The Handbook of Social Psychology*, Vol. II., edited by Daniel T. Gilbert, Susan T. Fiske, and Gardner Lindsey. New York: Academic Press.

Levy, Steven. 2007a. "Facebook Grows Up." *Newsweek*, August 28, pp. 41–42.

Lindau, Stacy Tessler, L. Philip Schumm, Edward O. Laumann, Wendy Levinson, Colm A. O'Muircheartaigh, and Linda J. Waite. 2007. "A Study of Sexuality and Health among Older Adults in the United States." *New England Journal of Medicine* 357(8):762–774.

Linden, Eugene. 1989. "The Death of Birth." *Time*, January 2, pp. 32–35.

Lindsey, Linda L. 2016. *Gender Roles: A Sociological Perspective.* 6th ed. New York: Routledge.

Linton, Ralph. 1936. *The Study of Man.* New York: Appleton-Century-Crofts.

Liska, Allen E., and Barbara D. Warner. 1991. "Functions of Crime: A Paradoxical Process." *American Journal of Sociology* 96(6):1441–1463.

Lorber, Judith, and Patricia Yancey Martin. 2013. "The Socially Constructed Body." Pp. 249–274 in *Illuminating Social Life: Classical and Contemporary Theory Revisited*, edited by Peter Kivisto. 6th ed. Thousand Oaks, CA: Sage.

———. 2017. "Television Talk Shows Construct Morality." Pp. 66–73 in *Social Problems: Constructionist Readings*, edited by Joel Best and Donileen R. Loseke. London: Routledge.

Luckerson, Victor. 2014. "Landline Phones Are Getting Closer to Extinction." *Time*, July 8. http://time.com/2966515/landline-phones-cell-phones/.

Maccoby, Eleanor E. 1980. *Social Development, Psychological Development: Psychological Growth and the Parent–Child Relationship.* New York: Harcourt Brace Jovanovich.

Macedo, Donaldo P., and Lilia I. Bartolomé. 1999. *Dancing with Bigotry: Beyond the Politics of Tolerance.* New York: St. Martin's Press.

Machlup, Fritz. 1988. "Are the Social Sciences Inferior?" *Society* 25 (May/June):57–65.

Mandelbaum, David G. (ed.). 1949. *Selected Writings of Edward Sapir in Language, Culture and Personality.* Berkeley: University of California Press.

Mangum, Garth L., Stephen L. Magnum, and Andrew Sum. 2003. *The Persistence of Poverty in the United States.* Baltimore: Johns Hopkins University Press.

Marshall, Nancy L., ed. 2003. "The Social Construction of Gender in Childhood and Adolescence." *American Behavioral Scientist* 46(10):1289–1295.

Martineau, Harriet. 1837. *Society in America.* Saunders and Otley.

———. 2015 [1838]. *How to Observe Manners and Morals.* Create Space Independent Publishing Platform.

Marx, Karl. [1867] 1967. *Capital: A Critical Analysis of Capitalist Production.* New York: International Publishers.

May, Hazel. 2000. "Murderers' Relatives: Managing Stigma, Negotiating Identity." *Journal of Contemporary Ethnography* 29(2):198–221.

McCall, George, and Jerry Simmons. 1979. "Social Perception and Appraisal." Pp. 66–78 in *Social Interaction: Introductory Readings in Sociology*, edited by Howard Robboy, Sidney L. Greenblatt, and Candace Clark. New York: St. Martin's Press.

McConnell, Campbell, Stanley Brue, and Sean Flynn. 2014. *Economics: Principles, Problems, and Policies.* New York: McGraw-Hill.

McCord, William. 1991. "The Asian Renaissance." *Society* 28 (September/October):50–61.

McElroy, Wendy. 1997. "Pornography Does Not Incite Violent Sexual Crime." Pp. 40–44 in *Pornography: Opposing Viewpoints*, edited by Carol Wekesser. San Diego: Greenhaven Press.

McGavin, George C. 2007. *Endangered: Wildlife on the Brink of Extinction.* Westport, CT: Firefly Books.

McGuire, Meredith B. 2008. *Religion: The Social Context.* 5th ed. Long Grove, IL: Waveland Press.

McKay and Fanning. 2016. *Self Esteem: A Proven Program of Cognitive Techniques for Assessing, Improving, and Maintaining Your Self Esteem* (4th ed.). Oakland, CA: New Harbinger.

McNeil, Elton B. 1969. *Human Socialization.* Belmont, CA: Brooks/Cole.

Mead, George H. 1934. *Mind, Self, and Society.* Chicago: University of Chicago Press.

Merton, Robert K. 1938. "Social Structure and Anomie." *American Sociological Review* 3(5):672–682.

Milkie, Melissa. 2007. "Media Images' Influence on Adolescent Girls' Self-Concepts." Pp. 50–64 in *Inside Social Life: Readings in Social Psychology and Microsociology*, edited by Spencer E. Cahill. 5th ed. Los Angeles: Roxbury.

Miller, Joanne. 1988. "Jobs and Work." Pp. 327–359 in *Handbook of Sociology*, edited by Neil J. Smelser. Newbury Park, CA: Sage.

———. 1956. *The Power Elite*. New York: Oxford University Press.

———. 1959. *The Sociological Imagination*. New York: Oxford University Press.

Moos, Bob. 2006. "The Gender Gap Endures, Even in Retirement." *Dallas Morning News*, June 18, p. 1A; 10A.

Myers, David G., and H. Lamm. 1978. "The Group Polarization Phenomenon." *Psychological Bulletin* 83:602–627.

Nack, Adina. 2000. "Damaged Goods: Women Managing the Stigma of STDs." *Deviant Behavior* 21(2):95–122.

Nam, Charles B., and Susan O. Gustavus. 1976. *Population: The Dynamics of Demographic Change*. Boston: Houghton Mifflin.

Namboodiri, Krishnan. 1988. "Ecological Demography: Its Place in Sociology." *American Sociological Review* 53(4):619–633.

———. 2017. "Children's Access to and Use of the Internet." *The Condition of Education*. May. https://nces.ed.gov/programs/coe/indicator_cch.asp.

National Center on Elder Abuse. 2015. "Elder Justice and Protection." *Department of Health and Human Services Newsletter* (June).

National Center for Transgender Equality (N.d.). http://www.nctequality.org.

National Children's Alliance. 2014. National Statistics on Child Abuse. https://www.nationalchildrensalliance.org/media-room/nca-digital-media-kit/national-statistics-on-child-abuse/.

National Hurricane Center. 2018. "Costliest U.S. Tropical Cyclones Tables Updated." *National Hurricane Center*. https://www.nhc.noaa.gov/news/UpdatedCostliest.pdf.

National Law Center on Homelessness and Poverty. 2015. https://www.nlchp.org/documents/Homeless_Stats_Fact_Sheet.

NBC News. 2015. "Things are Looking Up in America's Porn Industry. NBC News, Business, January 20. https://www.nbcnews.com/business/business-news/things-are-looking-americas-porn-industry-n289431.

Nelson, David Erik. 2012. *Online Pornography: Opposing Viewpoints*. Farmington Hills, MI: Greenhaven Press.

Newport, Frank. 2016. "Most Americans Still Believe in God." *Gallup News*, June 29 http://news.gallup.com/poll/193271/americans-believe-god.aspx.

Nichols, Mark. 1997. "Studies Show That Pornography Causes Violence." Pp. 45–47. in *Pornography: Opposing Viewpoints*, edited by Carol Wekesser. San Diego: Greenhaven Press.

Nierenberg, Danielle. 2003. "Factory Farming in the Developing World." *World Watch* 16(3):10–19.

Nisbet, Robert. 1970. *The Social Bond*. New York: Knopf.

Novak, Mark. 2018. *Issues in Aging*. 4th ed. London: Routledge.

Nuclear Energy Institute. 2015. World Statistics Nuclear Energy Around the World, 2015. http://www.nei.org/Knowledge-Center/Nuclear-Statistics/World-Statistics.

Ogburn, William F. 1922. *Social Change*. New York: Viking Press.

———. 1964. "Culture Lag as Theory." Pp. 86–95 in *On Culture and Social Change*, edited by William F. Ogburn. Chicago: University of Chicago Press.

Paden, William E. 1995. *Religious Worlds: The Comparative Study of Religion*. Boston: Beacon Press.

Parenti, Michael. 1992. *Make-Believe Media: The Politics of Entertainment*. New York: St. Martin's Press.

Parillo, Vincent N., ed. 2013. "Melting Pot." Pp. 575–576 in *Encyclopedia of Social Problems*, edited by Vincent N. Parillo. Thousand Oaks, CA: Sage.

Park, Robert E. 1916. "The City: Suggestions for the Investigation of Human Behavior in the Urban Environment." *American Journal of Sociology* 20:577–612.

———. 1928. "Human Migration and the Marginal Man." *American Journal of Sociology* 33 (May):881–893.

Parnell, Susan and Edgar Pieterse, eds. 2014. *Africa's Urban Revolution: Policy Pressures*. London: Zed Books.

Parsons, Talcott. 1951. *The Social System*. New York: Free Press.

Paterniti, Debora A. 2000. "The Micropolitics of Identity in Adverse Circumstance." *Journal of Contemporary Ethnography* 29(1):93–119.

Patterson, Karen. 2004. "Piling on the Violence: Link between Media and Aggression Clear, Experts Say." *Dallas Morning News*, April 12, p. 1E.

Pavlov, Ivan P. (1926). 2013. *Conditioned Reflexes and Psychiatry*. New York: Oxford University Press.

Payne, Brian. 2011. *Crime and Elder Abuse: An Integrated Perspective*. Springfield, IL: Charles C. Thomas.

Perrow, Charles. 2000. "An Organizational Analysis of Organizational Theory." *Contemporary Sociology* 29(3):469–476.

———. 2014. *Complex Organizations: A Critical Essay*. Battleboro, VT: Echo Point Books & Media.

Peterson, Richard A., and Roger Kern. 1996. "Changing Highbrow Taste: From Snob to Cultural Omnivore." *American Sociological Review* 61(5):900–907.

Pieterse, Edgar. 2009. *City Futures: Confronting the Crisis of Urban Development*. London: Zed Books.

Pike, Gary R. 2011. "Using College Students' Self-Reported Learning Outcomes in Scholarly Research." *New Directions for Institutional Research* 150:41–58.

Pirsig, Robert M. 1974. *Zen and the Art of Motorcycle Maintenance*. New York: Bantam Books.

Pollack, William S., and Todd Shuster. 2000. *Real Boys' Voices*. New York: Random House.

Population Reference Bureau. 2018. www.prb.org/publications/whatissheets/2014.

Powell, A. D. 2005. *"Passing" for Who You Really Are*. Palm Coast, FL: Backintyme.

Prewitt, Kenneth. 2013. "Fix the Census' Archaic Racial Categories." *New York Times*, August 21.

Quinn, James F., and Craig J. Forsyth. 2005. "Describing Sexual Behavior in the Era of the Internet: A Typology for Empirical Research." *Deviant Behavior* 26(3):191–207.

Quinney, Richard. 1975. *Criminology: Analysis and Critique of Crime in America*. Boston: Little, Brown.

———. 1980. *Class, State, and Crime*. 2nd ed. New York: Longman.

Reckless, Walter. 1961. "A New Theory of Delinquency and Crime." *Federal Probation* 25 (December):42–46.

Redfield, Robert. 1941. *The Folk Culture of Yucatan*. Chicago: University of Chicago Press.

———. 1953. *The Primitive World and Its Transformations*. Ithaca, NY: Cornell University Press.

Reiman, Jeffrey H. 2017. *The Rich Get Richer and the Poor Get Prison*. 11th ed. New York: Routledge.

Renzetti, Claire M., and Daniel J. Curran. 1995. *Women, Men, and Society*. Boston: Allyn & Bacon.

Rheingold, Harriet L. 1969. "The Social and Socializing Infant." Pp. 779–790 in *Handbook of Socialization Theory and Research*, edited by D. H. Goslin. Chicago: Rand McNally.

Rheingold, Howard. 2002. "The Virtual Community in the Real World." Pp. xxvii–xxviii in *The Internet in Everyday Life*, edited by Barry Wellman and Caroline Haythornwaite. Malden, MA: Blackwell.

Ridgeway, Cecilia L., and Shelley J. Correll. 2000. "Limiting Inequality through Interaction: The End(s) of Gender." *Contemporary Sociology* 29 (January):110–119.

Ridley, Matt. 2003. *Nature via Nurture: Genes, Experience, and What Makes Us Human*. New York: HarperCollins.

Ritzer, George. 1977. Working: Conflict and Change. 2nd ed. Englewood Cliffs, NJ: Prentice Hall.

———. 2007. *The Globalization of Nothing 2*. Thousand Oaks, CA: Pine Forge Press.

———. 2018. *The McDonaldization of Society*. 9th ed. Thousand Oaks, CA: Sage.

Robbins, Paul, John Hintz, and Sarah A. Moore. 2014. *Environment and Society: A Critical Introduction*. 2nd ed. Malden, MA: Wiley-Blackwell.

Robinson-Wood, Tracy. 2017. *The Convergence of Race, Ethnicity, and Gender*. 5th ed. Los Angeles: Sage.

Roethlisberger, Fritz J., and William J. Dickson. 1939. *Management and the Worker*. Cambridge, MA: Harvard University Press.

Rosenbloom, Stephanie. 2007. "Academics Flock to Facebook." *New York Times*, December 17.

Rosman, Abraham. 2017. *The Tapestry of Culture: An Introduction to Cultural Anthropology*. 10th ed. Lanham, MD: Rowman & Littlefield.

Ross, Robert J. S., and Kent C. Trachte. 1990. *Global Capitalism: The New Leviathan*. Albany: State University of New York Press.

Rossides, Daniel W. 2009. *Social Stratification: The Interplay of Class, Race, and Gender*. 2nd ed. Upper Saddle River, NJ: Prentice Hall.

Roy, Avik. 2011. "Why the American Medical Association Had 72 Million Reasons to Shrink Doctors' Pay." *Forbes*, November 28.

Ruggiero, Vincent Ryan. 2014. *The Art of Thinking: A Guide to Critical and Creative Thought*. 11th ed. Boston: Pearson.

Rykwert, Joseph. 2000. *Seduction of Place: The City in the Twenty-First Century and Beyond*. New York: Pantheon.

Sapir, Edward. 1929. "The Status of Linguistics as a Science." *Language* 5(4):207–214.

Savage, Mike, Gaynor Bagnall, and Brian J. Longhurst. 2005. *Globalization and Belonging*. Thousand Oaks, CA: Pine Forge Press.

Sawin, Janet L. 2003. "Water Scarcity Could Overwhelm the Next Generation." *World Watch* 16(4):8.

Schaefer, Richard T. 2015. *Racial and Ethnic Groups*. 14th ed. Boston: Pearson.

Scheff, Thomas J. 1988. "Shame and Conformity: The Deference-Emotion System." *American Sociological Review* 53(3):395–406.

Schlesinger, Arthur M., Jr. 1998. *The Disunity of America: Reflections on a Multicultural Society*. Rev. ed. New York: Norton.

Schlissel, Arnold. 2009. *Combating Desertification with Plants*. New York: Springer.

Schneider, Jennifer P. 2000. "Effects of Cybersex Addiction on the Family: Results of a Survey." *Sexual Addiction & Compulsivity* 7(1–2):31–58.

Schultz, Emily A., and Robert H. Lavenda. 2017. *Cultural Anthropology: A Perspective on the Human Condition*. 10th ed. New York: Oxford University Press.

Schumpeter, Joseph A. 2014. *Capitalism, Socialism, and Democracy*. 2nd ed. Kirkwood, MO: Impact Books.

Schur, Edwin M. 1971. *Labeling Deviant Behavior*. New York: HarperCollins.

Schwartz, John and Matthew L. Wald. 2003. "'Groupthink' Is 30 Years Old, and Still Going Strong." *New York Times*, March 9. https://www.nytimes.com/2003/03/09/weekinreview/the-nation-nasa-s-curse-groupthink-is-30-years-old-and-still-going-strong.html.

Scott, John. 1991. "Networks of Corporate Power: A Comparative Assessment." *Annual Review of Sociology* 17:181–203.

Sheehy, Gail. 1976. *Passages: Predictable Crises of Adult Life*. New York: Bantam Books.

———. 1993. *The Silent Passage: Menopause*. New York: Pocket Books.

———. 1996. *New Passages*. New York: Ballantine Books.

———. 2006. *Passages: Predictable Crises of Adult Life*. 30th anniversary ed. New York: Ballantine Books.

Sherif, Muzafer. 1936. *The Psychology of Social Norms*. New York: HarperCollins.

Shostack, Arthur. 2000. *Cyberunion: Empowering Labor through Computer Technology*. Armonk, NY: M. E. Sharpe.

Simmel, Georg. [1908] 1955. *Conflict and the Web of Group Affiliations*. New York: Free Press.

Simmons, Rachel. 2003. *Odd Girl Out: The Hidden Culture of Aggression in Girls*. New York: Harvest Books.

Simon, David R. 2018. *Elite Deviance*. 11th ed. New York: Routledge.

Singer, Eleanor. 1981. "Reference Groups and Social Evaluation." Pp. 66–93 in *Social Psychology: Sociological Perspectives*, edited by Morris Rosenberg and Ralph Turner. New York: Basic Books.

Smith, Allen C., III, and Sherryl Kleinman. 1989. "Managing Emotions in Medical School: Students' Contacts with the Living and the Dead." *Social Psychology Quarterly* 52(1):56–69.

Smith, Craig. 2002. "Beware of Cross-Cultural Faux Pas in China." *New York Times*, April 30, pp. 1–3.

Smith, Dorothy. 1989. *The Everyday World as Problematic: A Feminist Sociology*. Boston: Northeastern University Press.

Smith, Joel. 1991. "A Methodology for Twenty-First Century Sociology." *Social Forces* 70(1):1–17.

Sorokin, Pitirim. 1941. *The Crisis of Our Age*. New York: Dutton.

Sorokin, Pitirim, and Carle Zimmerman. 1929. *Principles of Urban-Rural Sociology*. New York: Holt.

Spanier, Bonnie B. 1997. "Sexism and Scientific Research." *National Forum* 77 (Spring):26–30.

Spencer, Sam. 2012. "How Big Is the Pornography Industry in the United States?" *Covenant Eyes*, June 1. http://www.covenanteyes.com/2012/06/01/how-big-is-the-pornography-industry-in-the-united-states/.

Spillsbury, Richard. 2009. *Deforestation: Can the Earth Cope?* New York: Hodder Wayland.

Spradley, James P. 1979. *The Ethnographic Interview*. New York: Holt, Rinehart & Winston.

———. 1980. *Participant Observation*. New York: Holt, Rinehart & Winston.

Stark, Rodney, and William S. Bainbridge. 1985. *The Future of Religion: Secularization, Revival and Cult Formation*. Berkeley: University of California Press.

Statistica. 2015. Number of Monthly Active Facebook Users Worldwide as of 1st Quarter 2015 (in millions). http://www.statista.com/statistics/264810/number-of-monthly-active-facebook-users-worldwide/.

Steitz, Jean A., and Tulita P. Owen. 1992. "School Activities and Work: Effects on Adolescent Self-Esteem." *Adolescence* 27(105):37–50.

Stephens, Lowndes F. 1994. "Children and Youth Audiences." Pp. 231–250 in *Handbook on Mass Media in the United States: The Industry and Its Audiences*, edited by Erwin K. Thomas and Brown H. Carpenter. Westport, CT: Greenwood Press.

Stillerman, Joel. 2015. *The Sociology of Consumption: A Global Approach*. Cambridge, UK: Polity.

Stonequist, Everett H. 1937. *The Marginal Man*. New York: Scribner.

Straus, Murray A., Richard J. Gelles, and Suzanne K. Steinmetz. 2006. *Behind Closed Doors: Violence in the American Family*. Somerset, NJ: Transaction Publishers.

Strossen, Nancy. 1995. *Defending Pornography: Free Speech, Sex, and the Fight for Women's Rights*. New York: Scribner.

Subrahmanyam, Kaveri, and Patricia Greenfield. 2008. "Online Communication and Adolescent Relationships." *The Future of Children* 18(1):119–146.

Sugiyama, Lawrence S. 2004. "Is Beauty in the Context-Sensitive Adaptations of the Beholder? Shiwiar Use of Waist-to-Hip Ratio in Assessments of Female Mate Value." *Evolution and Human Behavior* 25(1):51–62.

Sumner, William Graham. 1906. *Folkways*. Boston: Ginn.

Sutherland, Edwin, and Donald Cressey. 1978. *Principles of Criminology*. Philadelphia: Lippincott.

Swann, William B., Jr. 1998. "The Self Is Not a Bowling Ball." Pp. 399–407 in *Attribution and Social Interaction: The Legacy of Edward E. Jones*, edited by John M. Darley and Joel Cooper. Washington, DC: American Psychological Association.

Sykes, Gresham M., and David Matza. 1957. "Techniques of Neutralization: A Theory of Delinquency." *American Sociological Review* 22(6):664–670.

Tabery, James. 2014. *Beyond Versus: The Struggle to Understand the Interaction of Nature and Nurture (Life and Mind: Philosophical Issues in Biology and Psychology)*. Kindle ed. Boston: MIT Press.

Talmadge, Eric. 2007. "Quake-Damaged Nuclear Plant Closed." *Dallas Morning News*, July 19, p. 10A.

Taverner, William J. (ed.). 2009. *Taking Sides: Clashing Views on Controversial Issues in Human Sexuality*. 11th ed. Guilford, CT: McGraw-Hill Dushkin.

Tenore, Mallary Jean. 2008. "My First Web Site: Moms and Babies Discover Social Networking." *Dallas Morning News*, December 1, p. 1E.

Thau, Barbara. 2017. "Five Signs that Stores (Not E-Commerce) are the Future of Retail." *Forbes*, June 27. https://www.forbes.com/sites/barbarathau/2017/06/27/five-signs-that-stores-not-online-shopping-are-the-future-of-retail/#5399094e4641.

Thelwall, Mike. 2008. "Social Networks, Gender, and Friending." *Journal of the American Society for Information Science and Technology* 59(8):1321–1330.

Thomas, Kristy A. 2007. "Bicultural Socialization among Adoptive Families: Where There Is a Will There Is a Way." *Journal of Family Issues* 28(9):1189–1219.

Thomas, William I., and Dorothy Thomas. 1928. *The Child in America*. New York: Knopf.

Thompson, Mica L., and William E. Thompson. 2016. "Learning the Student Role Four Decades Later: A Sociological Analysis of 21st Century

Kindergarten as Academic Boot Camp." *Sociological Spectrum* 39(1):13–23.
Thompson, William E. 1986. "Deviant Ideology: The Case of the Old Order Amish." *Quarterly Journal of Ideology* 10(1):29–33.
———. 2012. *Hogs, Blogs, Leathers, and Lattes: The Sociology of Modern American Motorcycling*. Jefferson, NC: McFarland Press.
Thompson, William E., and Jack E. Bynum. 2017. *Juvenile Delinquency: A Sociological Approach*. 10th ed. Lanham, MD: Rowman & Littlefield.
Thompson, William E., and Jennifer C. Gibbs. 2017. *Deviance & Deviants: A Sociological Approach*. Malden, MA: Wiley Blackwell.
Thompson, William E., Joseph V. Hickey, and Mica L. Thompson. 2019. *Society in Focus: An Introduction to Sociology*. 9th ed. Lanham, MD: Rowman & Littlefield.
Thorne, Barrie. 1993. *Gender Play: Girls and Boys in School*. New Brunswick, NJ: Rutgers University Press.
———. 2007. "Borderwork among Girls and Boys." Pp. 317–325 in *Inside Social Life: Readings in Social Psychology and Microsociology*, edited by Spencer Cahill. 5th ed. Los Angeles: Roxbury.
Todorov, Alexander. 2017. *Face Value: The Irresistible Influence of First Impressions*. Princeton, NJ: Princeton University Press.
Toennies, Ferdinand. [1887] 1961. "Gemeinschaft and Gesellschaft." Pp. 190–201 in *Theories of Society*, edited by Talcott Parsons, et al. 3rd ed., vol. 1. Glencoe, IL: Free Press.
Tomasson, Richard F. 2000. "Reaching the Top." *Society* 37(5):9–18.
Tong, Rosemary Putnam. 2017. *Feminist Thought: A More Comprehensive Introduction*. 5th ed. London: Routledge.
Turk, Austin. 1969. *Criminality and Legal Order*. Chicago: Rand McNally.
Turkle, Sherry. 2005. *The Second Self: Computer and the Human Spirit*. 20th Anniversary ed. Cambridge, MA: MIT Press.
———. 2009. *Simulation and Its Discontents*. Boston: MIT Press.
———. 2011. *Life on the Screen: Identity in the Age of the Internet*. New York: Simon & Schuster.
———. 2016. *Reclaiming Conversation: The Power of Talk in a Digital Age*. New York: Penguin Press.
———. 2017. *Alone Together: Why We Expect More from Technology and Less from Each Other*. Rev. ed. New York: Basic Books.
Turner, Ralph H., and Lewis M. Killian. 1987. *Collective Behavior*. 3rd ed. Englewood Cliffs, NJ: Prentice Hall.
Tuxill, John. 1997. "Death in the Family Tree." *World Watch* 10(5):12–21.
Twenge, Jean. 2007. *Generation Me*. New York: Atria.

United Nations. N.d. *Climate Change*. https://www.un.org/en/sections/issues-depth/climate-change/index.html.

United Nations Development Report. 2017. *Human Development Report 2017*. New York: United Nations.

———. 2018. *Statistical Abstract of the United States, 2017*. Washington, DC: Government Printing Office.

Vaughn, Adam. 2012. "London Air Pollution at Record High." *The Guardian*, March 15. http://www.theguardian.com/environment/2012/mar/15/london-air-pollution-record-high.

Veblen, Thorstein. 1899. *The Theory of the Leisure Class*. New York: Macmillan.

Vold, George B. 2009. *Theoretical Criminology*. 6th ed. New York: Oxford University Press.

Wade, Lisa, and Myra Marx Ferree. 2015. *Gender: Ideas, Interactions, and Institutions*. London: W. W. Norton.

Wallace, Samuel E. 2017. *Total Institutions*. London: Routledge.

Walsh, Patrick. 2016. "Birds Learn Skills for Nest Building." *University of Edinburgh News Bulletin*, April 13.

Wang, Hasim Lo. 2018. "2020 Census to Keep Same Racial Categories." *NPR*. https://www.npr.org/2018/01/26/580865378/census-request-suggests-no-race-ethnicity-data-changes-in-2020-experts-say.

Warschauer, Mark. 2003. *Technology and Social Inclusion: Rethinking the Digital Divide*. Cambridge, MA: MIT Press.

Washington Post. 1997. "Day Care Doesn't Hurt Kids' Learning, Study Says." *Dallas Morning News*, April 4, pp. 1A, 19A.

Watson, John B. 1924. *Behavior*. New York: Norton.

Webb, R. K. 1960. *Harriet Martineau, a Radical Victorian*. New York: Columbia University Press.

Weber, Max.1946. *Max Weber: Essays in Sociology*. H. H. Gerth and C. Wright Mills (eds. and trans.). New York: Oxford University Press.

———. 1947. *The Theory of Social and Economic Organization*. New York: Free Press.

———. [1904–1905] 1958a. *The Protestant Ethic and the Spirit of Capitalism*. New York: Scribner.

———. 1978. *Economy and Society*, vol. 2. Guenther Roth and Claus Wittich (eds.). Berkeley: University of California Press.

Weeks, John R. 2016. *Population: An Introduction to Concepts and Issues*. 12th ed. Boston: Cengage Learning.

Wekesser, Carol (ed.). 1997. *Pornography: Opposing Viewpoints*. San Diego: Greenhaven Press.

Wells, Spencer Y. 2009. "Your Genetic Journey..." *TANTATA: Things (Often) Are Not As They Appear*, February 6.

Whiting, Robert. 2009. *You Gotta Have Wa*. New York: Vintage Books.

Whyte, William Foote. 1943. *Street Corner Society*. Chicago: University of Chicago Press.

Williams, Frederick, Robert LaRose, and Frederica Frost. 1981. *Children, Television, and Sex-Role Stereotyping*. New York: Praeger.

Williams, Robin M., Jr. 1970. *American Society: A Sociological Interpretation*. 3rd ed. New York: Knopf.

Willingham, A. J. 2018. "An Oil Spill You Never Heard of Could Become One of the Greatest Environmental Disasters in the U.S." *CNN*, October 24. https://www.cnn.com/2018/10/23/us/taylor-energy-oil-largest-spill-disaster-ivan-golf-of-mexico-environment-trnd/index.html.

Wilson, Brian. 2003. "The Canadian Rave Scene and Five Theses on Youth Resistance." *Canadian Journal of Sociology* 27(3):373–391.

Wilson, Edward O. 2000. *Sociobiology: The New Synthesis*. Boston: Belknap Press.

Wilton, Tamsin. 2005. *Sexual (Dis)Orientation: Gender, Sex, Desire and Self-Fashioning*. New York: Palgrave Macmillan.

Wirth, Louis. 1938. "Urbanism as a Way of Life." *American Journal of Sociology* 44(1):1–24.

Wishart, David J. 2016. *Great Plains Indians*. Lincoln, NE: University of Nebraska Press.

Wolman, Harold L., Coit Cook Ford III, and Edward Hill. 1994. "Evaluating the Success of Urban Success Stories." *Urban Studies* 31(6):835–850.

Wood, Erica F. 2006. *The Availability and Utility of Interdisciplinary Data on Elder Abuse: A White Paper for the National Center on Elder Abuse*. Washington, DC: National Center on Elder Abuse, May.

World Health Organization. 2018. http://www.who.int/en/.

World Resources Institute. 2018. http:// www.wri.org.

Worldwatch Institute. 2014. *State of the World 2014: Governing for Sustainability*. Washington, DC: Worldwatch Institute.

———. 2017. *State of the World 2017: Confronting Hidden Threats to Sustainability*. Washington, DC: Island Press.

Zabarenko, Deborah. 2006. "Global Warming Reaches a 'Tipping Point': A Report." Reuters online news service, March 15.

Zephoria. 2018. *The Top 20 Valuable Facebook Statistics*. February. https://zephoria.com/top-15-valuable-facebook-statistics/.

Further Readings

APA. 2015. "How Common Is Sexting?" *American Psychological Association*. http://www.apa.org/news/press/releases/2015/08/common-sexting.aspx.

Associated Press. 2009. "Teen 'Sexting' Spurs Charges." *Dallas Morning News*, February 5, p. 8A.

Bahjat, Mudhaffer. 2017. "Sources of Human Psychological Differences: The Minnesota Study of Twins Reared Apart (1990), by Thomas J. Bouchard Jr, David T. Lykken, Matthew McGue, Nancy L. Segal, and Auke Tellegen." *Embryo Project Encyclopedia* (October 19). ISSN: 1940–5030. http://embryo.asu.edu/pages/sources-human-psychological-differences-minnesota-study-twins-reared-apart-1990-thomas-j.

Boyle, Karen. 2005. *Media and Violence: Gendering the Debates*. Thousand Oaks, CA: Sage.

Broadhurst, Roderic. 2006. "Developments in the Global Law Enforcement of Cyber-Crime." *International Journal of Police Strategies and Management* 29(3):408–433.

Brownill, Sue. 1984. "From Critique to Intervention: Socialist-Feminist Perspectives on Urbanization." *Antipode* 16(3):21–34.

Burns, Ronald G., Keith H. Whitworth, and Carol Y. Thompson. 2004. "Assessing Law Enforcement Preparedness to Address Internet Fraud." *Journal of Criminal Justice* 32:477–493.

Carson, Rachel. 1962. *Silent Spring*. Boston: Houghton-Mifflin.

Craddock, Ashley. 1997. "Netwar and Peace in the Global Village." *Wired* (May):1–5.

Cuyvers, Ludo, and Pilip De Beule, eds. 2006. *Transnational Corporations and Economic Development: From Internationalisation to Globalisation*. Hampshire, England: Palgrave Macmillan.

Daly, Kathleen, and Meda Chesney-Lind. 1984. Feminism and Criminology. *Justice Quarterly* 5(4):497–538.

Driskell, Nathan. 2017. *Internet Addiction: Kicking the Habit*. Cypress, TX: Independent.

Ellis, Desmond. 1987. *The Wrong Stuff*. New York: Macmillan.

Ember, Carol R., and Melvin Ember. 2015. *Cultural Anthropology*. 14th ed. Boston: Pearson.

Engels, Friedrich. [1884] 1902. *The Origin of the Family.* Chicago: Charles H. Kerr.

Englehardt, Tom. 1986. "The Shortcake Strategy." Pp. 68–110 in *Watching Television*, edited by Todd Gitlin. New York: Pantheon.

Erikson, Erik H. 1963. *Childhood and Society.* New York: Norton.

———. 1994. *Identity and the Life Cycle.* New York: W. W. Norton.

Felson, Richard B. 1996. "Mass Media Effects on Violent Behavior." Pp. 103–128 in *Annual Review of Sociology 22*, edited by John Hagan and Karen S. Cook. Palo Alto, CA: Annual Reviews.

Gentile, Douglas A., ed. 2014. *Media Violence and Children.* Santa Barbara, CA: Praeger.

———. 1982. "Testing the Theory of Status Integration and Suicide Rates." *American Sociological Review* 47(2):227–237.

Goff, Karen G. 2009. "Watching Violent News Has Harmful Effects on Children." Pp. 141–145 in *Opposing Viewpoints: Media Violence*, edited by David M. Haugen. Chicago: Greenhaven Press.

Governors Highway Safety Association. 2017. *Distracted Driving Laws.* www.ghsa.org.

Graber, Doris A., and Johanna L. Dunaway. 2017. *Mass Media and American Politics.* 10th ed. Los Angeles: CQ Press.

Graves, Joseph L., Jr. 2004. *The Race Myth: Why We Pretend Race Exists in America.* New York: Penguin.

Gregory, Christine. 2018. "Internet Addiction Disorder: Signs, Symptoms, and Treatment." *Psycom*, February 14. https://www.psycom.net/iadcriteria.html.

Grimes, Thomas, James A. Anderson, and Lori A. Bergen. 2007. *Media Violence and Aggression: Science and Ideology.* Newbury Park, CA: Sage.

Grossman, Lawrence K. 1995. *The Electronic Republic.* New York: Penguin.

Hall, Peter. 2014. *Cities of Tomorrow; An Intellectual History of Urban Planning and Design Since 1880.* 4th ed. New York: Wiley-Blackwell.

Harris, David R., and Jeremiah J. Sim. 2002. "Who Is Multiracial? Assessing the Complexity of Lived Race." *American Sociological Review* 67(4):614–627.

Harris, Marvin. 2011. *Cows, Pigs, Wars and Witches: The Riddles of Culture.* New York: Vintage.

Hess, John. 1991. "Geezer-Bashing: Media Attacks on the Elderly." *Extra* (August/September):6–7.

Hoare, Carol H. 2002. *Erikson on Development in Adulthood: New Insights from the Unpublished Papers.* New York: Oxford University Press.

Holt, Thomas J., and Adam M. Bossler. 2014. "An Assessment of the Current State of Cybercrime Scholarship." *Deviant Behavior* 35(1):20–40.

Houghton, John. 2015. *Global Warming: The Complete Briefing.* 5th ed. Cambridge, UK: Cambridge University Press.

Ingraham, Christopher. 2017. "The Richest 1 Percent Now Owns More of the Country's Wealth Than Any Time in the Past 50 Years." *Washington Post*, December 6. https://www.washingtonpost.com/news/wonk/wp/2017/12/06/the-richest-1-percent-now-owns-more-of-the-countrys-wealth-than-at-any-time-in-the-past-50-years/?utm_term=.db3421d47ed8.

Johnston, Jerome, and James S. Ettema. 1986. "Using Television to Best Advantage: Research for Prosocial Television." Pp. 143–164 in *Perspectives on Media Effects*, edited by Jennings Bryant and Dolf Zillmann. Hillsdale, NJ: Erlbaum.

Kantrowitz, Barbara. 2005. "The 100 Best High Schools in America." *Newsweek*, May 16, pp. 50–59.

Kantrowitz, Barbara, and Claudia Kalb. 1998. "Boys Will Be Boys." *Newsweek*, May 11, pp, 55–60.

Kohlberg, Lawrence. 1981. *The Psychology of Moral Development: The Nature and Validity of Moral Stages.* New York: Harper & Row.

Koo, Richard C. 2003. *Balance Sheet Recession: Japan's Struggle with Uncharted Economics and Its Global Implications.* Singapore: John Wiley & Sons.

Levert, Natasha P. 2007. "A Comparison of Christian and Non-Christian Males, Authoritarianism, and Their Relationship to Internet Pornography Addiction/Compulsion." *Sexual Addiction & Compulsivity* 14:145–166.

Levinson, Daniel J. 1978. *The Seasons of a Man's Life.* New York: Knopf.

———. 2007b. "Social Networking and Class Warfare." *Newsweek*, August 6, p. 16.

Liazos, Alexander. 1972. "The Poverty of the Sociology of Deviance: Nuts, Sluts, and Perverts." *Social Problems* 20:102–120.

Loewen, James W. 1988. *The Mississippi Chinese: Between Black and White.* 2nd ed. Prospect Heights, IL: Waveland.

Lombroso, Cesare. 1911. *Crime, Its Causes and Remedies.* Translated by H. P. Horton. Boston: Little, Brown.

Lowney, Kathleen. 1995. "Satanism as Oppositional Youth Subculture." *Journal of Contemporary Ethnography* 23(4):453–484.

Lyng, Stephen. 2005. *Edgework: The Sociology of Risk-Taking.* New York: Routledge Taylor and Francis.

Maguire, Brendan, Diane Sandage, and Georgie Ann Weatherby. 2000. "Violence, Morality, and Television Commercials." *Sociological Spectrum* 20 (January–March):121–143.

Markey, Patrick M., Charlotte M. Markey, and Juliana E. French. 2015. "Violent Video Games and Real World Violence: Rhetoric versus Data." *Psychology of Popular Media Culture* 44(4):277–295. http://dx.doi.org/10.1037/ppm0000030.

McCaffrey, Shannon. 2003. "Ruling: Filter Internet Porn in Libraries or Forfeit Funding." *Dallas Morning News*, July 24:16A.

McGinn, Daniel. 2002. "Guilt Free TV." *Newsweek*, November 11, pp. 53–59.

———. [1949] 1976. "Discrimination and the American Creed." Pp. 189–216 in *Sociological Ambivalence and Other Essays*, edited by Robert K. Merton. New York: Free Press.

Mills, C. Wright. 1951. *White Collar: The American Middle Classes*. New York: Oxford University Press.

Milne, George R. 2003. "How Well Do Consumers Protect Themselves from Identity Theft?" *Journal of Consumer Affairs* 37(2):388–402.

Mishel, Lawrence, Josh Bivens, Elise Gould, and Heidi Shierholz. 2012. *The State of Working America*. 12th ed. Ithaca, NY: Cornell University Press.

Mittelstadt, Michelle, and Catherine K. Enders. 2000. "Postal Workers Get Bad Rap, According to Violence Study." *Dallas Morning News*, September 1, p. 4A.

Morgan, Glenn, Peer Hull Kristensen, and Richard Whitley, eds. 2003. *The Multinational Firm*. New York: Oxford University Press.

Myers, David G. 2014. *Social Psychology*. 11th ed. New York: McGraw-Hill.

National Center for Education Statistics. 2018. *Digest of Education Statistics, 2017*. Washington, DC: Government Printing Office.

Nee, Victor. 1989. "A Theory of Market Transition: From Redistribution to Markets in State Socialism." *American Sociological Review* 54(5):663–681.

———. 1991. "Social Inequalities in Reforming State Socialism: Between Redistribution and Markets in China." *American Sociological Review* 56(3):267–282.

Newsweek. 2009. "We Are All Socialists Now: The Perils and Promise of the New Era of Big Government." *Newsweek*, February 11.

Nimmo, Dan. 1978. *Political Communication and Public Opinion in America*. Santa Monica, CA: Goodyear.

Noggle, Gary, and Lynda Lee Kaid. 2000. "The Effects of Visual Images in Political Ads: Experimental Testing of Distortions and Visual Literacy." *Social Sciences Quarterly* 81(4): 913–927.

O'Keefe, Gwenn Schurgin, and Kathleen Clarke-Pearson. 2011. "The Impact of Social Media on Children, Adolescents, and Families." *Pediatrics* 127(4):800–804.

Perez, Christina. 2014. Revisiting Erving Goffman's Stigma: Notes on the Management of Spoiled Identity. *Social Analysis of Health Network (SAHN)*. July 1. https://sahncambridge.wordpress.com/2014/07/01/revisiting-erving-goffmans-stigma-notes-on-the-management-of-spoiled-identity-by-cristina-perez.

Phillips, David P. 1974. "The Influence of Suggestion on Suicide: Substantive and Theoretical Implications of the Werther Effect." *American Sociological Review* 39(3):350–354.

———. 1983. "The Impact of Mass Media Violence on U.S. Homicides." *American Sociological Review* 48(4):560–568.

Piaget, Jean. 1954. *The Construction of Reality in the Child*. New York: Basic Books.

Pierson, David. 2009. "Rapid Growth in Elderly Population a Challenge for China." *Dallas Morning News*, July 12, p. 17A.

Real, Michael R. 1989. *Super Media: A Cultural Studies Approach*. Newbury Park, CA: Sage.

Rideout, Vicky. 2011. *Zero to Eight: Children's Media Use in America*. San Francisco: Common Sense Media.

Roberts, Donald F., and Ulla G. Foehr. 2008. "Trends in Media Use." *The Future of Children* 18(1):14–37.

Robinson, William I. 2014. *Global Capitalism and the Crisis of Humanity*. Cambridge: Cambridge University Press.

Rose, Peter I. 2014. *They and We: Racial and Ethnic Relations in the United States*. 7th ed. Boulder, CO: Paradigm Press.

Schein, Elyse, and Paula Bernstein. 2009. *Identical Strangers: A Memoir of Twins Separated and Reunited*. New York: Random House.

Schor, Julia. 2000. *The Overspent American: Why We Want What We Don't Need*. New York: Harper.

Sebald, Hans. 1968. *Adolescence: A Sociological Analysis*. New York: Appleton-Century-Crofts.

———. 1986. "Adolescents' Shifting Orientation toward Parents and Peers: A Curvilinear Trend over Recent Decades." *Journal of Marriage and the Family* 48:5–13.

Skerry, Peter. 2000. *Counting the Census? Race, Group Identity, and the Evasion of Politics*. Washington, DC: Brookings Institution Press.

———. 2004. "Women's Perspective as a Radical Critique of Sociology." Pp. 21–34 in *The Feminist Standpoint Theory Reader*, edited by Sandra Harding. New York and London: Routledge.

Spalter-Roth, Roberta, and Nicole Van Vooren. 2008. "What Skills Do Sociology Majors Learn and What Is the Pathway to Using Them on the Job?." *ASA Footnotes* 37 (May/June):1, 8.

Spitzer, Steven. 1980. "Toward a Marxian Theory of Deviance." Pp. 175–191 in *Criminal Behavior: Readings in Criminology*, edited by Delow H. Kelly. New York: St. Martin's Press.

Stack, Steven. 1987a. "Celebrities and Suicide: A Taxonomy and Analysis, 1948–1983." *American Sociological Review* 52(3):401–412.

———. 1987b. "Publicized Executions and Homicide, 1950–1980." *American Sociological Review* 52(4):532–540.

———. 1990a. "Execution Publicity and Homicide in South Carolina: A Research Note." *Sociological Quarterly* 31(4):599–611.

———. 1990b. "New Micro-Level Data on the Impact of Divorce on Suicide, 1959–1980: A Test of Two Theories." *Journal of Marriage and the Family* 52(1):119–127.

———. 1994. "The Effects of Gender on Publishing: The Case of Sociology." *Sociological Focus* 27(1):81–83.

———. 2000. "Media Impacts on Suicide: A Quantitative Review of 293 Findings." *Social Science Quarterly* 81(4):957–971.

———. 2002. "Gender and Scholarly Productivity: 1970–2000." *Sociological Focus* 35(3):285–296.

Stack, Steven and Augustine J. Kposowa. 2008. "The Association of Suicide Rates with Individual-Level Suicide Attitudes: A Cross-National Analysis." *Social Science Quarterly* 89(1):39–59.

Stiles, Beverly L., and Howard B. Kaplan. 1996. "Stigma, Deviance, and Negative Social Sanctions." *Social Science Quarterly* 77(3):685–696.

Stockard, Jean, and Robert M. O'Brien. 2002. "Cohort Effects on Suicide Rates: International Variations." *American Sociological Review* 67(6):854–872.

Stone, Brad. 1998. "The Keyboard Kids." *Newsweek*, June 8, pp. 72–74.

Tannen, Deborah. 1998. "Interview." *Dallas Morning News*, April 12, pp. 1J, 10J.

Tester, Keith. 2000. "Between Sociology and Theology: The Spirit of Capitalism Debate." *The Sociological Review* 48(1):43–57.

Thompson, Kenneth W. 1990. "Ubiquity of Power." *Society* 28 (November/December):56–65.

Thompson, William E. 1981. "The Oklahoma Amish: Survival of an Ethnic Subculture." *Ethnicity* 8(4):476–487.

———. 1983. "Hanging Tongues: A Sociological Encounter with the Assembly Line." *Qualitative Sociology* 6(3):215–237.

———. 1984. "Old Order Amish in Oklahoma and Kansas: Rural Tradition in Urban Society." *Free Inquiry in Creative Sociology* 12 (May):39–43.

———. 1991. "Handling the Stigma of Handling the Dead: Morticians and Funeral Directors." *Deviant Behavior* 12(4):403–429.

———. 2009. "Pseudo-Deviance and the 'New Biker' Subculture: Hogs, Blogs, Leathers, and Lattes." *Deviant Behavior* 30(1):89–114.

Turnbull, Colin M. 1977. *Man in Africa*. Garden City, NY: Doubleday (Anchor Books).

U.S. Bureau of the Census. 2000. *Statistical Abstract of the United States, 2000*. Washington, DC: Government Printing Office.

Van Ausdale, Debra, and Joe R. Feagin. 2007. "Young Children's Racial and Ethnic Definitions of Self." Pp. 37–49 in *Inside Social Life: Readings in Social Psychology and Microsociology*, edited by Spencer E. Cahill. 5th ed. Los Angeles: Roxbury.

Van Gennep, Arnold. [1908] 1960. *The Rights of Passage*. Translated by M. B. Vizedom and G. L. Caffee. Chicago: University of Chicago Press.

Van Poppel, Frans, and Lincoln H. Day. 1996. "A Test of Durkheim's Theory of Suicide—Without Committing the 'Ecological Fallacy.'" *American Sociological Review* 61(3):500–507.

———. 2000. "Study: Violent Media Targeting Young Buyers." *Dallas Morning News*, August 27:7A.

Whitcomb, Dan. 2008. "O.J. Simpson's Luck Runs Out after 13 Years." *Reuters*, October 4.

World Watch. 2003. "Interviews with Rajendra Pachauri and Robert Watson." *World Watch* 16 (March/April):10–15.

Wright, Wynne, and Elizabeth Ransom. 2005. "Stratification on the Menu: Using Restaurant Menus to Examine Social Class." *Teaching Sociology* 33(3):310–316.

Index

A
Abominations of the Body, 161
achieved statuses, 115
acting crowds, 218
ad infinitum, 94
adultescence, 96
adult socialization, 97–98
affirmative action, 74
Affordable Care Act, 45, 201
Afro-American sociology, 18
Afrocentrism, 73
age and ageism, 196–201
Age Discrimination in Employment Act (ADEA), 197, 199
agents of socialization, 87–94
    family, 88–89
    media and technology, 93–94
    peers, 91–92
    religion, 90–91
    school, 89–90
    workplace, 92
Age of Enlightenment, 13, 149
Age of Reason, 13, 149
agrarian societies, 59
agricultural mismanagement, 249
Agricultural Revolution, 59
Akers, Ronald, 174
alternate truths, 33
alt-right, 77
American Association of Retired Persons (AARP), 198
American Sociological Association (ASA), 43
Americentrism, 74
androgyny, 195
anticipatory socialization, 92
anticult movement, 222
antithesis, 213
appeal to higher loyalties, 176
applied sociology, 18, 258
Aryan Brotherhood, 77
Asch experiment, 140
ascribed statuses, 114–15
assimilationist approach, 73
assumptions, analyzing, 9, 10

authoritarian leaders, 139
authoritative knowledge, 33–34
authority, 149–51
autokinetic effect, 139–40
availability sampling, 47

B
baby boom, 238
baby boom echo, 238
baby boomers, 238
Bainbridge, William, 148–49
barbarism, 210
beauty, standards of, 63
Becker, Carl, 212
Becker, Howard, 42, 166–67, 173
becoming human, process of, 77
becoming you: a social being. *See* social development
beliefs, 61–62
Benford, Robert, 224
Berger, Peter, 2, 4
Berkeley free-speech movement, 227
bias, avoiding, 51
biography, defined, 4
biological race, 187–88
biological theories of evolution, 211
Black Panthers, 77
Blau, Peter, 151–52
Blemishes of Individual Character, 161
bloc mobilization, 227
Blumer, Herbert, 24, 111
body language, 66
Bork, Robert, 74
bourgeoisie, 16, 22, 170
Bridgman, Percy, 42
Brown, J. David, 116
Buffet, Warren, 136
bureaucracies, 142–43
Burgess, Ernest, 246–47
Bush, George W., 254

C
Cable, Sherry, 228
capitalism, 152
career model of deviance, 173

case studies, 41, 50
Castells, Manuel, 128
casual crowds, 217–18
causation, 40
cause-and-effect explanations, 14, 34
cause-and-effect relationships, 40
Cavan, Ruth, 158–59
Challenger disaster, 140
charisma, 226
charismatic authority, 150, 151
Cheney, Dick, 254
Chernobyl nuclear plant, 252
Chicago School, 19, 52, 245
childhood socialization, 94–99
    criticism of theories, 97
    cultural differences in, 96
    18- to 30-year olds, 96–97
    generalized others, responding to, 95
    Mead's development stages, 95–96
    primary socialization, 95
    role taking, 95
    significant others, responding to, 95
Children's Rights Movement, 224
childsaver movement, 222
chlorofluorocarbons (CFCs), 255
Christian, meaning of, 147
Christian Identity Movement, 77
chromosomes, 193
cisgender, 193
civilization, 210, 238–39
Civil Rights movement, 4–5, 226
class ranking. *See* social class
class system, 181. *See also* social class
Clinton, Bill, 3
closed-ended questions, 47
closed systems, 181
clothing, symbolic, 64
Cloward, Richard, 169
Code of Ethics (ASA), 43
code words, 74
coercion, 123
coercive organizations, 142
Cohen, Albert, 169
collective behavior, 215–22

collectivities, 215–16
colors, symbolic, 64
Columbia disaster, 140
comfort zones, 107–9
common sense *versus* common nonsense, 10, 11–12
compensators, 149
competition, 122–23
composition of a population, 234
Comte, Auguste, 14, 15, 18, 210–11
concentric zone model, 246–47
concept, defined, 38
conceptual definition, 38
conclusions, 41
condemnation of the condemners, 175
conflict, as pattern of interaction, 123
conflict perspective, 19, 21, 22–23
  of age and ageism, 201
  of class conflict, 213–14
  conflict theorists differentiated from functionalists, 53
  of cultural values, 68
  of desocialization and resocialization, 101–2
  of deviance and conformity, 170–72
  economics and, 151–52
  feminist theories and, 24
  in integrated approach, 27
  Marxian approach and, 16, 22
  of media portrayals, 94
  neo-conflict approach and, 16, 22
  of power, 170–71, 182
  in quantitative research, 52–53
  of social interaction, 123
  of socialization over life course, 99
  of social networks, 121
conformity, 156–57
  overconformity, 159
  place of occurrence, 160
  positive sanctions to reward, 177
  situation of, 160
  sociological theories of, 167–76
  time in defining, 159
  underconformity, 159
consolidated metropolitan statistical areas (CMSAs), 240
conspicuous consumption, 152
consumption, 152
contagion theory, 216
containment theory, 174–75
content analysis, 50–51
conventional crowds, 218
convergence hypothesis, 7

convergence theory, 216
Cooley, Charles Horton, 86–87, 95, 133
cooperation, 122
core values, 67–68
correlation, 40
cosmology, 148
countercultures, 76–78
countermovements, 225–29
crime, deviance equated with, 163
critical thinking, 8–9
crowd psychology, 216
crude birthrate, 234
crude death rate, 234
cultural borrowing, 209
cultural eclecticism, 79
cultural innovation, 209
cultural lag, 75–76
cultural relativism, 71–75
cultural tradition, gaining knowledge through, 32–33
culture
  beliefs in, 67
  components of, 60–71
  defined, 60
  first evidence of, 63
  ideal *versus* real, 75–76
  language in, 65–67
  mores in, 69–71
  norms in, 68–69
  popular, 78–79
  symbols in, 61–65
  taboos in, 71
  values in, 67–68
cyberbullying, 167
cyberporn, 163–65
cybersex, 163–65

D

"damned if you do, damned if you don't" dilemma, 9
Darwin, Charles, 15, 62, 83, 211
data analysis and interpretation, 41
data collection, 41
death rates, 234
deductive reasoning, 36–38
Deepwater Horizon explosion, 250–51
definition of the situation, 25, 110
deforestation, 249
degradation ceremony, 101
democratic leadership style, 139
demographic transition theory, 236–37
demography, 209, 234–35
Denzin, Norman, 51

dependent variable, 46
descriptive research, 44
desertification, 249
desocialization, 99, 100–104
deterrence theory, 177
DeVault, Marjorie, 53
developmental socialization, 99
development stages. *See also* childhood socialization
  adult, 97–98
  Mead's, 95–96
deviance, 156–57, 161–62
  career model of, 173
  crime equated with, 163
  defined, 163
  deterrence theory, 177
  elite, 171–72
  extreme, 159
  medical model and, 166
  mental illness and, 166
  negative sanctions to punish, 177
  overconformity, 159
  place of occurrence, 160
  popular explanations of, 165–67
  pornography, 163–65
  power theories for explaining, 170–71
  primary, 172–73
  relativity of, 159–60
  secondary, 173
  situation of, 160
  sociological theories of, 167–76
  stigma and, 160–62
  time in defining, 159
  underconformity, 159
deviant identities, 116
differences, emphasizing, 180–203
  age and ageism, 196–201
  intersectionality, 201–3
  race, ethnicity, and minority groups, 187–92
  sex and gender, 193–96
  social class, 180–82
  socioeconomic status, 183–87
differential association theory, 173
differential reinforcement, 174
diffusion, 209–10
discovering sociology, 2–27, 259
  common sense *versus* common nonsense, 10, 11–12
  conflict perspective, 19, 22–23
  feminist perspective, 19, 23–24
  global society, life in, 6–11

overview of sociological wisdom, 3–4
science, importance of, 12–20
sociological imagination, 4–5
structural functionalist perspective, 19, 20–21
symbolic interactionist perspective, 24–27
discrimination, 192
Disneyization, 79
distribution, 152
doing sociology, 30–55, 259–60
   ethical issues in sociological research, 42–43
   research types, 43–55
   scientific method, 40–42
   sociology and scientific knowledge, 35–36
   theory-building process, 36–40
   things are not what they seem, 30–35
dominant emotion, 217
Donne, John, 149
double jeopardy, 201
doubling time, 235–36
Dowd, James and Laura, 78
dramaturgical analysis, 25–26, 111
dramaturgy, 111–12
Dubois, William E. B., 18
Durkheim, Émile, 16–17, 36, 130, 147–48, 157, 168, 211–12, 244–45
dyad, 137
dysfunctional aspects of society, 21
dystopian societies, 130

E

Eagle Forum, 225
Eagleton, Terry, 78–79
ecological model, 246–47
ecological perspective, 248
ecology and the environment, 244–54
economic determinism, 22, 151
economic system, 152
economy, 151–54
   capitalism, 152
   consumption, 152
   distribution, 152
   mixed, 153
   production, 152
   socialism, 152–53
ecosystem, 245
education, 145–47
ego, 85
Ehrlich, Anne, 236
Ehrlich, Paul, 236–37

18- to 30-year olds, development of, 96–97
elder abuse, 200
Elder Justice Act of 2003, 201
Elder Justice Coalition, 201
elite deviance, 171–72
emergent norm theory, 216
empirical verification, 34
English as official language of United States, 74
environment, ecology and, 244–54
environmental causes, 254–56
Environmental Protection Agency, 252, 254
ethical issues in sociological research, 42–43
ethnic group, 189–90
ethnicity, 187–92
ethnocentrism, 71–75, 192
ethnographic interview, 41, 48–49
ethnography, defined, 49
ethnomethodology, 113
Eurocentrism, 73–74
evaluation research, 44–45
evolution, theory of, 62
exchange, 122
exchange theory, 151–52
experience, gaining knowledge through, 31
experimental method, 46
expertise, 150
explanatory research, 44
exploratory research, 43–44
expressive crowds, 218
expressive relationships, 133–34
extinction of plants and wildlife, 249–50
extreme deviance, 159
Exxon Valdez, 250–51

F

Facebook, 129
face-to-face interaction, 27, 109, 111, 129, 134, 136, 244
fads, 219–20
faith, gaining knowledge through, 33
family, as agent of socialization, 88–89
family, defined, 144–45
family of marriage, 145
family of orientation, 145
farming societies, 59
fashions, 220
Federal Bureau of Investigation (FBI), 45, 197

femininity, 193, 194
feminist perspective, 19, 23–24. *See also* feminist theory
feminist research, 53–55
feminist theory
   defined, 23–24
   deviance-conformity and, 176
   focus of, 27
   gender research and, 54–55, 98–99
   gender roles and, 98
   social change and, 215
   Standpoint Theory, 53
Ferree, Myra Marx, 202
fertility, 234
financial exploitation, of elderly, 200
Fine, Gary, 219
folklore, 32, 34, 259
folkways, 69
formal organizations, 141–42
formal sanctions, 69–70
formal social control, 244
frame alignment, 224
Franklin, Benjamin, 237
free-rider problem, 216, 226
Freud, Sigmund, 85
frustration–aggression hypothesis, 192
full participation, 50

G

game stage, 95–96
Gamson, William, 227
Garfinkel, Harold, 113
Gates, Bill, 136, 185
Gemeinschaft, 244
gender, defined, 193
gender identity, 193
gender research, 54
gender roles, 24, 98, 103, 176, 194–95
general deterrence, 177
generalizations, 5, 8, 41, 47
generalized beliefs, 217
generalized others, 95
gerontology, 266
Gesellschaft, 244
Gilligan, Carol, 98–99, 194, 195
Giordano, Peggy, 194
global awareness, 7
global climate change, 248–49, 253–54
global greenhouse buildup, 249
globalization, defined, 7, 58
global society, life in, 6–11
global village, 59
global warming, 253–54

Index

Goffman, Erving, 102, 111, 112, 117, 161–62
Goldberg, Robert, 224, 227–28, 229
googling, 67
Gore, Al, 254
government, 149–51
Gray Panthers, 198–99
Great Depression, 18
Green Party, 254
group polarization phenomenon, 141
groupthink, 11, 140
growth rate, 235

H
Hall, Edward, 107–8
Harley-Davidson motorcycles, 64–65
Harris, C. D., 247–48
Harris, Diana, 196
hate crimes, 162
"haves" and "have-nots," 16
Hawthorne effect, 46
heresies, 33
high culture, 78–79
hippie movement, 77
Hirschi, Travis, 174
history, defined, 4
history makers, 4
Homans, George, 136, 151–52
homogeneity, 211
homosexuality, 42–43
Hornsby, Anne, 130
How to Observe Manners and Morals (Martineau), 15
Hoyt, Homer, 247
human ecology, 245
Human Group, The (Homans), 136
human instincts, 83
human-interest stories, 219
human nature, 144
Humphreys, Laud, 42–43, 50
hunting-gathering societies, 59
Hurricane Harvey, 232–33
Hurricane Katrina, 232, 233
Hurricane Maria, 233
hypotheses, 41

I
I component in self, 85–86
id, 85
ideal culture, 75–76
idealistic mentality, 214
ideal type, 17–18, 42, 134, 143

ideational mentality, 214
imitative stage, 95
immigration, 13
immorality, 162–63, 172
impression management, 26, 112
Inconvenient Truth, An (Gore), 254
independent variable, 46
inductive reasoning, 36–37
industrialization, 13
Industrial Revolution, 13, 15, 59, 76, 210, 214, 245
industrial societies, 59
informal sanctions, 69
informal social control, 177–78, 244
informal socialization, 92
informant, 49
information processing, 59–60
information technologies, new, 9–10, 59, 78
in-group–out-group distinction, 134–35
injury, denial of, 175
inner containment, 174
instrumental behavior, 134
integrated approach to sociological wisdom, 26–27
interacting in everyday life, 106–30, 261–62
 media and technology, social interaction and, 125–30
 personal space and nonverbal communication, 106–13
 social interaction, patterns of, 122–25
 social networks, 119–21
 statuses and roles, 114–19
interactionist perspective. *See* symbolic interactionist perspective
International Treaty on Global Warming, 254
internet addiction, 163–65, 167
Internet Society, 128
internet use, abuse, dependency, and addiction, 165
interpretive paradigm, 48
intersectionality, 201–3
intervening variable, 46
interview, 47–49
intimate distance, 107
Iowa School, 52
iron cage, 142
Irwin, John, 102

J
Janis, Irving, 140
justice perspective on morality, 99

K
Kashiwazaki, Japan nuclear power plant, 252
Kennedy, John F., 22
Kennedy, Robert, 22
Keystone Pipeline, 254
kidults, 96
Killian, Lewis, 216, 218
King, Martin Luther, Jr., 22, 206, 215, 217, 226
Kitatani, Katsuhide, 255
knowledge
 authoritative, 33–34
 gaining, 31–33
 methodological flexibility in quest for, 42
 scientific, 34, 35–36
 theory-building process, 36–40
 types, 30–31
Koresh, David, 219
Kozol, Jonathan, 90
Kroc, Ray, 215
Kuhn, Maggie, 198–99
Ku Klux Klan, 227
Kusch, Polykarp, 42
Kushner, Jared, 121
Kyoto Protocol, 254

L
labeling approach, 26
labeling perspective, 42
labeling theories, 172
laissez-faire–style leaders, 139
language, 65–67
latent functions, 20–21
laws, 70–71
leaders and leadership styles, 138–41
Leavitt, Robin, 88
LeBon, Gustav, 216
legal-rational authority, 150, 151
legitimate power, 150
Lemert, Charles, 60
Lemert, Edwin, 172–73
Lenski, Gerhard and Jean, 212–13
liberation hypothesis, 176
life course, 94
life theme, 90–91

life theme, development of, 90–91
limited participation, 50
Linton, Ralph, 116
Loeb, Paul, 226
Lofland, John, 217
looking-glass self, 25, 86
lower class, 186–87
lower middle class, 186

M
Machlup, Fritz, 35
macro-changes, 208
macro-level analysis, 20, 21, 52–53
Magellan, Ferdinand, 6
manifest functions, 20
marginality, 77–78
marginal status, 114
marriage, 144–45
Martineau, Harriet, 14–15
Marx, Karl, 16, 17, 22, 23, 151, 170, 213
masculinity, 193, 194
mass behavior, 219
mass hysteria, 221
mass society, 62, 212, 221
mass suicide, 219
master status, 115, 173
material culture, 60–62
Matza, David, 175–76
McDonald brothers, 215
McDonaldization of society, 215
Mead, George H., 25, 85, 95–96
meaningful symbols, 25
mechanical solidarity, 17, 211, 245
me component in self, 85–86
media
    as agent of socialization, 93–94
    portrayals, 9–10
    power of, in social behavior, 162–63
    social interaction and, 125–30
medicalization of society, 166
medical model, 166
Medicare, 23, 198
megalopolis, 241
mental illness, deviance and, 166
Merton, Robert, 169
metaphysical stage, 210–11
metropolis, 240–41
metropolitan statistical areas (MSAs), 240
micro-changes, 208
micro-level analysis, 25
migration, 209, 234

migration rate, 234
millennials, 96–97, 238, 267
Mills, C. Wright, 4, 23, 55, 172, 208
minority, defined, 190–92
minority groups, 187–92
mixed economy, 153
mob, 218
mob behavior, 218
mobilization for action, 217
modernization, 208
Monju plant, 252
moral crusade, 167
moral entrepreneurs, 166–67
morality, 71, 90, 99, 147, 162–63
moral panic, 167
mores, 69–71
Morris, Aldon, 226
mortality, 234
Mothers Against Drunk Driving (MADD), 75
multiculturalism, 72–74
multiple-nuclei model, 247–48
multiracial look, 63
Myers, Norman, 250
myth, 148

N
Nader, Ralph, 254
NASA space shuttle disasters, 140
National Association for the Advancement of Colored People (NAACP), 18, 225, 226
National Audubon Society, 225
National Center on Elder Abuse, 200–201
National Geographic, 71
National Organization for Women (NOW), 225, 227
natural disasters, 232–34
natural resources, depletion of, 249
nature and nurture, 83–84
negative sanctions, 177
neglect, of elderly, 200
neo-conflict approach, 16, 22, 23
neo-evolutionary theories, 212
neurological research, 59–60
neutralization, techniques of, 175–76
New Age groups, 214, 222
New Money families, 185
Newsweek, 63
Nisbet, Robert, 122–23
nonmaterial culture, 60–62

nonparticipation, 49–50
nonverbal communication, 109–13
normative approach, 157
norm of reciprocity, 122
norms, 61–62, 68–69
    prescriptive/proscriptive, 157
norm-violating behavior, 174
nuclear reactors, 252–53
numerical minorities, 190

O
Obama, Barack, 201, 226, 254
objective method, 183
Odd Girl Out (Simmons), 195
Office of Adult Protective Services, 201
Offices of Elder Justice, 201
Ogburn, William, 75
Ohlin, Lloyd, 169
Old Money families, 185
Old Order Amish, 91, 178
On the Origin of Species (Darwin), 15, 62, 83
open-ended questions, 47
open systems, 181
operational definitions, 38–39
organic analogy, 15, 168
organic solidarity, 17, 211–12, 245
organizing our social world, 131–54
    bureaucracies, 142–43
    formal organizations, 141–42
    leaders and leadership styles, 138–41
    social groups, 132–38
    social institutions, 143–54
ostracism, 178
outer containment, 174
Outsiders (Becker), 42
overgeneralizations, 5, 132
overgrazing, 249
overpopulation, 249
ozone layer, damage to, 253–54

P
panic, 218–19
paradigms, 19
Park, Robert Ezra, 245
Parks, Rosa, 5, 215, 226
Parsons, Talcott, 151
participant observation, 41, 49–50
Passages (Sheehy), 97–98
peers, as agent of socialization, 91–92
people's methods, 113

People's Temple, 219
personal distance, 107–8
personality, development of, 77, 85
personal power, 182
personal space, 106–13
personal troubles, 5
physical abuse, of elderly, 200
physical environment, 209
Pickering Nuclear Power Plant, 252
Pirsig, Robert, 36–37, 38
planet, sustaining, 232–56
    demography, 234–35
    ecology and the environment, 244–54
    environmental causes, 254–56
    nature, forces of, 232–34
    population growth, 235–38
    urbanization and socialization, 238–44
play stage, 95
pluralist perspective, 182
Poland's Solidarity movement, 228–29
political correctness, 8
pollution, 250–53
popular culture, 78–79
population
    data, 45, 144, 187, 199, 237, 240
    defined, 47
    demography and, 234–35
    density, 234–35
    growth, 235–38
    sampling, 47–48
Population Bomb, The (Ehrlich), 236
Population Explosion, The (Ehrlich and Ehrlich), 236
pornography, 163–65
Positive Philosophy (Comte), 14, 15
positive sanctions, 177
positivism, 14
positivistic stage, 210–11
postindustrial societies, 59
poverty, 242
power
    in class ranking, 182
    of social institutions, 149–51
    theories for explaining deviance, 170–71
Power, Martha, 88
Power Elite, The (Mills), 23
precipitating event, 217
prejudice, 191–92
prescriptive norms, 69, 157
prestige, 182

primary deviance, 172–73
primary group, 133–34
primary socialization, 95
production, 152
profane, sacred distinguished from, 147–48
professional ex-s, 116
proletariat, 16, 22, 170, 186
proposition, 40
proscriptive norms, 69, 157
Protestant ethic, 61–62
pseudo-scientific explanations, 34
psychological abuse, of elderly, 200
public distance, 108
pull factors, 234
pure sociology, 18, 258
push factors, 234
Pyrrhic defeat theory, 171

Q

qualitative research design
    case studies in, 50
    ethnographic interview in, 48–49
    interactionist perspective in, 51–52
    participant observation in, 49–50
    in scientific method, 41
quantitative research design, 45–48, 52
    conflict perspective in, 52–53
    experimental method in, 46
    in scientific method, 41
    secondary analysis in, 45–46
    structural functionalist perspective in, 52
    survey research in, 46–48
quasi-experimental design, 46
questionnaires, 47

R

race, 187–92
racial purity, 77
racism, 22, 191, 195, 201, 226, 263
random sampling, 48
range of tolerance, 157–59
real culture, 75–76
Reckless, Walter, 174–75
Redfield, Robert, 212
reference groups, 135–36
reform movements, 224
Reiman, Jeffrey, 170–71
relative deprivation theory, 135–36, 223
relative gratification, 135
reliability, 39
religion

    as agent of socialization, 90–91
    life theme and, 90–91
    as social institution, 147–49
    symbols in, 148
remedial work, 113
reputational method, 183
research
    ethical issues in, 42–43
    questions, 40, 41, 51
    rights and responsibilities of researchers in, 43
research designs and methods, 43–55
    combining, 50
    descriptive, 44
    evaluative, 44–45
    explanatory, 44
    exploratory, 43–44
    feminist research, 53–55
    qualitative, 48–50
    quantitative, 45–48, 52
    scientific method, 40–42
resistance movements, 225–29
resocialization, 99, 100–104
resource mobilization, 223
responsibility, denial of, 175
revolutionary change, Marx's model of, 213
revolutionary movements, 224–25
revolutions, 218
Rheingold, Harriet, 88
Richardson, James, 221
ridicule, 177
riot, 218
rites of passage, 148
rituals, 148
Ritzer, George, 58, 215
Roaring Twenties, 18
Roe v. Wade, 70–71
role conflict, 118–19
role distance, 117
role embracement, 117
role engulfment, 173
role merger, 117–18
role models, 93
role performance, 117
roles, 114–19
role set, 118
role strain, 118, 119
role taking, 95, 117
Rossides, Daniel, 180
ruling class, 16, 22, 170
rumors, 220–21

S

sacred, profane distinguished from, 147–48
sacred commandments, 70
sacredness, 148
sampling, 47–48
sanctions, 69
Sapir–Whorf hypothesis, 66
Satanists, 222
savagery, 210
scapegoat, 192
Schlafly, Phyllis, 225
scholars in contemporary sociology
    Comte, Auguste, 14
    Dubois, William E. B., 18
    Durkheim, Émile, 16–17
    Martineau, Harriet, 14–15
    Marx, Karl, 16
    Spencer, Herbert, 15–16
    Ward, Lester, 18
    Weber, Max, 17–18
school, as agent of socialization, 89–90
Schur, Edwin, 173
science
    evidence based, 34
    explanations based, 13
    importance of, 12–20
    knowledge based on, 34, 35–36
scientific method, 40–42
Scott, John, 121
scripts, 117
secondary analysis, 45–46
secondary deviance, 173
secondary group, 133, 134
second-generation immigrants, 77–78
second self, 94
self, concept of, 85–87
sensate mentality, 214
sex, defined, 193
sex and gender, 193–96
sexism, 24, 53, 195–96
sex-linked differences, 193–94
sex offenders, 116, 164
sex ratio, 235
shame, 177
Sheehy, Gail, 97–98
Sherif, Muzafer, 139–40
Shostak, Arthur, 206–7
significant others, 95
Silent Passage, The (Sheehy), 98
Simmel, George, 136–37
Simmons, Rachel, 195

situated self, 87
Skocpol, Theda, 213
small group dynamics, 136
small groups, 136–37
Smelser, Neil J., 216
Smith, Dorothy, 53
Smith, Joel, 42
Snow, David, 224
social behavior. *See also* deviance
    controlling, 156–78
    power of media, 162–63
    range of tolerance, 157–59
    social control, 177–78
    sociological theories of, 167–76
social bond, 174
social bond theory, 174
social boundaries, 134–35
social change, 206–29
    collective behavior, 215–22
    defined, 207–9
    resistance to, 225–29
    social movements, 222–25
    sources of, 209–15
social class. *See also* social stratification
    Burgess's view of, 246
    deviance-conformity and, 160
    economics and, 151
    exploitation and, 16
    globalization and, 8
    Hoyt's view of, 247
    identifying, methods of, 183
    importance of, 180–82
    intersectionality and, 201–2
    lower class, 186–87
    lower middle class, 186
    Marx's view of, 16, 22, 170
    nonverbal communication and, 109
    personal space and, 106, 108
    popular culture and, 79
    social interaction and, 121, 124, 128, 129
    socialization and, 98, 99
    social networks and, 121
    socioeconomic status and, 183–87
    stereotypes and, 5, 124
    suicide rates and, 36
    underclass, 187
    in United States, 184–87
    upper class, 184–85
    upper middle class, 185–86
    value orientation and, 68

    Weber's view of, 182
    working class, 186
social clocks, 196
social contract, 149
social control, 177–78
social control factors, 217
social Darwinism, 15
social development, 82–104, 261
    desocialization and resocialization, 100–104
    nature and nurture, 83–84
    socialization, agents of, 87–94
    socialization over life course, 94–99
    social self, developing, 85–87
social differentiation, 212
social distance, 108
social equilibrium, 20
social groups, 132–38
    defined, 132–33
    group size, 136–38
    in-group–out-group distinction, 134–35
    primary group, 133–34
    reference groups, 135–36
    secondary group, 133, 134
    social boundaries, 134–35
social identity, development of, 90
social imperative, 4
social influence effect, 139
social institutions, 143–54
    defined, 143
    economy, 151–54
    education, 145–47
    family, 144–45
    government, 149–51
    religion, 147–49
social integration, 17
social interaction
    defined, 121
    patterns of, 122–25
    redefining, through media and technology, 125–30
socialism, 152–53
social isolationism, 7
social issues, 5
socialization, 238–44
    agents of, 87–94
    over life course, 94–99
social learning theories, 93, 173
social loafing, 138
social movement organizations (SMOs), 225–26, 227, 228

social movements, 215, 221–25
social networks, 119–21, 227
social pathology, 168
social perception, 124
social power, 182
Social Security, 23, 196–97, 198, 199–200
social self, developing, 85–87
social solidarity, 16–17, 211
social stratification. *See also* social class
   among elderly, 199
   defined, 180
   in Europe and America compared, 15
   natural disasters and, 233
   organizations" role in shaping, 142
   power and, 182
   prestige and, 182
   social change and, 207
   socialism and, 152–53
   socioeconomic status and, 183–84
   types of, 181
   wealth and, 181–82
social structure, 113
society and culture, 58–79, 260–61
   components of culture, 60–71
   ethnocentrism and cultural relativism, 71–75
   ideal *versus* real culture, 75–76
   popular culture, 78–79
   subcultures and countercultures, 76–78
   types of societies, 59–60
Society in America (Martineau), 15
society types, 59–60
sociobiology, 36, 84
sociocultural evolution, 60
socioeconomic status, 183–87
sociological imagination, 4–5
sociological research. *See* research; research designs and methods
sociological theory, 51
sociological wisdom
   integrated approach to, 26–27
   overview of, 3–4
sociologists
   goal of, 5
   role of, 3
sociology
   declining enrollments in sociology departments, 258
   defined, 3–4
   development of, 12–13, 18–19
   majors, 258–59
   misconceptions in, 258, 264–65
   origin of term, 14
   scientific knowledge and, 35–36
soft-porn, 164
soil erosion, 249
Sorokin, Pitirim, 214, 244
Soul of a Citizen (Loeb), 226
specific deterrence, 177
Spencer, Herbert, 15–16, 18, 168–69, 211
spurious relationship, 40
Standpoint Theory, 53
Stark, Rodney, 148–49
statement of research objectives, 41
statuses, 114–19
status inconsistency, 114
status set, 114
stereotypes, 5, 94, 124–25, 192
stigma, 161–62
stratified organizations, 142
stratified random sampling, 48
Street Corner Society (Whyte), 50
strong ties, 120
structural conduciveness, 216
structural functionalist perspective, 19, 20–21
   of desocialization and resocialization, 100
   of deviance and conformity, 167–70
   Durkheim and, 16
   economics and, 151–52
   ethnocentrism and, 74–75
   functionalists differentiated from conflict theorists, 53
   in integrated approach, 27
   in quantitative research, 52
   of religious socialization, 90
   Spencer's organic analogy and, 15
structural or strain theories, 169
structural strains, 217
subcultures, 76–78
subjective method, 183
subordinate, 123
suburbs, 241, 243–44
suicide, 17, 36, 38–40, 126, 167, 169, 219, 242, 246
Suicide (Durkheim), 17
superego, 85
superordinate, 123
survey research, 46–48
"survival of the fittest," 15, 62, 211
sustaining the planet. *See* planet, sustaining
Sutherland, Edwin, 173

Swann, William, 111
Sykes, Gresham, 175–76
symbolic interactionist perspective, 24–27
   of developing a social self, 85, 86–87
   of deviance and conformity, 172–76
   in qualitative research, 51–52
   of social change, 214–15
symbols, 61–65, 148
Sztompka, Piotr, 229

T
taboos, 71, 157
taste cultures, 78–79
Taylor, Verta, 229
Taylor Oil Spill, 250–51
team field research, 50
Tearoom Trade (Humphreys), 42–43, 50
techniques of neutralization, 175–76
technology
   as agent of socialization, 93–94
   defined, 209
   social interaction and, 125–30
telephone, invention of, 62
text speech, 66
theodicies, 149
theological explanations, 13
theological stage, 210–11
theoretical perspectives, 19
theory
   building, 36–40
   defined, 36
   development of, 19
thesis, 213
things are not what they seem, 30–35, 258, 259
Thorne, Barrie, 194
"Thou shalt nots," 70
Three Mile Island, 252
Toennies, Ferdinand, 211, 215, 244–45
total institutions, 100–102
total resocialization, 102
total uniformity, 216
traditional authority, 150, 151
traditional societies, 212
transgender, 193
transsexual, 193
triad, 137
triangulation, 50
Tribal Stigma, 161

Trump, Donald, 74, 121, 126, 232, 254
Trump, Donald, Jr., 121
truths, 33
Turkle, Sherry, 94
Turner, Ralph, 216, 218
tweens, 96
twixters, 96

U
Ullman, Edward, 247–48
underclass, 187
Uniform Crime Reports (FBI), 45
unilineal evolution, 210
United Nations Population Division, 255
United Nations Population Fund, 255
U.S. Bureau of the Census, 45, 144, 187, 199, 237, 240
untruths, 33
upper class, 184–85
upper middle class, 185–86
urban decay, 242–43
urbanism, 245–46
"Urbanism as a Way of Life" (Wirth), 245
urbanization, 13, 238–44
urban legends, 221
urban sociology, 244
utilitarian organizations, 142
utopian movements, 224

V
validity, 39
value-added theory, 216
value-free, 17
value orientation, 67, 68, 244
values, 61–62, 67–68
variables, 40
Verstehen, 17, 18, 260
victim, denial of, 175
voluntary organizations, 142
vulgarity, 78

W
Wade, Lisa, 202
Ward, Lester Frank, 18, 258
weak ties, 120
wealth, defined, 182
Weber, Max, 17–18, 61, 142–43, 150, 181–82, 215, 260
welfare, 11–12, 15, 68, 74, 135, 187
Western Electric, 46
White, Ryan, 219
Whyte, William Foote, 50
Williams, Robin, 67
Wilson, E. O., 250
Wirth, Louis, 245, 246
women's movement, 22, 206
working class, 16, 22, 170, 186
workplace, as agent of socialization, 92
World Conference on Women, 215
World Elder Abuse Awareness Day, 201
World War II, 18

Y
youthhood, 96

Z
Zen and the Art of Motorcycle Maintenance (Pirsig), 36–37
Zero Population Growth (ZPG), 236
Zimmerman, Carle, 244
Zuckerberg, Mark, 129, 185

Credits

Chapter 1

p. 1 iStock/PhotoTalk
p. 3 www.cartoonstock.com/Mike Shapiro
p. 6 iStock/Creative-Family
p. 8 iStock/Tom Merton
p. 10 iStock/ferrantraite
p. 14 iStock/CREATISTA
p. 19 iStock/CaseyHillPhoto
p. 21 iStock/diane39
p. 26 iStock/Moussa81

Chapter 2

p. 29 iStock/sekulicn
p. 32 iStock/MaytheeVoran
p. 34 www.cartoonstock.com/Jason Love
p. 37 iStock/D-Keine
p. 39 iStock/shironosov
p. 44 iStock/mokee81
p. 49 iStock/MissHibiscus
p. 51 iStock/Rawpixel
p. 54 iStock/bernardbodo

Chapter 3

p. 57 iStock/bluecinema
p. 59 iStock/jovan_epn
p. 59 iStock/BrandyTaylor
p. 61 www.cartoonstock/Guy & Rodd
p. 65 iStock/Tiago_Fernandez
p. 68 Michael Zagaris/Contributor
p. 72 iStock/AlxeyPnferov
p. 76 iStock/Art Wager
p. 78 iStock/Roberto Galan

Chapter 4

p. 81 iStock/Morsa Images
p. 83 www.cartoonstock.com/Naf
p. 86 iStock/ronstik
p. 89 iStock/SolStock
p. 91 iStock/helenaak
p. 93 iStock/ViewApart
p. 97 iStock/Rawpixel
p. 101 iStock/mediaphotos
p. 104 iStock/B&M Noskowski

Chapter 5

p. 105 iStock/LightFieldStudios
p. 107 iStock/epicurean
p. 109 iStock/ferrantraite
p. 110 www.cartoonstock/Todd Condron
p. 112 iStock/pidjoe
p. 116 iStock/Willowpix
p. 119 iStock/svetikd
p. 125 iStock/J. Michael Jones
p. 128 iStock/grinvalds

Chapter 6

p. 131 iStock/urfinguss
p. 133 iStock/VladGans
p. 135 iStock/Julian J Rossig
p. 138 iStock/Image Source
p. 141 www.cartoonstock.com/Mike Flanagan
p. 145 iStock/wavebreakmedia
p. 147 iStock/shaunl
p. 151 Fair Use
p. 153 iStock/RedDaxLuma

Chapter 7

p. 155 iStock/Rapideye
p. 158 iStock/avid_creative
p. 162 iStock/Yuri_Arcurs
p. 165 www.cartoonstock.com/John McPherson
p. 168 iStock/Purpleimages
p. 171 iStock/Bastiaan Slabbers
p. 174 iStock/imagesource
p. 176 iStock/CREATISTA
p. 178 iStock/LightFieldStudios

Chapter 8

p. 179 iStock/Thomas_EyeDesign
p. 181 www.cartoonstock.com/Richard Dall
p. 183 iStock/ALotOfPeople
p. 185 iStock/msymons
p. 185 iStock/MattStansfield
p. 188 iStock/kate_sept2004
p. 191 iStock/Cerchi
p. 194 iStock/svetikd
p. 198 iStock/vectorarts
p. 202 iStock/eyecrave

Chapter 9

p. 205 iStock/Tassii
p. 207 iStock/PhonlamaiPhoto
p. 208 www.cartoonstock.com/Fran
p. 212 iStock/Lingbeek
p. 217 iStock/shironosov
p. 220 iStock/Peopleimages
p. 223 iStock/David Tran
p. 228 iStock/Bastiaan Slabbers

Chapter 10

p. 231 iStock/KariHoglund
p. 233 iStock/Jodi Jacobson
p. 237 iStock/Andrey Shevchuk
p. 239 iStock/Vivvi Smak
p. 242 iStock/zetter
p. 246 iStock/Rachel_Web_Design
p. 248 iStock/MsLightBox
p. 251 iStock/Phonix_a
p. 253 www.cartoonstock.com/Jon Carton

Chapter 11

p. 257 iStock/EtiAmmos
p. 259 www.cartoonstock.com/Marty Bucella
p. 265 iStock/kali9